You Don't Always Get
What You Pay For

You Don't Always Get What You Pay For

The Economics of Privatization

Elliott D. Sclar

A Century Foundation Book

Cornell University Press

Ithaca and London

The Century Foundation, formerly the Twentieth Century Fund, sponsors and supervises timely analyses of economic policy, foreign affairs, and domestic political issues. Not-for-profit and nonpartisan, it was founded in 1919 and endowed by Edward A. Filene.

Copyright © 2000 by The Century Foundation, Inc.

First published 2000 by Cornell University Press

Printed in the United States of America

Library of Congress Cataloging-in-Publication Data

Sclar, Elliott.
    You don't always get what you pay for : the economics of privatization / Elliott D. Sclar.
        p.   cm.
    Includes bibliographical references and index.
    ISBN 0-8014-3733-4 (cloth)
    1. Privatization—United States. 2. Privatization—United States—Case studies.
I. Title.
HD3888 .S35 2000
338.973'05—dc21   99-055904

Cornell University Press strives to use environmentally responsible suppliers and materials to the fullest extent possible in the publishing of its books. Such materials include vegetable-based, low-VOC inks and acid-free papers that are recycled, totally chlorine-free, or partly composed of nonwood fibers. Books that bear the logo of the FSC (Forest Stewardship Council) use paper taken from forests that have been inspected and certified as meeting the highest standards for environmental and social responsibility. For further information, visit our website at www.cornellpress.cornell.edu

Cloth printing   10 9 8 7 6 5 4 3 2 1

Contents

Foreword   vii

Acknowledgments   xi

Chapter 1   The Urge to Privatize: From the
            Bureaucratic State to the Contract State   1

Chapter 2   What Is the Public Buying? Identifying
            the Contracted Public Good   20

Chapter 3   Public vs. Private Production:
            Is One Better and How Would You Know?   47

Chapter 4   What's Competition Got to Do with It?
            Market Structures and Public Contracting   69

Chapter 5   All in the System: Organizational Theories
            and Public Contracting   94

Chapter 6   Restructuring Work: The Relational
            Contract ·   130

Chapter 7   The Privatization of Public Service:
            Economic Limits of the Contract State   151

            Bibliography   169

            Index   177

Foreword

Political discourse is seldom notable for the precision of its language. Abstraction and impressionism rather than realism have been the rhetorical model for candidates of all persuasions since time beyond recall. Politicians routinely use words in symbolic fashion, seeking to create in the minds of voters attractive approximations of reality and lyrical visions of the future. The specifics of political diction, to be sure, do change over time, reflecting new issues and alterations in the culture and character of the polity. Those gifted at political conversation seem to have the ability to co-opt the most potent contemporary language and put it to use in support of their particular set of arguments. During the 1980s and 1990s, many politicians built a dialect of immense appeal around phrases that celebrated the market and disparaged government. At the heart of this popular vocabulary was a word of especially great power: *privatization.*

Like most useful political words, privatization has deep roots in society. Americans fought a revolution in part to defend private property. Through the dangerous years of the Cold War, they served, in effect, as "Defender of the Faith" for belief in free enterprise and limited government. Actually, faith may be the wrong word because it implies the absence of empirical proof. For U.S. citizens, the evidence that capitalism works best, occasional depressions aside, has been all around them for two centuries. As the United States' role in the world expanded, the propagation of the "faith" assumed a new importance. During the second half of the twentieth century, for example, U.S. policy abroad was animated most of all by the core tenets of Western-style free enterprise. With markets in place, Americans believed the risks of a country "going Communist" or starting wars would disappear.

Although all "good" Americans are expected to love capitalism, it is perfectly acceptable for them to be anything but fond of their own government. The strong central government that Madison and Hamilton had in mind was a long time coming. But, propelled largely by war, economic depression, social causes, and internationalism, it did arrive, and Washington, D.C., in fits and starts, became the capital of a modern nation-state. In terms of public support, the federal government probably reached its peak in the aftermath of the Great Depression and World War II. For a time, citizens came to see the national government as generally benign and competent—a force for constructive change and a healthy offset to market failures. Beginning in the 1960s and 1970s, though, these positive attitudes toward government began to evaporate. Polls and politics confirm that support for government has been steadily declining for a generation.

One consequence of the present coincidence of exaltation of the market and cynicism about government has been a powerful surge of support for the privatization of public services. In other nations, privatization often refers to the sale of government-operated "businesses," such as airlines, telephone companies, and commodity monopolies. Because the U.S. public sector has always been very limited in scope, however, here the term "privatization" ordinarily refers to expansion of the already widespread practice of providing public services and goods by contracting with private entities. Over the past decade, this sort of arrangement has had special political cachet at the state and local level, with its appeal crossing ideological boundaries.

The argument for more privatization is normally based on the conviction that profit motive and competition are necessary to provide the proper incentives for efficiency and quality. That view, however, is a bit simplistic, ignoring, for example, the powerful discipline imposed by elections and the media on the operations of government. Virtually all officeholders, after all, seek ways of gaining popularity and avoiding taxes—and of providing a high level of services at a reasonable cost in terms of taxation in order to stay in power. The pressure of public scrutiny and competitive elections is, in many cases, more relentless and ruthless than the market itself.

Whatever the real virtues of public versus private service provision, experiments with expanded privatization continue to proliferate around the nation. Although there has been a good deal of superficial journalism about this activity, there is remarkably little in-depth analytical work in the area.

Elliott Sclar, a professor of planning and public policy at Columbia University, has tracked these developments with a keen eye and exceptional commitment to empirical evidence and analytical objectivity. In the pages that follow, he examines the pluses and minuses of privatization in several specific cases and provides a general framework for evaluating these and other examples of the practice. He considers these blueprints for privatization both in terms of the experience of actual communities and with reference to the inevitable complexities implied by governmental reliance on private monopolies or oligopolies. He analyzes the dynamic process that transforms public contracting from something akin to competition into sole source monopoly. The privatization debate needs precisely the sort of grounding in fact and close examination of real-world conditions marshaled by Sclar in analyzing the consequences of the limits of competition.

Sclar's overall conclusion is clear: privatization, although useful, is easily overworked. It is not a solution to the problem of providing public goods when both costs and benefits are hard to measure. Without good public management, contracting does little to enhance public value. Perhaps the most important contribution of *You Don't Always Get What You Pay For* is its grouping of public and private provisions for services in the context of the organizational *reality* of local government rather than the abstract theory of market competition. Although theory may help to guide us to the best approach, it is no substitute for looking at the evidence drawn from actual case studies. Theory must be informed by experience.

The Century Foundation has supported a number of studies on privatization in recent years. In 1995, it sponsored *Privatization and Public Hospitals*, which focused on New York City's hospitals; in 1996, it sponsored *Hard Lessons: Public Schools and Privatization*; and more recently, it supported a white paper by Dean Baker examining the issues involved in the privatization of Social Security.

Elliott Sclar's work adds greatly to our ongoing effort to help clarify these issues. Of course, the debate about privatization will not, and indeed should not, be finally settled. The truth is that, at least in the United States, there is no one "system" that works best for every community or the nation as a whole. Only an ideologue tries to fix for all time one specific mix of governmental and private sources for the provision of public goods. Therefore, plain old U.S. practicality remains the best guide for action. We have strong beliefs about capitalism and government, but we seldom let them get in the way, for long, of the most reasonable solution to specific problems. In these circumstances, the one constant political goal should be discourse that truly provides more clarity and knowledge in our public debates. Because of this book's important contribution to that goal, on behalf of the Trustees of The Century Foundation, I thank Elliott Sclar for his efforts.

RICHARD C. LEONE, President
The Century Foundation
August 1999

Acknowledgments

Book covers can be misleading. They hint at the notion that the author alone is responsible for whatever value lies inside. But that is just not true. The process of writing a scholarly work is always something of a "group" effort. Ideas do not exist in social vacuums. They come alive and take on meaning from the give and take between writer and the larger community of critics and supporters that precede putting pen to paper, or more contemporaneously, fingers to keyboard. I have been especially fortunate to be able to write this book amidst an exceptionally able community of others. I want to take this opportunity to acknowledge many of the people who created the intellectual context from which this book emerged. This book has value because of the people whose names would otherwise not appear. Needless to say, despite their best efforts to the contrary, if this book falls short of its goal, the fault is entirely mine.

The sponsorship of The Century Foundation (formerly the Twentieth Century Fund) and the support of its president, Richard C. Leone, were crucial to getting this project off the ground. In particular, I thank my first project officer at the Foundation, Harry Ozeroff. It was Harry who led me through the initial stages of proposal writing. Greg Anrig and David Smith read and critiqued the several drafts. Ken Emerson, my opinion editor at the now defunct *New York Newsday*, appeared at the Foundation and helped me through the penultimate draft. Beverly Goldberg and Jason Renker shepherded this book from the Foundation to the right publisher, Cornell University Press. Frances Benson is my supportive and wise editor, and for that I am most grateful. In the final stages of production, Melissa Nelson of Textbook Writers Associates put a great deal of time, competence, and care into copyediting my manuscript.

At Columbia University, I have been fortunate to have colleagues and graduate students who patiently sat through my working and reworking of many of the ideas that found their way into this text. Peter Marcuse, my colleague on the planning faculty, has been a constant source of support and challenge that I deeply treasure. I also especially acknowledge Brendan (Dan) O'Flaherty, my colleague in the School of International and Public Affairs, and C. W. Ada Lee, a graduate student in the economics department, for giving this manuscript a rigorous and thoughtful read. Two of my own graduate students, Caroline Suh and Kil Huh, served as research assistants at different crucial points. Caroline catalogued and sorted all the information collected on my various field trips, and Kil went well beyond the call of duty to track down references and fact check as the final draft of the book went to press.

This book originates in work I undertook for the Economic Policy Institute in Washington, D.C. It was there that my interest in the larger implications of public-service privatization began to take shape. My colleagues at the institute contributed in ways large and small as the book moved forward. My very dear old friend Jeff Faux was always a source of inspiration and keen insight. Larry Mishel and Max Sawicky have read and commented on various portions of this book in various stages of the process.

I regret that another dear friend, the late Bennett Harrison, was not here to see the completion of the project. His enthusiasm buoyed me for the final push. More importantly, his knowledge of American music was instrumental in helping me avoid a mistaken song title in the first chapter. Bruce Wallin, Jane Holtz Kay, and Michael Zweig provided critical and thorough readings of the manuscript at different points along the way. Philip Webre helped me think through the initial ideas for this project and has been supportive at every stage.

In my research travels, I met many public officials and public union leaders who helped me to appreciate the power of institutional complexity in the issue of privatization. At the Amalgamated Transit Union I acknowledge the help and advice received from Jim LaSala, Robert Molofsky, Michael Rucker, and Bill Jones. At the old AFL-CIO Public Employees Department, Al Bilik, Laura Ginsberg, and Paul Hughes were very helpful in getting me access to local public officials and union leaders to conduct my research. Along the way, they became friends.

In Indianapolis, Deputy Mayor Charles "Skip" Stett took the time to talk to me and thoughtfully read my drafts on that experience. John Mc-Corkhill, the administrator of the Indianapolis Fleet Service, provided time and data to help keep this account accurate. On the union side, Steve Fantauzzo, Executive Director of AFSCME State Council 62, Bernie Ahaus, the current president, and Dominic Mangine, the past president of Local 3131, were unstinting of their time. In Albany, City Comptroller Nancy Burton and Albany County Comptroller and former City Department of Public Works Commissioner Mike Connors helped to paint for me the larger picture. Steve Alviene, Fred Pfeiffer, Tim Stewart, and Ken Larkin of AFSCME DC 66 gave me the view from the shop floor. In Massachusetts, my thanks go to Frank Borges and Tim Dean of SEIU Local 285 and John Parsons of the Office of the State Auditor.

Last, but never least, Nancy Aries has been an abiding source of support, wisdom, and insight throughout the entire process. To my children, Corey, Gia, Jennifer, Jason, and Hannah, and my grandson, Noah, who always saw less of me for the time spent at the keyboard, I thank you all for your patience and love.

ELLIOTT D. SCLAR

You Don't Always Get
What You Pay For

1 The Urge to Privatize

From the Bureaucratic State to the Contract State

The More Things Change, the More They Remain the Same

The dawning of the twentieth century brought a widespread belief in the power of government to serve as an agent of positive social change. Through the application of rational analysis to social problems, it was believed that plans and programs would be developed that could overcome those problems. This notion of rational public action taken in the name of the people (progressivism) evolved in response to social dislocation, overcrowding, environmental pollution, and wrenching poverty, which were byproducts of the new era of urbanization and industrialization brought on by the prior century. The laissez-faire capitalism that transformed society and created unprecedented levels of wealth also produced severe destabilization. Not only was a belief in public intervention *widely* held, it was *deeply* held, too. It was embedded in ideologies throughout the political spectrum. State power was the only countervailing force capable of checking the antisocial excesses of the emergent class of economic oligarchs or "robber barons" spawned by the new industrialization. Hierarchically organized and professionally trained bureaucrats would exercise this state power. It was believed that such a system of public service was capable of imposing necessary order and stability where markets left only disorder and instability.

For a good part of the twentieth century, the only real debate among reformers concerned how much intervention would be sufficient. In the extreme, it was believed the state itself should run the entire economy in the name of "the people"—socialism. For socialist advocates, this through-going reform was the only way to permanently end the social problems caused by capitalism. For more moderate reformers, the "third way" involved some variant of the social democratic welfare state that came to characterize all the world's industrialized nations for much of the century. It is noteworthy that no less an admirer of the virtues of unbridled capitalism than the brilliant Joseph Schumpeter, standing at almost the midpoint of the century, observed that it was only a matter of time before capitalism succumbed completely to socialism.

> Can capitalism survive? No. I do not think it can. But this opinion of mine, like that of every other economist who has pronounced upon the subject, is in itself completely uninteresting. What counts in any attempt at social prognosis is not the Yes or No that sums up the facts and arguments which lead up to it but those facts and arguments themselves. (Schumpeter 1947, 61)

The essence of his argument was that capitalism was a wonderful system for generating wealth and encouraging creativity. However, it was not capable of equitably distributing the fruits of its effort. Accordingly, even though capitalism had solved society's production problem, socialism, although it would never produce great art or music, would come to dominate the world because it was better prepared to tackle the distribution problem. The widespread belief in either the inevitability of socialism or the continuation of some form of welfare state capitalism persisted halfway into the final quarter of the twentieth century.

But then things quickly changed. By the beginning of the 1980s, political and economic cracks in the foundations of the structures of Eastern European socialism became gaping holes. By decade end, the entire structure imploded. Simply put, although production and distribution are distinctive economic acts, they are not unconnected. In the aftermath of this seismic shift, governments everywhere, even democratic ones, were no longer viewed as the logical solution for the world's social problems. Indeed, they were increasingly viewed as an important source of these problems. As a new century begins, the alternative to government direction and the employment of public bureaucracy to carry out its commands is a fresh belief in the social beneficence and effectiveness of the marketplace.

While in the extreme, the differences in the stylized political conventional wisdom at the beginning and end of the century appear as distinct polar opposites; the distance that actual policy debates can traverse almost invariably falls short of these ends. The activist and expansionist consensus about government that dominated American politics for much of the century, compared with the contemporary debate, merely allowed for more regulation and intervention in what has always been a predominately market-oriented society. Contemporary debate, although marked by far fewer politically viable options for active government but many more for market-sustaining programs, is far more nuanced in reality. Indeed, disgruntled conservatives mutter that in the two decades or so since they ascended to real political power with the election of Ronald Reagan as president, regulation of society has increased not decreased. Evidence exists in every area of social life, from the environment to the right to bear arms. It does not appear to matter whether the conservatives politically control the White House and/or Congress. At the same time, liberals are forced to confront the reality that there is no effective political interest in the types of large-scale interventions, such as urban renewal and public housing, that marked the middle decades of the century. On balance, it is fair to say that while the range of policy choices has shifted more in the direction of nonintervention, it has not been and is not a straightforward move. The notion that government is still the proper bulwark to contain social distress abides. People merely expect government to do more with less. Now the public believes that markets can shoulder far more of the burden than they have been permitted to do in the past.

Consistent with this newfound belief in the efficacy of the market, the question of how government should organize to provide public service is prominent on the policy agenda. In the U.S. political context, this question is characterized as "privatization." The term, as used here, describes initiatives to introduce market relationships into the bureaucratic production of public services. The intention is to force public bureaucracies to be governed by the same competitive forces that make private markets socially beneficial. Conversely, it is important to remember that the welfare state, which evolved under progressive and New Deal political philosophies earlier in the century, assumed that government programs must be staffed by government employees. Consequently, every expansion in state activism was matched by expansion in the public payroll. This was especially the case among the professionals who were needed to deliver the more complex services created by social policies intended to invest in society's human capital, particularly its poorest members. Thus, not only did the public sector require professional police officers, fire fighters, corrections officers, and school teachers, but it also began to need social workers, an expanded public university professorate, doctors, nurses, lawyers, and accountants, among many others. All these professions began to have sizable numbers of members who earned their livelihoods as public servants.

Because the services provided by these workers remain valuable, their continued public employment seriously impedes the larger laissez-faire goal of shrinking both the size and role of the state in society. Advocates for smaller government have been more successful in convincing the citizenry that the *size* of the public sector could be diminished than they have been in convincing them that its *responsibilities* also could be reduced. Privatization, in the form of public contracting with private parties to deliver public services, has much to offer in this regard. If the size of the public workforce could be diminished, then the second half of the chore, namely, gathering popular support for a diminished level of public responsibility, would be easier to achieve in the future.

The case for privatization is built on the assertion that contractual relationships will give the public sector all the advantages of the market without undermining the level of public service. If laissez-faire advocates could demonstrate that private sector employees working under contract and disciplined by market imperatives provide comparable or better service at equal or lower cost, at least a first step could be taken to diminish government activism. In contrast, if the case is not as open and shut as hoped by these proponents, then the role of government in the life of society will not be reversed easily. Consequently, the political debate about privatization is significantly more than a discussion of pragmatic issues in public service management. Although that element does exist and is important—indeed it is the principal focus of this book—it is not the driving force in this debate. Ideology that places market concerns ahead of those of equity and access animates the larger political discourse in which privatization is advocated.

To the extent that shrinkage of government itself is the ultimate goal of a number of the proponents of privatization, I believe they will be disappointed in their quest. By now the notion that government is central to the life of society is deeply rooted and will only expand with the scope of the global marketplace. To the extent that the goal is to make government more cost-effective, a proper use of contracts does have much promise. But it must be a use based on an understanding of the limits of contracting and the value of creating good public organizations. More narrowly, the question is one of how we are to make decisions about the relative costs and benefits of contracts and enhancement of direct service provision. If we fail to address this admittedly less ideological but more practical question, then we run the risk of moving further into an arena of ambiguous contractual arrangements that will be neither discernibly better nor worse than present ones.

To say that not much will change one way or the other does not mean that we won't pay a price. We risk losing a valuable opportunity to meaningfully improve public service. The debate initiated by the change in attitudes toward government presents us with a rare chance to move the issue of improving the efficiency and effectiveness of public service provision from the policy back burner to the front. Indeed, with changes in communications and information technologies we have many more ways to solve public management problems and enhance public services. When I worked for the federal government, we obtained our office supplies from a central government store. One of our employees had to go "shop" and bring back supplies. In an age when large private firms such as Staples and Office Max can ship overnight at low prices, the rationale for using a public agency to store and track a large inventory is difficult to sustain. It is equally difficult to justify using valuable employee time to physically shop for needed items. On the other hand, there are many public functions that are similar to private functions, which are still better done directly. But, how do we know which to contract out and which to retain?

In the following chapters, it is my intention to outline the concerns that must be part of any policy decision to reorganize public service. In too much of the present debate there is an implicit assumption that contracting is identical to organizational reform. Privatization is often presented to public workers with a "shape up or ship out" set of choices. Officials in essence say to their employees, "You figure out how to meet the price of an outside competitor or give up your job." But, as every good manager knows, organizational change is neither a bottom-up nor an easily mandated initiative. By the same token, every good manager also knows that contracting is not an automatic blessing. It takes much hard work and planning to avoid the serious problems and expenses inherent in the misuse of this option. Contrary to near conventional folk wisdom that privatization almost invariably represents improvement, this is simply not true. If we want our public services to really improve, then it is important to combine the judicious use of contracting with a strategy of internal agency reform.

I propose to scrutinize the economic reasons why privatization as a reform strategy in the form of public contracting often bogs down. By understanding the problems, it is possible to construct solutions—the

aim of Chapters 6 and 7. My goal is to present readers with a better understanding of the approaches that we might take to balance the use of
contracting and internal reform to enhance the operation of public
agencies. No one can predict when or how the political pendulum may
shift in the future. Regardless of when or how, it is important to the sur-
vival of the values of a humane and progressive democracy that public
services be as efficient, responsive, and democratically administered as
possible.

Since the early 1980s, with the backing of newly empowered conservative political leaders, many ambitious attempts have been made to transform public service from direct to contract provision. Results have fallen
far short of promises. However, they have not been the abject failure predicted by opponents. This outcome should not have been surprising. Privatization American style is essentially old-fashioned public contracting
writ very large. Privatization inherits and aggravates difficulties already
present with this genre of public management. Similarly, it also extends
the advantages. Despite approximately twenty years of agitation for more
contracting, the proportion of public money spent via contracting is
about the same as it has always been—one-half. The underlying problem
is the sometimes useful but always limited way that contracting achieves
public policy goals. The reasons for this are similar to the reasons why private organizations find outsourcing useful but limited.

The Standard Market Model

To begin to understand the strengths and weaknesses of public service
privatization, it is necessary to understand the theory behind the policy.
The competitive contract market generally envisioned by privatization
advocates is derived from modification of the standard market model,
the core element in neoclassical economic theory. A quick review of its
essential components is the proper starting point for evaluating the role
of privatization as a method of providing public service.

The standard market model envisions a world of markets, each of
which is composed of a large number of unrelated buyers and sellers.
Each is assumed to be pursuing his or her own gain independent of the
others. All are sufficiently small relative to the size of the market to ensure that any individual actions have little or no appreciable impact on
the price, quantity, or quality of the product, which are shaped by the ag-
gregation of individual decisions made by the larger market. From the

perspective of individual buyers or sellers, these market conditions are viewed as uncontrollable givens on which they base individual decisions to buy, sell, or leave the market. There are no appreciable impediments to the entrance or exit of any buyer or seller from the market in question. Hence, no concentration of market power can accrue because of such barriers. All buyers and sellers are assumed to share equally all relevant knowledge (or ignorance) about the key factors determining product quality and prices in the market. Thus, the aggregate key market characteristics of price, quantity, and quality change only through the concerted action of the equally informed participants. The quality of goods traded in such a market is assumed to be sufficiently uniform and known so that buyers need merely to seek out the lowest priced seller.

On the production side, the pressures of many sellers vying for the dollars of the most buyers leads sellers to discipline their production methods to keep costs as low as possible. Sellers seek to keep their individual production costs low to achieve maximum gain, regardless of the ups and downs of market price. It is assumed that every producer is aware of and has access to all the technical possibilities for producing the goods in question and that each chooses the least costly means to do so.

If all these conditions hold, the market is said to be competitive. A competitive market is similar in many respects to an election: no single vote carries the day, but the collective weight of all votes is decisive. From a social standpoint, the collective interests of buyers and sellers generate countervailing pressures that ensure the sale of products that consumers wish to buy. Prices are determined, not by any coercive power on the part of an individual or small group, but by underlying production costs. Production costs, in turn, reflect the most technically efficient production methods.

It is but a small conceptual step to move from this model of a single competitive market that gives customers what they want at prices that cover legitimate costs to an economy that is an infinite aggregate of such markets. It is a world in which knowledge, technology, product, prices, and costs are all givens. Hence, the profit-maximizing position for each producer and the satisfaction-maximizing position for each consumer become highly predictable. The complexities, uncertainties, and ambiguities of imperfect information, inadequate distribution of existing information, barriers to market entry, and product differentiation are all assumed to be either nonexistent or trivial. In such a world, economic decision-making essentially reduces to a technical matter—a mere mathematical algorithm.

Textbooks of economic theory usually present this standard model, with more or less mathematical sophistication depending on their intended audience, as the starting point for the rest of their analysis. If the conditions for such a competitive market economy hold, then society can attain a state of being in which all individuals are as well off as they can be, given their initial endowment of wealth (i.e., labor skills, capital, raw materials). The standard market model makes no judgments about the quality of initial endowments. The model merely demonstrates that, given each individual's initial wealth, the state of technology, and the state of market prices, the optimal amount of output will be created at the lowest possible cost. At that point, no rearrangement of production or markets can make any individual better off unless another becomes worse off. Labeled a "Pareto optimum," after the early twentieth-century economist Vilfredo Pareto, who first articulated the notion, the idea is quite powerful. Following the teachings of Adam Smith, it implies that not only will a competitive market society enhance material wealth, but that as each individual acts in pursuit of his or her own gain, everyone is in fact helping to create the optimal possible amount of material satisfaction for everyone else in society. The individual optima are, of course, constrained by the initial distribution of wealth. Any change in the distribution of wealth would lead to a recalculation of the optimal result.

Since the standard market model makes no judgments about the fairness of any wealth distribution, it has nothing to say about the fairness of any Pareto optimal outcome. It merely asserts that, given the initial wealth distribution, a society of competitive markets ensures the best possible deal for everyone given their resources. As the Nobel prize winning economist Amartya Sen has succinctly put it, "A society or an economy can be Pareto optimal and still be perfectly disgusting" (Sen 1970, 22). Any policy change that induces a redistribution of wealth is a question of values and not efficiency, according to the model's designers, who have never claimed any special expertise on such matters.

The extent to which one views the standard market model as a more or less complete description of an actual market-oriented economy typically correlates with the strength of one's belief that privatization is more efficient than direct public service provision. The critical issues here pertain to the accuracy of assumptions about the ease of seller access to the contract market and the ready and inexpensive availability of relevant contract information. The first assumption speaks directly to the existence of sustainable competition, and the second pertains to the ability to obtain low cost and effective contract enforcement. To the extent that these conditions hold, contracting in a market-oriented society can typically be expected to be more efficient and effective than the work done by public employees.

However, the extent to which one questions the validity of the presumption that market entry barriers are sufficiently low that many *qualified* sellers will appear and the extent to which one believes that public officials have relevant market information correlate strongly and directly with the strength of individual skepticism about the relative efficiency of public contracting. The higher the barriers to market entry for additional sellers and the greater the lack of inexpensive access to good information on the part of public purchasers, the less likely it is that contracting will provide meaningful improvement. In this case, the notion that privatization is a quick and easy way to overcome bureaucratic inefficiency and move us closer to a state of Pareto optimality is seriously compromised.

Competition and Privatization

The standard market model grossly oversimplifies many important connected issues of economic and political power. This is of special concern when the focus of our analysis is a process of public contracting. There are numerous ways in which arm's-length relationships between government buyers and outside contractors may be breached. Unlike the standard market model, the real economy is not a flat playing field on which a host of atomistic and more or less equally endowed economic agents perpetually compete with one another in pursuit of wealth. The economic playing field is more realistically conceived as mountainous terrain that includes several high peaks from which well-endowed corporate and individual warriors swoop down to seize targets of opportunity. Among these high peaks are some flat areas where market battles akin to the competitive ones described by the standard market model do occur. But the players are not always as equal as the model assumes, and these comparatively level plateaus are seldom where the real economic action takes place.

Because privatization policy emphasizes these small, flat interstices and neglects the dominant peaks, it does not concern itself with the existence and persistence of powerful economic and political concentrations, nor is it able to explain why they would disappear if government increased its use of contracting. By sidestepping the issue of how concentrated economic power arises and sustains itself in the actual operation of contract markets, privatization advocacy often amounts to little more than an endorsement of changing rather than correcting the problems we face with public agency performance.

Atomistic competition almost invariably gives way to concentrated economic power because the competitive market is not a desirable or sustainable long-term condition for sellers. Sellers seek to end this distasteful condition as quickly as possible. Why eke out a marginal profit while battling an unending string of challengers in a style akin to a "good guy" against a host of "bad guys" in a martial-arts movie? To counteract this, sellers continually attempt to attain a strategic high ground from which to drive away their competitors. Although it is possible to conceive of economic situations in which all contractors survive endless rounds of competition, that is not the typical state of the contract market in either the public or the private sector. The more typical situation is one in which success is achieved by driving rivals out of the market or absorbing them through mergers and acquisitions. Sellers try to undermine competition because monopolistic situations are significantly more profitable. In competitive situations, sellers slug it out with each other for slim to nonexistent profit margins. Diminished competition increases profits for the remaining firms. The greater the market power achieved by a seller, the more easily he or she can maintain market prices significantly above production costs. It is also important to remember that in the real world, unlike the standard market model, all competitors do not start from a more or less equal position. Consequently, the probability that any particular market will either sustain competition or trend toward it, as the standard market model assumes, is unlikely.

In general, the tendency for erosion of competition in individual contract markets is exacerbated in the public realm because economics and politics are not separate spheres. Instead, there is a strong tendency for the imbalance between the public and those who stand to gain from anticompetitive behavior to increase because the winners use their advantage to exert political leverage. Although, collectively, taxpayers stand to gain the most through sustained market competition, they have less individual incentive to politically defend competitive public contracting than sellers have to undermine it. Thus, even though competitive contracting seemingly promises more choice and better prices, the potential benefit for individual taxpayers is often insufficient for them to justify the investment of time and money to enforce sustained competition. Contractors, on the other hand, typically stand to reap a great deal individually by ensuring that the public market structures work to their advantage. Therefore, they are willing to invest the necessary resources to shape public markets in anticompetitive ways.

Replacing the assumption that markets are level playing fields with a more realistic and complex political and economic topography yields a clearer view of the possibilities and limitations of privatization. Clarity comes at the price of certainty, however. Although one can find instances in which particular markets bear some resemblance to the standard market model, more often than not they are exceptions to the rules of engagement used by public buyers and private sellers.

The Economic Ideology of Privatization

Depending on where one looks, virtually every public service is now considered a candidate for privatization, including public schools, public hospitals, social services, penal institutions, police and fire departments, and transit systems. All these initiatives are proposed or implemented in the name of managerial efficiency and effectiveness. The most vehement advocates of privatization believe that government should, indeed could, be all but put out of business. In 1991, when Stephen Goldsmith first ran for the office of mayor of Indianapolis, he asserted that he could run the entire city with just four contract managers (Fantauzzo n.d., 2). His bold assertion was the practical elaboration of an idea popularized eleven years earlier by Robert Poole, architect of the libertarian Reason Foundation, which has been perhaps the staunchest proponent of privatization in the United States. In his 1980 book, *Cutting Back City Hall*, Poole envisioned a city run entirely via contractual arrangements between a small government and a host of private providers.

The case for privatization made by Poole and others (Savas 1987; Osborne and Gaebler 1992) always rests on an appeal to a theory of competitive contractual behavior derived from the standard market model. The notion rests on an assumption that contracting takes place in a competitive market environment. Based on that assumption, it is possible to construct a rationale that endows the cause of privatization with a strong political and economic legitimacy in the context of U.S. values. Politically, the existence of competition assumes an environment in which anyone wishing to vie for the right to contract can freely enter the fray and obtain public work. Moreover, the notion implicitly assumes that the barriers to market entry are either nonexistent or so minimal that this freedom of entry is not notional but real. Hence, political legitimacy is achieved because the existence of contract competition essentially sweeps away the need to address the problem of political favoritism, which in practice often dogs public contracting.

Economically competitive contracting sets incentives in place that ensure production of the best possible product for the lowest possible price. The action of many bidders seeking to win the government's business leads each of them to try and deliver the product most desired by the government at the lowest price consistent with costs. To do otherwise could risk loss of the business to a lower priced competitor.

However, privatization and competition are not as inevitably linked as are love and marriage in the 1950s song "Love and Marriage": you *can* have one without the other. Only in a highly constrained set of conditions is it possible to sustain competitive contracting. When competitive contracting cannot be sustained, neither can the automatic case for the *intrinsic* political and economic superiority of privatization compared with direct government service provision. A case may still be made for private contracting, but it is a very different case. It must be sustained on the basis of unique situational factors, not because competition ensures that there are incentives to make it the best possible outcome (Sappington and Stiglitz 1987).

Because of the strong intuitive appeal of the simple competitive market model as adapted to the case for privatization, many of the richest insights of modern economic and organizational theory regarding the relationship between organizational performance and contracting have been notably absent from the privatization debate to date. Most of the resultant claims for the superiority of private contracting borrow little from modern social science literature beyond the crude notion that competition is preferable to monopoly. This truism is then generalized into an abstract theory of organizational behavior in which contracting is either typically competitive or easily made competitive and, therefore, intrinsically efficient. By inference, anything else is just monopoly and inefficiency by another name. To the extent that the case for the ease of competitive contracting can be sustained, it is then possible to pursue privatization as a matter of general public policy. Situations of direct service provision can then be reduced to the status of anomalies. However, if the case cannot be sustained, then each proposed privatization must be examined on its individual merits. The conservative desire to diminish the role of government in society via the easy adoption of a policy of widespread privatization becomes a far more elusive goal.

Experience demonstrates that not only is sustaining competitive contracting for complex services difficult, but other factors also prove to be far more crucial for the ultimate success or failure of the venture. Contracting for services, regardless of whether a public agency or private firm undertakes the task, involves elaborate and generally difficult to anticipate relationships between purchasers and vendors. Much hinges on the institutional and historic context that defines the parameters of relationship between the organizations bound together by contract. Absent a broader analysis of these contextual complexities, the privatization policy debate largely has been little more than dueling anecdotes. Those favoring privatization tell their favorite stories, and those opposed peddle theirs. Like the blind men who each touch a single part of an elephant and self-assuredly contradict each other, they extrapolate their narrow experiential evidence into general descriptions of entirely different creatures.

If we are truly concerned about the long-term efficiency and effectiveness of the public sector, then we need to move the analysis beyond anecdotal assertions. Regardless of number, they do not make a case one way or the other. They become useful only when integrated into a comprehensive conceptual frame of reference that enables analysis of the potentials and limits of contracting for fulfilling the mission of the public sector. To the extent that this frame of reference diminishes the superficial generality of the appeal of privatization as a management strategy, it serves two beneficial social purposes: we can bring more powerful management tools to bear on the challenge of (1) efficient and (2) effective public agency operation.

The Limited Condition of Contractual Competition

Unlike hiring a contractor once every few years to paint the family house over a few days, privatization usually requires establishing a long-term relationship between a government agency and an outside service provider. Because of the complex nature of most public services, privatization contracts are typically written for multiyear periods. Therefore, they foreclose easy competitive access to alternative providers if the product is not up to par. As a result, the characteristics of the contractor–agency relationship principally determine service quality and cost savings, not the competitive marketplace. The longer the term of the contract and the more complex the service provided, the smaller the role played by market competition in the costs and benefits of privatization.

If, for example, a local government must decide whether to replace its own management of a wastewater treatment plant with an outside operator, three factors structure the outcome. The first factor is the nature of the contracting process used to choose the manager. If there are many potential providers operating in an environment of no collusion, hard bargaining for any work, and an agency knowledgeable about all that the work entails, it is possible to envision structuring a management contract highly favorable for the agency. When there is only a handful of professionally interconnected providers with the relevant expertise and the agency is disadvantaged by a lack of relevant internal know-how, the agreement is likely to be more advantageous for the winning provider.

Regardless of the level of competition in the contracting process, once the deal is signed, its success depends critically on the second and third factors: the technological constraints of the work itself and the interpersonal skills of the agency personnel and contractor personnel. Wastewater treatment, for instance, is inherently a monopolistic operation. Because a wastewater treatment plant represents an enormous fixed capital investment, it is most economical to construct a single plant large enough to serve an entire community. A municipality does not build lots of small plants. Since sewer hookups are fixed and rigid, even if there were lots of small plants it would be prohibitively expensive for customers to deliver their wastewater to competitive providers for small price incentives. Once an operator is in place, the learning curve is such that the transaction costs, both financial and in service quality, of frequently changing management effectively reduce outside competition to a theoretical possibility. In practical terms, it would take severe mismanagement to compel the public agency to switch operators once the contract is in place.

Finally, the ultimate success or failure of the arrangement depends in no small measure on the quality of the long-term relationship that develops between the contractor and the public agency. The noncompetitive nature of wastewater treatment means that replacement of the public plant operator with a private one effectively equals the choice of a monopolist with whom the community will coexist for the long haul. No one can foretell the future, and no contract can take every contingency into account. Thus, the dollar amount of a contractor's initial bid may matter less than the contractor's reputation for honest dealing and technical expertise. Although price competition becomes a minor factor in the wastewater treatment decision, this does not necessarily mean that the local government is making a mistake by converting from public to private operation. It does mean that the long-term decision implicit in privatization must be made on a far more complex basis than a belief in the beneficence of competitive markets.

Organizations and Markets

Fundamental to the rationale for privatization is the belief that external competition either reforms the internal workings of public agencies to make them as efficient as possible or puts them out of business. The catalytic agent in this theory of organizational change is external competition. The power of competition lies in its ability to threaten the jobs of public employees. Absent the threat, according to the theory, public employees have no incentive to produce as efficiently as possible. Indeed, if anything, incentives work the other way around. Public employees are typically remunerated in terms of the length of time they work, not the extent of their accomplishments during that time. Although there is certainly a powerful element of truth in the notion that the threat of losing one's job may commit one to work as efficiently as possible, it does not comprise a satisfactory theory of organizational change; it is a theory of individual behavior. Regardless how diligently and efficiently any individual works, his or her ability to enhance organizational productivity is constrained by the institutional arrangements under which their agency functions. A fuller theory of organizational change is needed.

The standard market model, which is the basis for this individualized theory of organizational change, in fact has no inherent theory of organizational behavior. The standard market model is a powerful theory about the operation of a decentralized system of resource allocation but has nothing to say about the operation of organizations (Demsetz 1993). The firm, to the extent that it is considered at all in economics textbooks, is essentially a proxy for an individual entrepreneur who is assumed to manage the firm's resources to maximize profits. Neoclassical economic theory provides no rationale for any organizational size larger than a single individual. It is the ultimate contract society. In the world as articulated by the theory, we all should be contracting with each other for everything we need—but we don't. Instead, we work in firms, public agencies and not-for-profit businesses. We are members of families, clubs, religious groups, and other voluntary organizations. In all these roles, we act not in response to contracts and market prices but in ways determined by other more complex social pressures. The market is such a circumscribed institution because, contrary to the assumptions of the standard market model, it is not cost-free to use. Because there is a cost in terms of time and money to get relevant information to use the market well, it is often more efficient to use organizational bureaucracies and hierarchies to get things done. In fact, the theory of the firm as it has evolved in contemporary economics is at odds with the standard market model. It argues that firms exist because the costs of using contracts and markets, called transaction costs, often exceed the bureaucratic costs of maintaining an organization (Coase 1937).

Organizations respond to incentives in more complex ways than do individuals because organizations must respond to multiple agendas both from within and outside the organization (Hirschman 1970). They accumulate and process larger amounts of information than any one individual could assimilate (Arrow 1974). To evaluate the role of contracts in providing public services, we thus need a more sophisticated understanding of organizational behavior than the one provided by the standard market model.

The "Make-Buy" Decision

When is it less expensive to expand the size of an organization to accomplish tasks necessary for a firm's mission? When is it more economical to purchase needed goods or services from outside vendors? Together these questions comprise the essence of what is known as the "make-buy" decision. From an organizational perspective, when are the internal bureaucratic costs that accompany larger size less than the external transaction costs of using the market?

The wrenching tragedy of the explosion and crash of a ValuJet flight in the Florida Everglades in 1996 transformed a mundane organizational make-buy determination into front-page news. In its drive to establish itself as a low-price and low-cost air carrier, ValuJet relied heavily on a strategy of outsourcing as much as possible of its operation in order to avoid high fixed overhead costs. Aircraft maintenance, an expensive part of daily operation and a task vital to the organizational mission of the airline, was outsourced. The Federal Aviation Agency (FAA) determined that the explosion of spent oxygen generators that were improperly stored in the cargo hold by the aircraft maintenance contractor, Sabretech, caused the crash. The FAA has since imposed new rules that explicitly prohibit such shipments in the future. However, even before these explicit rules were effected, the shipment of such generators, long classified as hazardous materials, in the enclosed cargo holds of aircraft was well known to be potentially dangerous. The generators are the property of the airline, not the contractor. Consequently, contractors are eager to return such hazardous materials to the rightful owner as quickly as possible, which is apparently the situation that predicated that fateful day. In the day-to-day rush of activity between ValuJet and Sabretech, the remote risk posed by the shipping decision seemed less important than other tasks. As a result, no one appeared to be in a position to clearly stop the loading of these generators into the cargo hold of the plane. Each party blamed the other for the mix-up as the heirs of the crash victims wended their way through legal proceedings to collect liability damages. In May 1998, the Federal Aviation Administration levied a record fine of $2.25 million against Sabretech.[1] In the fall of 1999, the justice department charged Sabretech and several of its employees with criminal negligence.

It is not my wish to second-guess this tragedy, but the experience does starkly point out the full range of transaction costs that properly should be considered in the use of contracting for such a day-in and day-out type of service. The crash may have been avoided if ValuJet had invested significantly more personnel resources in supervising its maintenance contractor's activity in greater detail. Or ValuJet simply may have avoided the entire problem of such transaction costs by establishing in-house maintenance. But either decision would have been more costly and diametrically opposed to the company's business plan for maintaining low overhead in order to maintain low prices. In the aftermath of the crash, ValuJet decided to switch to in-house maintenance balanced by some outsourcing, which is more typical in the commercial airline industry.

---

[1]Sabretech Inc., was found guilty of improperly handling the oxygen generators that caused a ValuJet DC-9 to crash nearly three years ago, killing all 110 people on board. Sabretech delivered the oxygen generators to a ValuJet ramp agent, who put them on a plane bound from Miami to Atlanta. The generators activated after takeoff, resulting in a fire that caused the plane to crash on May 11, 1996 (Braggs 1999).

Whether this is a more fully costed decision in terms of the full risks that the company bears or merely a public relations ploy is difficult to know from the outside. The larger issue here is the range of tangible and intangible but potentially real costs involved in make-buy decisions. Different firms in the same industry may come to very different decisions depending on their business plans, market position, and resource base. Such decisions do not lend themselves to simple formulaic rule making. Privatization decisions, if driven by management concerns and not ideology, are essentially just a class of make-buy decisions. As such, they too need similar detailed analyses.

When an organization decides to buy rather than make a product, it must go shopping in either a spot market or a contract market. Spot markets are analogous to "buying off the rack," and contract markets are similar to custom tailoring. Spot markets are typically used to acquire products such as office supplies and motor vehicles, which come in sufficiently standardized forms that commercial vendors routinely maintain inventories that are virtually impossible for the firms to make for themselves. However, some long-term services that organizations can readily perform themselves also fit in this spot market category. A business may prepare its payroll internally in its own bookkeeping office or hire an outside payroll service. A periodical publisher may process its own subscriptions and mail its own journals or hire an outside fulfillment company.

When the choice is between spot purchases of standardized products or internal production, the decision rule is essentially a matter of comparative direct production cost analysis. The organization must compare its internal production costs with the cost of purchase. The transaction costs are virtually zero as a result of the standard units in which the product is traded and used. Learning the price often entails little more than two or three phone calls. Typically, goods available in spot markets are sold in competitive environments. Product quality is usually obvious to all buyers and sellers. Competition ensures that retail prices hover just above the level of wholesale prices and that average quality suits the taste of average buyers.

Such simplicity is not the rule when the make-buy decision involves contracting for ongoing specialized services. The choice of sellers is more limited, and both product quality and the relation of contract price with underlying costs are governed more vaguely by market competition. Consequently, decisions to contract out usually involve complex transaction costs related to the specification of product, the negotiation of prices, the close monitoring of quality, and the need to anticipate unforeseen contingencies. In such cases, the managerial decision process involves analyzing not only the comparative production costs typical of spot markets but also the transactions costs associated with contract design and monitoring. In such situations, obtaining all the relevant information can be difficult or require considerable time and money.

Much of the privatization debate in the political sphere ignores such costly transactional complexity. The contracting process is treated as a trivial modification in essentially a spot market. All one need do is announce the availability of the contract through a request for proposals, or RFP, specify the relevant contract contingencies and terms to all the potential bidders, and allow the bidders to set the price competitively. Typically, the lowest bid wins. When the process is that simple and straightforward, contracting for the long term is identical with spot market purchasing. But when contracts are sought for less-standardized outputs with less readily discernible quality and under conditions of greater uncertainty, a more complex managerial calculus is needed. That is typically the case with privatization.

It is also important to remember that privatization via contracting relies heavily on the belief that most contracts can be almost self-enforcing. Yet, the necessity for a written contract arises because each party of a transaction fears that the other party or parties may fail to deliver or perform. Thus, contracts contain descriptions of the future behavioral obligations of all parties to the extent that such behavior can be anticipated and the sanctions to be imposed if any party fails to hold up its end of the bargain. Such future-oriented obligations, created in an atmosphere of uncertainty, place parties in a far different relationship with each other than the cut-and-dried transactions of either the spot market or the idealized contract market cum spot market envisioned by privatization advocates. The extent of this divergence of market types is critical in determining the comparative efficiency of the privatization option.

2

What Is the Public Buying?
Identifying the Contracted Public Good

Apples, Oranges, and Postal Delivery

Morningside Heights is home to several of the most important educational and religious institutions in New York as well as a major hospital complex. Not surprisingly, the density of people and activities generates a large volume of mail and package traffic, which is why the U.S. Postal Service (USPS) maintained a substation at the corner of West 115th Street and Amsterdam Avenue, catty-corner to one of the two main gates to the Columbia University campus where I teach. With the exception of a few post office boxes, no mail was delivered from this substation. Its primary mission was to process the outgoing letters and packages for the neighborhood. It was packed with customers from the moment it opened at 9 A.M. until it shut its doors at 5 P.M. Indeed, to get a jump on the daily rush, some customers began queuing up outside as early as 8:45 A.M.

All day, a long and unrelenting line of customers waited for the next available clerk. Although there were five window stations, other postal duties and occasional breaks meant that four—but usually only three—windows were staffed at any one time. Around midday, when most of the local employees and students were on lunch break, demand expanded but supply contracted because postal clerks are entitled to lunch just like everybody else. Thus during the busiest time of the day, the post office often operated with just two windows open for business. Even though the clerks on window duty worked diligently and efficiently, visiting this facility was generally frustrating and time-absorbing. Conducting a two-minute transaction typically required a wait in line of fifteen minutes to a half hour.

On the other side of the Columbia campus, on West 116th Street, just across from the Broadway gate, is an office of the privately owned Federal Express package delivery service. Like the publicly owned postal service substation, this is a parcel and letter intake facility. One or two clerks routinely staff its counter. The wait for service is seldom more than three to five minutes. Usually, customers can walk up to an available clerk immediately after filling out the necessary forms. Payment is promptly accepted by charging a company account or credit card, but there are no cash transactions. The dramatic difference in the speed of service between the two establishments is not lost on most patrons. The curtness of the harried but better compensated postal clerks is no match for the more relaxed demeanor of the FedEx employees.

Undoubtedly every reader could provide a similar example of a public service contrasting poorly with a private one. The most common horror story is that of a state Department of Motor Vehicles office, where a hapless applicant waits for untold hours in line A only to be informed by an unsympathetic clerk that she or he must move to the end of even longer line B. American folk wisdom holds that by and large, public service is uncaring, unbending, bureaucratic, and expensive, whereas competitively supplied private services such as FedEx are efficient and responsive.

If we are to weigh the true costs and benefits of exchanging public for private service, fact, not folk wisdom, must tip the scales one way or the other.

The post office in the small town of Ghent, New York, where I lived for several years, was a small, one-story, white, wood-frame building, perhaps a total of 900 square feet. At the edge of a rutted and unpaved parking lot, it was a full-service post office. The employees not only collected mail and packages but also delivered them to the entire town through post-office boxes and rural delivery routes. Three of the eight employees worked full-time in that cramped facility sorting mail, selling stamps and money orders, receiving packages, and handling all the other transactions undertaken by the USPS. Although there was only one service window, the wait was never more than two or three minutes, if there was one at all.

The service was high quality. Virtually everyone was greeted by name. Once I mailed a letter without a stamp. The postmaster added the necessary postage and left a note in my box asking me for the additional few cents the next time I came in. Whenever an Express Mail parcel (the overnight delivery service provided by the USPS) arrived for me, I received a call asking whether I would be stopping by or would like someone to run it up to my house, about four miles outside town. Every weekday, the building shut down from noon to 1 P.M. so all the employees could go to lunch. Ghent residents knew that they had to transact their business before noon or after one.

Everyone in town was more than happy with this post office. It was a vital civic center. The local food pantry collected goods there to feed the hungry. Every important community announcement was posted outside the building. When I inadvertently locked my keys in my car, the postmaster loaned me his car to go home and retrieve a spare set. The USPS in Ghent, New York, is a model for a responsive public service that functions as well as, if not better than, FedEx.

Some may argue that the Ghent post office is an inefficient, overstaffed facility. Poor service in locales such as Morningside Heights subsidizes good service in the "Ghents" of the United States. But, there was no place to hide from public view in the small white building, and no one ever appeared to be sitting around and doing nothing. Thus, an equally strong argument could be made that the Ghent post office represents adequate staffing rather than overstaffing.

It is also important to remember that FedEx provides a highly specialized service efficiently and responsively but with a high price tag. It is exclusively a high-quality package-delivery service. The least expensive service offered by FedEx—three-day guaranteed and tracked delivery of a letter—costs between $9.45 and $12.75, depending on distance to the destination. The USPS will deliver a first-class letter anywhere in the United States for a flat fee of 33 cents. The letter is neither guaranteed nor tracked but, nine times out of ten, it arrives at its destination within the same three-day period.

FedEx is not a public service. The USPS is. The primary corporate mission of FedEx is to serve the best interests of its shareholders. The management of FedEx believes that a market composed of business firms and affluent creditworthy individuals is the best way to achieve that goal. The USPS has an overriding public mission to provide low-cost mass-based letter and parcel delivery services to all U.S. residents. To that end, it offers a broad menu of delivery options and ancillary public services such as money orders and passport applications. These wide-ranging services, including certified mail and priority mail, do not necessarily cover the full cost of providing them, let alone make a profit. On the other hand, taken together, the public services that the USPS delivers throughout the United States are highly valued for both their direct and indirect benefits. Although first-class mail, the centerpiece of the USPS, is no match for the signature next-day delivery service provided by FedEx, it is generally an adequate and low-cost vehicle for many of the nation's important communication needs. Although the goals of profit maximization and mass-based services are not inherently incompatible, they also are not inherently compatible. Although the USPS is similar to a profit-making firm in that it has a marketable product and is required by law to cover its costs through user fees, its management decision calculus is not the same as that governed by the need to provide only profitable services capable of adding value to share prices.

Given these service and motivational complexities, it is impossible to draw simple conclusions about the relative efficiency and effectiveness of public versus private letter and package delivery services. The USPS and FedEx are apples and oranges. As we examine the comparative efficiency of private versus publicly provided services, we must be careful to fully describe the service or product in question. It is here, at the very beginning, that contracting out often falters, at the initial and obvious stage of defining the public good or service to be privatized.

Is It a Matter of the Public Supply of Private Goods or the Private Supply of Public Goods?

Why are some services supplied publicly and others privately? The answer is one part historic (we have always done it that way), one part political (special interests do not allow change), and one part economic. Some services can be adequately supplied only through public action. Markets will undersupply or not supply them at all. To appreciate the privatization potential of public services, the relative factors that shape supply decisions need to be conceptually clear.

From an economic point of view, there are three categories in which all goods and services can be placed: private, public, and publicly provided. The private category contains the vast majority of products that we encounter every day. Economists distinguish these private goods on the basis of two characteristics: excludability and "rivalrousness." The access and use of excludable goods are relatively easy to control. For example, a theater ticket designated for a specific performance is an excludable good. When I wear my shoes, everyone else is excluded from using them.

Indeed, even when I take them off, I retain sufficient control of them to keep anyone from using them—except, of course, my younger daughter who occasionally sneaks them out of the closet and delights in clopping around the house in them! The second characteristic of private goods is their rivalrous consumptive quality. If I eat a bowl of soup, no one else can. If I purchase a ticket and then sit in my seat and watch the show, no one else can sit in that particular seat at that time. Essentially these two characteristics make these goods easily amenable to private market supply. There is virtually no rationale or need for public intervention to stimulate the supply of the large panoply of goods and services that define our daily lives. These goods, by and large, strongly exhibit these ordinary characteristics. Private markets do a good job of adjusting the supply of them to the amounts demanded by consumers.

At the other end of the spectrum are goods and services that possess little or none of one or both of these two characteristics. These products could be called "pure" public goods. There are very few of them, and their use is strongly nonexcludable and nonrivalrous. A classic textbook example is a lighthouse that warns ships away from dangerous coastal rocks. It would be very difficult, if not impossible, to find a private supplier for this highly valued service. Because the light is available for all to see, it is not possible to exclude "free riders" from navigating the dangerous shoals with the help of the light. Moreover, even as the light guides them, its consumption or use is virtually always nonrivalrous. Unless the shipping channel becomes as congested as a Los Angeles freeway at rush hour, use by some does not preclude use by others. Although it is possible to conceive of ways in which private supply might work (Coase 1960), the transaction costs of creating sufficient exclusion to ensure the feasibility of a private supply and absence of free riders are higher than the costs of direct public provision for all maritime users. A pertinent contemporary example is national defense. Everyone in the nation presumably benefits from the existence of powerful armed services. But no one would have any incentive to individually purchase that expensive product. Through collective nonmarket action, we create the good, in this case defense.

In the middle is the (larger) group of publicly provided goods, which is more often the principal focus of the inquiry into privatization than is the smaller class of pure public goods. Publicly provided goods are often sufficiently excludable and rivalrous so that they are almost always provided to some degree by private markets (e.g., USPS and FedEx). What then is the factor that moves such products from the category of private goods to that of publicly provided ones? These types of goods typically have a third characteristic: they generate externalities. Mail service is provided publicly because the benefits of a good, low-priced, mass-based package and letter delivery system redound not only to its direct users but also to society at large in terms of the larger efficiency concerns of a market economy and the equity concerns of a democratic society. In terms of efficiency, a high-quality and low-cost delivery system lowers the general costs of the economy. To the extent that equality of opportunity is a vital social concern, access to inexpensive information and means of communication is essential. These indirect and unquantifiable but real impacts on society by the postal service are called external benefits.

There are also goods in which there are external costs distinct from benefits. A completely private system of automobile transportation for densely populated urban locations could be disastrous in terms of both degraded air quality and extensive street and road congestion. Consequently, publicly subsidized systems of public transportation typically are introduced as an alternative to mitigate these external costs. In general, when a product creates significant external benefits or costs, society (in the guise of government) intervenes to ensure that more of the beneficial goods are produced and that the goods responsible for negative impacts are produced less frequently or not at all.

Public intervention into the supply process becomes necessary because the impacts are external to the marketplace in which buyers and sellers engage one another. Consequently, these larger concerns do not play a role in their private market calculations. The amounts traded are sufficient to satisfy the private calculations of costs and benefits, regardless of whether they are excessive or inadequate from a social point of view. Hence, FedEx works well for its comparatively small target market segment. To induce this package deliverer to expand its volume to that of a mass-based carrier, public subsidies would be necessary. Alternatively, government can and does spend money directly to produce the mass-based alternative that generates vital external benefits. The degree to which society deems the externality of a good or service worthy of expanding or suppressing beyond the amount created by private activity is crucial for the political determination to transform it from a private to a publicly provided good.

There are many examples of goods that can be produced privately for a specific group of people but are so valued in terms of their external impacts that they are publicly provided to foster wider use. Primary and secondary education is the most obvious and salient example. Private schools for the small segment of the population that is able to pay the full cost of education do not contribute to national productivity and social equity in the same way as publicly provided education. City dwellers benefit greatly from the provision of publicly provided and subsidized transportation for both urban riders and suburban commuters. Public transportation helps to lessen air pollution and facilitates more rapid movement around our great metropolitan centers.

To say that a good is publicly provided is not the same as saying that it must be *directly* provided. It just means that for whatever political or civic reason, society has calculated that it values the external benefits of expanded consumption far more than the costs of producing the good in question. Especially when the good falls in that middle category between purely public and purely private, how the good is produced is not a simple matter. There are many valid answers to the question of how the good should be produced. In the next section, we explore the complexity of this issue.

Fire Protection: The Evolution of a Publicly Provided Good

Fire protection is popularly considered a typical public service. Eighty percent of the U.S. public receives its fire-protection services from full-time professional firefighters, almost all of whom work for the nation's municipalities as public employees. These full-time professionals comprise only about one-third of the nation's firefighters (United States Department of Commerce, Bureau of the Census 1992; National Fire Protection Association 1992). Most are volunteers working in the rural and suburban portions of the country. Although popularly considered as a pure public service, it is more accurately characterized as a publicly provided service. A very small number of municipalities even contract with profit-making firms for their publicly provided product. In addition to being publicly provided, fire protection, like private schooling, also exists as a private good. It is typically supplied to a handful of airports and private industrial sites, often by the same for-profit professional fire companies that provide the small amount of municipal service.

To understand the factors that delineate fire protection as a publicly provided good from fire protection as a private one, it is necessary to understand the nature of the product in relation to the places being served. Consider life in the United States as a spatial continuum that runs from sparse rural settlement to dense urban living. In a rural community where homes are far apart from each other, it is easy to conceive of fire protection as a purely private service. A homeowner averse to risk in such a community might enter into a contract with a private fire-protection firm, which agrees to respond immediately with a fully equipped professional fire-fighting team should the insured property catch fire. A more risk-tolerant resident might choose to forego such an expense and rely instead on the slower, voluntary response of community members who would need to be called away from other obligations. If the risk-tolerant neighbor's house burns to the ground, it is of little material consequence to the risk-sensitive household up the road.

As the proximate distance between structures decreases, as in suburbs and cities, the risk of fire caused by a spreading conflagration increases exponentially. The best protection for all under such circumstances is a quick response to every fire, regardless of location. Because of this external benefit, fire protection invariably is transformed from a private and frequently voluntary service to a publicly provided and compulsory good as settlement density increases. It is impossible to envision an urban society physically constructed on a spatial basis in which some buildings received fire protection but abutting structures did not. Indeed, the impetus for the establishment of municipal fire departments in the nineteenth century was the series of conflagrations that regularly burnt large swathes of U.S. cities to the ground. Who in the United States does not know the tale of Mrs. O'Leary's cow and the great Chicago fire?

As a publicly supplied good, fire protection is enjoyed equally by all. A fire on the property of a risk-tolerant individual brings the same response from firefighters as one at a location owned by a more risk-averse individual. I need my neighbor's house to be protected, regardless of his risk tolerance, to protect my home and my family. To discourage free riders—individuals who enjoy the benefits of around-the-clock professional fire protection but do not voluntarily pay their fair share of the costs—the services are financed through taxes. Of course, fire protection, even as a publicly provided good, does not need to be supplied by public employees. Private firms under contract to local government, rather than individual property owners, could provide it. We examine the merits of this alternative in Chapter 4.

The important point here is that by converting fire protection from a private to a publicly supplied service, aggregate consumption increases to a level where society as a whole enjoys broader external benefits than those of a strictly private service. In instances such as this, private markets fail to achieve sufficiently high levels of social benefits and we transform private goods into publicly provided ones. By collectively taxing ourselves and providing services such as these in amounts that exceed what we would individually purchase, we expand both individual and collective well-being beyond that created by private markets alone.

This helps to explain why we produce certain goods and services through public action rather than private markets, but it does not explain why we need to directly produce them publicly. To understand this, we must move from the rationale for publicly provided goods to the actual process of providing them. Many problems of privatized public services arise because the contracted commodity is either not clearly understood by the officials creating the contract or not easily delineated. Sometimes the make-buy decision is made with little understanding of the precise services contracted out by the government and even less knowledge of exactly how much it costs government to provide those services directly.

Haste Makes Waste on Massachusetts Highways

Ideally the decision to privatize a publicly provided service should turn on the comparative cost effectiveness of the contracting option. Comparative cost effectiveness is easy to define but actually difficult to measure because choosing the time span over which to consider costs and outputs and the cost items needed to analyze the alternatives requires making assumptions with less than complete information. These choices mean that there can be no formulaic objective analysis. All comparative cost models involve judgment and choice in their creation and use. We more fully consider the implications of this measurement problem in Chapter 3.

This problem is exacerbated when a public official who is also an advocate for privatization carries out the analysis. Elected officials who come to power motivated by a strong ideological policy agenda tend to discount pragmatic concerns about the existence of cost savings. They typically believe that history will vindicate them regardless of present difficulties. Since, as a practical matter, the bulk of public services fall into that large gray area of publicly supplied goods, there is often both public and private sector precedence for alternative models of service delivery. The experience with privatization to date indicates that the magnitude of actual overall cost difference between contracting out and direct service provision, regardless of the direction of the savings, is typically measured in single-digit percentages (Rehfuss 1989). With such slight cost differentials, choices can be and often are based on politics, not economics. In the bygone days of the welfare state, the dominant political presumption was to favor in-house supply. Contemporary logic is reversed: When in doubt, contract it out. This willingness to conflate ideology with economics—even at the margin where most action exists—effectively muddles the case for privatization as a way to improve public service through increased efficiency. To evaluate it in economic terms, we must first disentangle the two elements. Political and ideological preferences simply do not command as powerful and compelling a reform imperative as do choices grounded in a more solid and pragmatic economic analysis.

All these concerns surfaced when the Commonwealth of Massachusetts completely privatized its state highway maintenance program in selected regions. The maintenance of roads and streets is an unquestioned publicly provided service that historically has involved a great deal of public contracting. The decision of where the public providers (typically states and municipalities) should draw the line between direct public provision and the use of contracts has always been fluid. In all fifty states, the dominant supplier of highway maintenance is the state highway department. But, all fifty states also supplement this work in varying degrees with the help of outside contractors. Unlike the area of police protection, where exclusive direct public provision is an historic and strong tradition, it is far easier politically to expand contracting in this service area. Private firms can do much of the work, such as repairing potholes and mowing grass. Highway maintenance appears to pass what privatization proponents call the "yellow pages" test by being one of the categories of potential sellers found in local telephone directories. Such listings are considered to be substantive evidence that an external competitive market exists to supply the desired service. Monitoring contractor performance also appears to be visually straightforward: either the potholes are filled or they are not; either the grass has been mowed or it is too high.

Yet, when William Weld, a combative laissez-faire advocate, was elected governor of Massachusetts in November 1990 on a promise to establish "entrepreneurial government," highway maintenance was not high on the wish list initially compiled by his privatization task force. After considering the service, the task force concluded that road conditions among the state's maintenance districts vary widely and no reliable historic information existed about comparative performance standards for either the potential contractors or the highway department's own personnel. The task force also acknowledged that departmental personnel take considerable pride in their work, whereas private contractors are bound only by the terms of their contracts, possibly making their performance inconsistent and difficult to verify. In light of these comparative cost and performance difficulties, the task force sought to move on to more visible targets of opportunity (Harvard University, John F. Kennedy School of Government 1993).

Despite the difficulties and the task force's caution, highway maintenance moved to the top of the Weld administration's list because the big-ticket items that were more ideologically appealing, such as privatizing Logan Airport, were also more controversial and required legislative approval. What appears to have tipped the balance in favor of highway maintenance privatization was the plausible chance of success and, perhaps more importantly, the realization that it would never be a clear-cut failure. So long as contracted-out highway maintenance did not fail egregiously, it could not undercut Weld's more ambitious and wide-ranging, but politically riskier, privatization agenda.

Highway maintenance privatization began in 1992 in Massachusetts. In light of subsequent events, it appears that the governor's task force was prescient. The inability of the commonwealth's highway department, MassHighway, to describe accurately and fully the maintenance service to be subjected to privatization made it impossible to ever evaluate definitively its success or failure relative to the preexisting situation. Credible and voluminous evidence gathered after the fact suggests that the hasty implementation effort resulted in an inadequate delineation of the privatized work. This, in turn, made it impossible to know if the state made a wise decision in terms of cost or service quality. The state has probably been losing money but is suffering neither a cash hemorrhage nor sufficiently inadequate contracting to compel the state to reverse direction.

The initial highway maintenance privatization efforts were analyzed in a series of official reports or officially sponsored reports prepared by the Weld administration, the Office of the State Auditor (OSA), and the state legislature, called the General Court. Essex County, in the north-eastern section of the state, was chosen as a pilot region for what rapidly became a statewide effort. In July 1992, MassHighway released a Request for Proposals (RFP) for state highway maintenance in that county based on a proposed contract that, at first glance, appeared sufficiently extensive to address the complex issue of service definition. Covering all district services except snow and ice removal (85 percent of which had historically been contracted out to small local vendors) and first emergency response, the contract was noteworthy for its comprehensive approach. It envisioned a single contractor who would be responsible for the myriad of tasks that comprise highway maintenance in that area. These included the cleaning, repair, and maintenance of highways, bridges, signage, traffic control, and lighting systems; roadside mowing and tree trimming; and the operation of drawbridges. The RFP described in detail the repair methods, material specifications, quality standards, and safety precautions; stipulated limitations on the value of subcontracts; included provisions for minority employees and subcontractors; and required at least 80 hours of training for new operators of drawbridges because of lack of experience in the private market. Despite the wealth of detail in the contract, as it turned out, it still was not detailed enough.

MassHighway estimated that purchasing the comprehensive service package for Essex County should cost approximately $4.08 million—an estimate not disclosed to potential bidders. MassHighway arrived at that estimate by costing out each of the specific tasks on a per unit basis and then multiplying that cost by the number of units it needed for the duration of the contract. Thus, if it cost Z per linear mile to sweep the roads and the roads would, on average, be swept Y times during the contract, the estimated price for that service component would be $Z \times Y \times$ the number of linear miles of road. Although service items such as road cleaning and signage maintenance are sufficiently simple to allow many small firms to undertake the work, because the contract required the contractor to bundle a number of tasks, only large operators with access to a network of subcontractors could effectively bid the job. The market was limited further because tasks such as bridge washing were entirely unique to the public sector. Although the individual tasks were often straightforward, the need to schedule and supervise them made the contract more complex. In essence, the winning bidder was being asked to convert at least a portion of his or her business into a mini–highway department. Given this complexity, the firms that ultimately qualified to bid as prime contractors were drawn from the highway construction industry. They had expertise with heavy equipment and, more importantly, the experiential know-how of state highway contracting processes.

The complexity of the challenge illustrates why the yellow pages test is often misleading. When broken into individual tasks, the small maintenance firms listed in the yellow pages could, in fact, accomplish many of them. But the key element here was not contracting out singular tasks. It was seeking to contract out such a wide array of tasks that it was in effect contracting out the management of a public agency. Although the contractual language of the RFP appeared to be describing a bundle of predetermined tasks that the commonwealth sought to have accomplished, that was not the case. The state essentially desired to transfer both the administration and execution of highway maintenance from public to private hands. Small yellow-pages firms that could undertake highly specific tasks in an on-demand outsourcing situation were not capable of performing the complex management assignment implicit in the contractual bundling of all the tasks. As a result, the universe of effective participants in the actual bidding situation was small. Only the interconnected community of politically networked major highway construction contractors who already dominated highway construction contracting were able to submit credible bids. The Commonwealth of Massachusetts sought to have them provide some services that they already provided, but more importantly the commonwealth asked them to enter into an entirely new business, one found in no known yellow pages: public highway administration.

Because the commonwealth prequalified all bidders, MassHighway's bottom line was price, and ultimately it received six qualified bids. Not surprisingly, bids ranged widely, reflecting the high degree of uncertainty among the bidders about the actual work that this new business entailed. Submitted bids ranged from $3.7 million to $8.1 million, and MassHighway awarded the contract to the lowest bidder, the Middlesex Corporation of Chelmsford, Massachusetts. The contract went into effect in October 1992.

The winning firm, founded in 1972, is typical of the construction/highway maintenance firms that contract with state highway departments. It is a privately owned company that expanded from paving to heavy construction and asphalt manufacturing. At the time of the initial contract, the Middlesex Corporation employed about 350 nonunion workers. Public works projects accounted for most of its business, and the company held more than 30 public contracts, twelve of which were with MassHighway. Most of the other contracts were with the neighboring states New Hampshire and Connecticut (ibid., 40).

Five months later, the Weld administration abruptly announced that it was sufficiently pleased with the preliminary results in Essex County and intended to extend the privatization program immediately to the rest of the commonwealth. Because there had been no formal evaluation of the effort and given the governor's ideological predilections, the decision most likely reflected the Weld administration's eagerness to expand privatization as quickly as possible. Nothing untoward appeared to be occurring in the Essex County endeavor, so the risk of moving ahead appeared to be minimal.

The Weld administration quickly and continually proclaimed the initial effort to be an overwhelming success in terms of cost savings and enhanced work quality. That opinion was not shared widely by other knowledgeable parties. Two outside independent examinations that were completed in later years, one by the Audit and Oversight Bureau of the General Court (state legislature) and the other by the OSA, strongly challenged this conclusion.

In May 1994, the House Post Audit and Oversight Bureau released the *Interim Report Review of Essex County Privatization,* an exhaustive study of the first year of the Essex County privatization effort. The reported data came from a review of internal departmental documents, testimony from officials in charge of the operation, and an on-site audit of the contractor's performance. In addition, the bureau conducted interviews with outside highway maintenance experts "to ascertain from a technical standpoint the rationale for particular maintenance functions as well as the cost-benefit rationale for each of the items that could be identified as necessary highway maintenance" (Commonwealth of Massachusetts, House Post Audit and Oversight Bureau 1994, 8). Given the amount of public infrastructure at risk in terms of existing bridges and roads, the bureau was particularly concerned with those maintenance measures that most directly related to capital preservation strategies.

On a most basic level, the report indicated concern that privatization was never a pragmatic pilot project but rather the initial implementation of a predetermined strategy. Charles Kostro, Transportation Secretary James Kerasiotes' principal aide in this matter, testified that his boss told him to "make sure it works and you better do a good job" (ibid., 2). George Ward, the Essex County supervisor for the privatization, testified that he was given a similar instruction (ibid., 3). Although such comments may have been nothing more than innocuous pep talk to subordinates, it is also plausible, in light of Weld's ideological goals, to read this less benignly as a directive to make sure that problems were either explained away or concealed.

In more specific terms, the bureau report found problems in the areas of contract management and comparative costs. The management problems fell into three general categories: oversight, delegation, and actual performance. Oversight is a classic problem in public contracting: maintaining an arm's-length relationship between the contractor and the state employees charged with supervising the contractor's performance. The bureau found that George Ward had been, along with other MassHighway employees, an overnight guest of the Middlesex Corporation as part of its annual Christmas festivities at the Marriott Long Wharf, a high-priced Boston hotel. As noted in Chapter 1, it is always in the interests of the contractor to form an external amicable relationship with the agent designated by the state to supervise him or her. Although nothing that was presented impugned Mr. Ward's professional behavior, in light of his testimony that he was expected by his supervisors to make the relationship work, there is reason to be concerned about the impact of such actions upon the ostensible arm's-length relationship required for competitive public contracting. Incidents such as these rarely become public knowledge. For that reason, awareness about the existence of even one such situation is cause for concern.

More structurally, the terms of the contract itself made the nature of oversight vague. Typically, in a contract situation with wide-ranging tasks, principals seek to maintain tight control over the work process, including the sequencing and timing of tasks. But that comes at a price. It increases supervision costs for the state and coordination costs for the contractor. The less expensive alternative is to permit the contractor to set internal working priorities and judge the decisions and payments by the outcomes. The bureau found that this latter approach characterized the structure of contract oversight. Because MassHighway was apparently predisposed to privatization, that conclusion should not surprise us.

However, the bureau indicated several serious problems with this laissez-faire approach. First, the contractor was a large asphalt paving and construction company with many government contracts around

New England. Given all the demands on its personnel and equipment, how could the state ensure that the company would always be available on an as-needed basis in the district as specified in the contract? Given this inherent conflict between the needs of the state and the multiple interests of the company, permitting the contractor to set priorities left the state at a serious disadvantage. This dilemma is known in the contract literature as a principal–agent problem, which is discussed in greater detail in Chapter 4. This is a situation in which the interests of the principal (in this case the Commonwealth of Massachusetts) and the interests of the agent (in this case the Middlesex Corporation) can diverge. The interests of the principal are potentially compromised as the agent pursues its best interest. This contractual deficiency was of special concern to the bureau because one of its goals was to ascertain the degree to which the maintenance program was conserving the state's bridge and road capital. It is not difficult to envision situations in which the contractor deems certain work that fits with its complex contractual pressures to be a higher priority than other work that may most maximize the long-term value of the state's assets.

In their field and record audit of the program, the bureau uncovered several instances of problems caused by this hands-off approach to setting priorities. Litter should be collected before grass mowing commences. "The Bureau observed shredded litter all over the medians and roadways after grass cutting. The Bureau does not believe that the total number of mowings claimed by [MassHighway] were performed" (Commonwealth of Massachusetts, House Post Audit and Oversight Bureau 1994, 21). The contractor was permitted to defer road sweeping until the end of the contract. The contract also permitted the contractor to clean catch basins before sweeping. The net effect of this was to nullify the cleaning effort as the catch basins fill with debris from the sweeping (ibid., 14). More importantly, after inspecting 700 catch basins in the spring of 1993, the bureau concluded that there was "little evidence that they were cleaned in the recent past" (ibid., 14). MassHighway reported that by May 23, 1993, 95 percent of all drainage structures were cleaned. The bureau concluded, on the basis of its own photos and inspections, that the claim was inaccurate (ibid., 14).

To evaluate the comparative cost effectiveness of highway maintenance privatization, it is necessary to have a clear understanding of the relationship between capital costs and operating costs. The former, which consist of items such as construction of new lane mileage or major refurbishment of existing mileage, is typically the province of the capital budget. Maintenance represents operating cost and comprises the ongoing work of keeping the existing highway infrastructure in good and safe working order. A good maintenance program minimizes the need for capital spending to preserve existing infrastructure. Therefore, to properly determine the level of requisite maintenance work, a maintenance plan must address obvious immediate needs, such as snowplowing in the winter and pothole filling in the spring, and it must also involve service programs to prolong the life of the state's highway infrastructure.

Despite the obvious need for such comprehensive planning in the initial preparation of an outside contract, the bureau discovered that the Weld administration never systematically investigated the linkage and its cost implications. Instead, the Weld administration reduced the problem to a crude single-year cost comparison with the previous year. According to Mr. Kostro, they "took figures for FY '92 for personnel, overtime, police expenditures, contract work materials, administrative costs, a whole series of things we felt were the kind of functions that were covered under a maintenance operation, and we tallied up what the cost was of that and it came to about $6.6 million" (ibid., 9). The bureau's objections to this costing methodology can be summarized as four points (ibid., 10 and 11).

1. *Any single year is inherently idiosyncratic.* An appropriate cost comparison must span several years.
2. *There was a great deal of arbitrariness as to what was included or not included in the package of maintenance work.* Under the terms of the Essex County privatization effort, the bureau found that pothole filling is a contractual service, but crack sealing is excluded. In discussions with outside experts, the exclusion of this labor intensive but highly effective method of road surface preservation emerged as a serious omission. In past years, it had been part of the standard public maintenance package.
3. *There was a lack of backup information on the calculation of past cost as done by MassHighway.* As a result, the method described by Kostro was at best subjective and not replicable by the bureau's staff. There was no systematic cost identification method used to actually price the internal maintenance activity.[1] Items such as the value of contract supervision or the value of state-owned equipment provided to the contractor under the terms of the agreement were not even quantified.

[1]The defense of this lack by Kostro is that at the time of the privatization the necessary costing procedure was not required (Kostro 1994).

4. *To highlight the accomplishments of the contracted work, MassHighway understated the amount of actual maintenance accomplished by state workers prior to privatization.* MassHighway asserted that no bridge washings were done in the year before privatization. The bureau found that washings had been completed. More generally, MassHighway was unable to provide any documentation to substantiate what was actually done or not done in the previous year.

Lacking a substantial base of information on precisely what the task required and a systematic, consistent internal cost accounting system, it is impossible to know the actual cost of the state doing the necessary work in-house. Because of this lack of a comparative base, it is impossible to know what any savings claim really means. Is it truly lower cost or just less work? Perhaps less work even at higher cost? This problem became even more complex because of the structure of the contract itself. It is an open-ended document. Prices offered by the various bidders were not the final prices. Their prices were for doing the work as itemized in what was in effect a model contract. The nature of road maintenance work and weather conditions is such that more or less work could be required depending on actual conditions and administrative decision-making by the state. Because the state had the right to order less work than described by the model contract, the state always had the ability to keep the final cost below the offered price. The bureau concluded that any reduction in the actual contract cost represented expense deferrals, not cost savings (Commonwealth of Massachusetts, House Post Audit and Oversight Bureau 1994, 16).

The nature of the contract was such that the state could hide a great deal of cost as well as defer it. MassHighway retained a maintenance crew in the county for emergency responses and supervisory work. The terms of the contract were such that when the crew was not occupied with its own duties, it could use state equipment to perform tasks that the contractor was obligated to fulfill. The bureau was concerned that the value of the use of state employees and state equipment in carrying out contractual tasks was understated. The bureau observed state workers performing contracted chores such as grass cutting, litter pick up, and rest area maintenance. Mr. Kostro conceded the fact but asserted that the contractor was still doing 90 to 95 percent of the work (ibid., 16 and 17). However, after auditing the actual work hours for the state crew the bureau found that 1,988 out of 5,631 hours during their test period "were committed to work performed on functions that were supposed to be privatized" (ibid., 29). That amounts to 35 percent of their work. The bureau also uncovered evidence that the department was either understating the amount of time devoted to supervising the contract or undercounting the time. "The amount of time spent on contract supervision was 12.4%. The bureau believes that this figure should have been much higher if proper oversight was being performed" (ibid., 28). The bureau also found that the state was shifting maintenance costs, such as for carpenters, tree surgeons, and line painters, to the snow and ice account, an open-ended account that was not part of privatization. In all, 86 percent of overtime across all categories of work was charged to snow and ice removal (ibid., 30). The bureau believed that these costs were shifted to make the direct costs of privatization appear lower.

The bureau concluded that the contract as written failed to provide for regular and continuous district maintenance. Because of the political context in which it was fashioned, it provided incentives for both the state and the contractor to engage in deferred maintenance. For the state, the goal was to keep costs below the contract price. The flexibility of the arrangement permitted the contractor to perform the most profitable work, sometimes by deferring the most useful work. The bureau's on-site inspections revealed that even the supervision, which was supposed to be supplied by the state, was lax. Much of the work allegedly done was actually either not done or poorly done. State employees did much of the work that was actually done.

The problems caused by the imprecision of the allocation of tasks between state workers and the contractor and the problems with defining the nature of the work itself, which were identified by the Post Audit and Oversight Bureau's analysis, came into sharper financial focus when the state auditor attempted to verify the financial claims made by MassHighway for the Essex County Privatization. Using the methodology previously described by Charles Kostro, the state estimated that its FY'92 costs for privatization would have been $6.6 million. The state auditor calculated the cost at $4.1 million. The difference of $2.5 million represents a discrepancy of almost 40 percent. The major difference between the auditor's preprivatization cost calculation and MassHighway's estimate is salaries. MassHighway estimated that it spent $5.2 million on personnel costs. It derived this estimate by taking base salaries for one week in December 1991 and multiplying that by 52 weeks. That amount was then increased by 25 percent to account for fringe benefits. As with the Post Audit and Oversight Bureau, MassHighway was unable to supply the list of the employees and base salaries used to derive their estimate to the

Table 1. Comparative Analysis of In-House and Privatized Costs of Essex County Highway Management

Cost Item	In-House Cost	Privatization Cost	Difference
Salaries	$2,920,467	$1,078,524	$1,841,943
Overtime	266,705	150,000	116,705
Police	200,000	210,000	(10,000)
Materials	24,975	6,000	18,975
Vehicle maintenance	91,520	26,415	65,105
Administrative costs	257,700	183,925	73,775
Contract costs	419,709	3,687,158	(3,267,449)
Contingency	—	250,000	(250,000)
Subtotal	$4,181,076	$5,592,022	$(1,410,946)
Equipment savings	—	255,000	255,000
Total costs	$4,181,076	$5,337,022	$(1,155,946)

Source: Data from State Auditor's Report on the Privatization of the Maintenance of State Roads in Essex County October 7, 1992, to October 6, 1993, Report No. 93-5015-3, July 19, 1995.

state auditor. The state auditor calculated the salary cost by taking the actual salaries paid in calendar year 1991 as reported to the Internal Revenue Service on W-2 forms, increasing them by the state's official fringe rate for the year, 33 percent, and then subtracting the proportion of salary costs used for tasks that were not privatized. The state auditor found, on the basis of departmental time sheets, that those hours represented just over 32 percent of the total hours worked in Essex County. Similarly, the overtime estimate was reduced by the proportion of overtime spent on duties not privatized. The vehicle maintenance costs were reduced to reflect the portion related to snow and ice removal, a non-privatized function.

The state auditor then adjusted MassHighway's estimate of the costs of privatization from $5.8 million to $5.6 million to account for the overestimation by the department of the actual costs of the remaining 31 employees in the district. With those adjustments, the state auditor was able to compare the costs of in-house production with the costs of privatization. These results are presented in Table 1.

The state auditor estimated that the department actually *lost* approximately $1.4 million as a result of privatization before an adjustment for equipment savings; that amount was reduced to $1.1 million after adjustment.

If allowed to stand, these findings by the state agency charged with independently auditing all the financial activities of the state are a powerful indictment of the privatization effort. Hence, the Weld administration retained the management-consulting firm of Coopers and Lybrand

Table 2. Comparison of Pre-Privatization (FY '92) Versus Privatization (10/92–10/93)

Direct Costs	Pre-Privatization	Privatization 10/92–10/93	Savings	% Cost Difference
Personnel	$5,581,738	$1,552,191	$4,029,546	−72.2%
Materials	24,974	0	24,974	−100.00%
Contract service	419,709	2,605,719	(2,186,010)	520.8%
Other direct costs	1,135,808	545,204	590,604	−52.0%
Total	$7,162,229	$4,703,114	$2,459,114	−34.3%

Source: Data from Coopers & Lybrand, "Independent Assessment of Massachusetts Highway Maintenance Privatization Program," prepared for the Executive Office of Transportation and Construction, June 1996.

Table 3. Comparison of Coopers & Lybrand's Post-Privatization Costs with Those of the Office of the State Auditor

Direct Costs	C & L	OSA	Difference
Personnel	$1,552,191	$1,228,524	$(323,667)
Materials	0	6,000	6,000
Contract service	2,605,719	3,687,158	1,081,439
Other direct costs	545,204	670,340	125,136
Total	$4,703,114	$5,592,022	$888,908

Source: Data from Coopers & Lybrand, "Independent Assessment of Massachusetts Highway Maintenance Privatization Program," prepared for the Executive Office of Transportation and Construction, June 1996, and State Auditor's Report on the Privatization of the Maintenance of State Roads in Essex County October 7, 1992, to October 6, 1993, Report No. 93-5015-3, July 19, 1995.

to reanalyze the data on the Essex County privatization. Coopers and Lybrand concluded that the state not only did not lose money on the privatization, but also actually saved $2.5 million. Table 2 summarizes their analysis.

The major difference between the two estimates is in the area of personnel costs. Within the area of other direct services, differences pertain to the calculation of the value of closed facilities, which Coopers and Lybrand set at $475,164. Table 3 compares the postprivatization cost analyses of Coopers and Lybrand and the OSA.

The major discrepancy in postprivatization costs relates to the cost of the contracted services. The state auditor used the original estimated price; Coopers and Lybrand used the actual expenditures.

The discrepancy about the cost of personnel will never be resolved to everyone's satisfaction. There are two areas of contention: the size of the preprivatization workforce and the allocation of personnel to tasks covered by privatization. In a rejoinder letter to Secretary Kerasiotes regarding the Coopers and Lybrand review, State Auditor Joseph DeNucci pointed out that MassHighway provided their consultant with an additional 44 names of employees "who were not originally considered by the highway department as preprivatization costs or part of the scope of the privatization contract at the time of our audit" (DeNucci 1996). The state auditor estimated the value of these additional workers at around $1 million. In addition, the Coopers and Lybrand study never adjusted its personnel costs to reflect the actual jobs done by the employees in relation to the work to be done by the private contractor. Given the loose interpretation of the shifting of tasks between contractor and state workers by MassHighway, this, too, is an area of unresolved contention.

Conversely, it is clear that the contract did come in at a final cost that was $1 million less than the initial estimate used by the state auditor in his report. Hence, on a cash basis true loss is invisible because the approximate loss of $1 million found by the auditor is effectively offset by the lower final price on the contract. However, what this means in terms of the cost of the services actually rendered is unclear. It should be remembered that MassHighway originally priced the work at about $4 million. The low bid was $3.7 million. If the final price was $2.6 million then, as the House Post Audit Bureau found, any saving is essentially the result of diminished quantity and/or quality of the service delivered. Hence, any comparison of the state auditor's data and the Coopers and Lybrand analysis has no value; the two organizations analyzed different outputs.

The ongoing problem with highway maintenance results from the lack of ground rules established prior to the privatization that delineated the nature of the service. Therefore, there is no way of ever knowing whether or not privatization added value for the citizens of the commonwealth. However, as long as MassHighway can limit costs by not purchasing all the services included in its budget, the problem will remain hidden in the financial data. Undermaintenance problems will become apparent only if there is a major mishap. Even if the resultant, implied deferred maintenance hastens the deterioration of roads and bridges, it did not occur on Weld's watch and is hard to trace back to him.

The state is now divided into fourteen highway maintenance districts, and the work is evenly divided among state workers and private contractors. The unions representing the remaining state workers believe that they have proven that they provide a better product at lower

Table 4. Comparison of Union Bids with Lowest Contractor Bids, Massachusetts Highway Maintenance, June 1996

District	Union Offer	Lowest Contractor	Difference
2A	$1,420,480	$2,132,970	50%
2B	1,420,480	2,009,769	41%
3A	1,360,480	2,059,300	51%
3B	1,400,480	1,515,575	8%
3C	1,375,480	1,617,290	18%
4A	1,743,500	1,961,339	–11%
4B	3,174,720	3,527,164	11%
4C	3,211,800	4,118,646	28%
4D	4,836,880	5,169,442	7%
5A	3,224,366	2,174,350	–33%
5B	4,250,880	3,858,008	–9%
5C	2,040,104	1,968,758	–3%
Total	$29,459,650	$32,112,611	9%

Source: Data from Local 285, SEIU.

cost (Local 285, SEIU 1995). The Weld administration continued to aggressively deny the claim (Kostro 1995). Given the inherently vague nature of much of the work, the lack of strong contract supervision, the use of state workers to perform work for the private contractors, and the department's ability to permit the deferral of maintenance, it is impossible to know the truth of what the union claimed in a timely manner. Certainly, the results of the Essex County experience indicate that there is a strong likelihood that the state is losing money, however slightly. Further evidence for this conclusion may be gleaned from a comparison of union bids with the lowest outside bids in the 1996 round of bidding. The state asked unions to submit their bids for doing the work when it lets a new round of contracts. The unions complied because their only other option was to lose the work entirely.[2] Table 4 compares these bids for the work in the twelve maintenance districts then up for bid.

[2]Although it might appear that permitting the unions to bid against outside contractors is a progressive step in the direction of healthy competition, that is misleading. There are two problems. The issue is not one of unions versus outside contractors but of existing agency staff, including middle management versus outside contractors. As we will see in Chapter 7, when a positive program of employee cooperation is established, it can lead to meaningful savings in a cooperative environment. In Massachusetts, the ideological coloration of the state officials makes this an adversarial process. The second problem is that as the union loses bids, it loses workers so that over time this so-called competition is really a shell game that hides the larger intention to eventually convert the entire operation to contract work with private providers.

The unions were the lowest bidders in nine of the twelve districts. Union bids were on average 9 percent less than those of the outside bidders. In absolute terms, the difference between bids is $2.6 million, a sufficiently large amount that suggests privatization is the endpoint for the administration, not efficient service. These numbers make a strong suggestive case that a far more innovative labor–management cooperation program could be put into place that would save significant amounts of money for the state but would not be privatization. The Weld administration continued to approach such possibilities with great diffidence. To the extent that the present (Cellucci) administration is committed to the ideological policies of its predecessor (Weld), the future is one in which the department will be nothing more than a contract manager for a group of politically connected suppliers who from time to time change places. However, because of the powerful negative political reaction to such a sudden overt move, the goal of both the Weld and Cellucci administrations appears to be one of gradual phase-in.

Although correspondence from the state to the unions in the closing days of the Weld administration continued to vaguely refer to maintaining "the partnership that has been established between labor and management," it also warns that "we will no longer be able to provide the 'slack' we have given the union workers" (Kostro 1995). By 1996, there was no longer any pretense on either side that the goal was about working toward improvement of the quality of public-sector work. Instead, the unions were resigned to the fact that they would almost automatically be given half the work, regardless of the merits of all their bids; the other half would be contracted out. But, this was always seen as a stop-gap measure. The unions and Secretary Kerasiotes both knew it was all a waiting game because the remaining workers were aging. Although some new equipment had been purchased, the state did not intend to remain in the highway maintenance business. Indeed, Kerasiotes said as much.

> The unions must also recognize that hiring new employees and purchasing large quantities of new equipment are not realistic under the present fiscal circumstances, *circumstances that are not likely to change in the foreseeable future.* If the present trends continue, over time and through attrition the unions are going to find their employees replaced by private contractors. Making their workers competitive with private contractors will, at the very least, slow this trend. (n.d., 114; emphasis added)

The strongest carrot the secretary seemed willing to hold out was that employee acquiescence in this waiting game would buy them a slower rate of downsizing.

Conclusions

Successful public contracting requires three preconditions. First, the service to be contracted must be carefully specified. Only within the context of service specification can a contract for actual work be developed. Because publicly supplied goods are often generated because of their external as well as direct benefits, both qualities must be evaluated in relation to production choices. Many seemingly straightforward public services are, in fact, more subtly complex in terms of outcomes. The importance of this precondition is often far easier to state than fulfill. In the case of the USPS, despite the many calls for its privatization and the obvious competition from private package-delivery services, no profit-maximizing firm would step in to take over the broad range of publicly supplied services that this self-financing public agency provides to all Americans. If its full range of services was carefully delineated, how many independent contractors around the country (after all, we would not want to create a new private monopoly) could provide them at a lower price? None, in all likelihood, and that is perhaps the main reason privatizing the postal service has never become a mainstream issue despite the current popularity of laissez-faire economic ideas in contemporary political discourse.

It is important to conduct a thorough preprivatization cost accounting of the work to be contracted out. Regardless of whether the privatization of highway maintenance in Massachusetts was a political success for the Weld administration—for all anyone knows, it may have been an economic failure—economic success was the principal rationale for undertaking it in the first place. The decision to privatize a public service should not be based on ideological considerations but rather on economic merits. The danger of such decision-making is the loss of the opportunity to integrate contracting into public production as an effective tool in our collective approach to improve public-sector performance.

Many of the highway-maintenance tasks that comprised the contract were actually easy to contract and supervise in isolation from one another. But, the privatization contract was not for the isolated delivery of individual services, it was for the coordinated and comprehensive delivery of them all. More importantly, although they were isolated acts, they were not easy to separate and render in isolation from one another. Sequencing significantly affects their value. If catch basins are cleaned before leaves are cleared or grass mowed before litter is collected, improper sequencing creates a significantly degraded service. Yet, under the terms of the originally written contract, it was possible for the contractor to assert that the terms had been fulfilled. This highlights the importance of careful service delineation. In this case, the real added value sought by the public agency derived not from the completion of the most obvious tasks but rather was created through the effective management and coordination of many tasks. Thus, organizational ability was effectively the product purchased by the Commonwealth of Massachusetts, not—as the state officials believed—a straightforward bundle of singular tasks. Because the theory that motivated their rush to the market does not account for organizational response, these officials were in a sense caught flat-footed by the management and coordination problems ultimately uncovered by outside evaluators.

Finally, the Massachusetts highway-maintenance experience illustrates one other important lesson: history matters. If governments have been providing a service for a long time, outsiders rarely have the knowledge or expertise to do the job done by the public agency. It is, therefore, not surprising that government agencies have a difficult time finding or organizing qualified bidders. Even when private firms provide similar services, they may not have the expertise to operate at the scale or with the scope of service required by the government. Moreover, public agencies are often repositories of valuable expertise gathered over the years that we essentially risk discarding in the name of innovation. Consequently, the experiential advantages of reorganizing government work should be compared with the additional "learning-curve costs" of hiring inexperienced outsiders. It might well be the case that if we were starting from scratch, a strong conceptual case could be made that contracting is superior to direct production. But, real life never starts from scratch. Whenever we seek to reform a public agency, we inherit a complex organizational history, for better and worse. Discarding it without considering reform can be a costly choice. Indeed, as the comparison between the bid prices of outside contractors and public employees in Massachusetts suggests, differentials can be sizable.

Fulfilling these preconditions in the most dispassionate of reform efforts is difficult enough. In the case of Massachusetts, where the political leadership was not ideologically disposed to consider such subtlety, the problem was worse. Unfortunately, former governor Weld is not alone in this regard. He is prototypical of a class of politicians who have risen to power recently. They lose sight of the goal of more efficient and effective government even as they become overly attached to the means—privatization. In Chapter 6, we consider what happens when such a libertarian politician moves from a doctrinaire privatization stance to a pragmatic position on the question of public agency reform.

3

Public vs. Private Production
Is One Better and How Would You Know?

The conceptual bottom line of the economic case for privatization is the assertion that the public sector can deliver publicly supplied services at a lower cost via more extensive use of contracting than it can via direct production. This conclusion is rooted in the standard market-model formulation of competitive market-based economic behavior. The public sector, which is allegedly sheltered from the competitive cleansing power described by this formulation, is presumed to be awash in inefficiency. Private suppliers, by way of contrast, are under constant market pressure to keep down their costs. Moreover, thanks to this same competitive pressure, they are continually forced to pass efficiency-generated savings on to their customers in the form of the lowest possible prices.

The gaping intellectual hole in this formulation is that it is too simple. As long as we conceptualize economic actors—buyers and sellers—as autonomous units out to maximize their individual gain and relevant market knowledge as complete, price alone conveys all the information and incentives needed to modify behavior. But, in a world where market information is less than complete, markets are less competitive than the ideal, and market participants are complex organizations instead of individuals, the model provides no way to predict how these complex actors will respond to any given market signal (Holstrom and Triole 1989; Milgrom and Roberts 1988; Williamson 1988). This shortcoming is more than an intellectual quibble. Basing a policy intended to change organizational behavior on a theory that disregards all real-world complexity can and, as we saw in the case of highway-maintenance privatization in Massachusetts, does lead policy makers to use public contracting inappropriately.

To make the case for privatization as a means to more efficiently obtain publicly supplied services, privatization advocates began to publish a voluminous spate of comparative cost studies in the 1970s. The basic methodological strategy of all these studies is the identification of a service for which there are existing alternative models of direct public and privately contracted delivery and then cost comparison. If the private service appeared to be less expensive, as was almost invariably the case in these studies, the authors concluded that this was because of the unseen spur of competitive market pressures stimulating an ongoing search for efficiency in the private sector that was absent in the public sector. By logical extension, if the contracting option was expanded to other services, government could potentially save vast amounts of taxpayer money while preserving public services (Savas 1987). The policy pitfall here is the implied conclusion that the act of public contracting effectively injects the lubricating power of private competition into the creaky joints of public bureaucracy. It means either forcing public service providers to compete via enhanced efficiency with private firms or disbanding them entirely in favor of private suppliers. Although many services were investigated to some degree, the most popular target of opportunity was solid-waste collection (Kemper and Quigley 1976; Kitchen 1976; McDavid 1985; Savas 1977). This service lent itself most easily to quantitative comparative analysis because in both Canada and the United States there were sufficient observations of several styles of public and private trash collection.

The weight of evidence from these studies makes a strong and plausible a priori case for the argument that contracting should be considered (certainly for trash collection). However, even in that arena, much relevant information was overlooked. In addition to the places where small, low-cost haulers provide good and inexpensive service, there were (and still are) many places where the dynamic of small company size and competitiveness has been transformed into collusion, price-fixing, and monopolization.

The latter markets are perennial targets for prosecutorial investigators and public regulators (Bubrick 1997; Crooks 1993). Even when prosecution has been occasionally successful, effective regulation has invariably proven itself to be easier to propose than it is to implement. In the late 1950s, the City of New York privatized all commercial solid-waste collection and has been fighting an uphill battle ever since to make its commercial trade waste-collection system behave more like a competitive market rather than a protection racket. New York City is not unique in this regard. Awareness of the problem is now conventional wisdom. A recent political cartoon in a suburban New York newspaper entitled "Folkloric Legends" (Davies 1999, 10B) contained drawings of three mythic creatures: Big Foot, the Loch Ness Monster, and the Unindicted Garbage Hauling Co. Inc., Westchester Co., N.Y.! By focusing only on isolated segments of the industry instead of the industry as a whole, these comparative studies are limited as a basis for more general policy conclusions. Taking into account the entire picture, it is not possible to sustain the simple assertion that "private" (in this case) almost invariably equals "efficient" whereas "public" means "inefficient." Indeed, according to one estimate, the $1.5 billion trash bill paid by New York City businesses for private trash collection is about $500 million higher than it should be (*Crain's New York Business* 1995, 8).

Busing in Canada

To understand why these types of comparative studies with their presumption of private competitive efficiency are often not well grounded in the complex nature of the services that they purport to analyze, we consider two of them in detail in the next two sections.

A recent comparative study of urban transit in Canada claimed that if "all urban transit service [in Ontario, Canada between 1982 and 1990] . . . had been delivered by private-sector operators . . . governments and taxpayers would have saved over $850 million" (Kitchen 1992). To arrive at that staggering sum, the study author estimated average total cost per revenue vehicle hour for publicly run and privately contracted systems in the province for each of the nine years in his study. (A vehicle revenue hour is an hour in which a bus is in service on its assigned route.) He found the private contractors to be, on average, 12 percent less expensive each year. He then multiplied the difference between his estimated average public and private hourly costs by the number of revenue vehicle hours of annual provincial operation and summed the resultant annual amounts to arrive at an $850 million estimate (ibid., 14).

There are two obvious problems with such a gross estimating procedure. First, the aggregate saving is an artifact of the author's arbitrary choice of 1982 and 1990 as the endpoints for his inquiry. Beyond a rationale of convenience of data collection, the number has little meaning as a motivational basis for public-policy decision-making. More importantly, the study makes two strong assumptions. To achieve that much in savings, *all* the costs of public operation had to disappear when private-contract operators took over. It also assumed that private-contract operation on such a scale would incur no new difficulties and that there were no public costs for administering the contract system and monitoring performance. Neither assumption is correct. Presumably, a public-administrative structure had to remain for contract supervision, maintenance of the contracting process, and enforcement of the policy mandates governing the provision of a public service. U.S. transit experience suggests that, even when the direct service is contracted out, overhead costs remain substantial, ranging from 16 percent to one-third of total costs,[1] depending on system size and complexity. If we take 20 percent as a conservative, "back-of-the-envelope" estimate and assume that the new costs of contract administration and supervision (estimated at about 6 percent [Gomez-Ibanez and Meyer 1993, 68]) are subsumed in that 20 percent figure, Kitchen's average savings of 12 percent provides no offset at all and actually represents an 8 percent loss. Even at the low end of our overhead estimates, this means a 4 percent loss.

But, if we take a closer look at the pattern of direct public provision and contracting provision of public transportation in Canada, there are actually more complex structural issues that need to be addressed. To better understand the actual situation in terms of public and private transit costs in Canada, I analyzed all the Canadian transit systems. The data came from the Canadian Urban Transit Association's national database for 1992[2] (Sclar and Watkins 1994). Table 5 demonstrates the distinct size pattern associated with the variations between public and contract service.

Contracted operations cluster tightly among the very smallest service areas (less than 25,000 people) where 70 percent of the service is privately provided. Conversely, only two of the thirty-one contract systems serve areas with a population greater than 100,000. The average area served by private contractors, including the large areas of contract operations, contained 77,187 people whereas the average service area for public providers was 215,851, almost three times more.

---

[1]For a higher estimate, see San Mateo County California Transit District Budget Department 1993. A lower estimate can be found in KPMG Peat Marwick 1991.

[2]There were 93 systems in all. But, in the analysis that follows, various systems were excluded because of missing data in various categories. Hence, the number of systems scrutinized varies from 77 to 89. These data do, however, provide a picture for the entire nation.

Table 5. Service-Area Characteristics: System Operation and Service-Area
Population, 1992

Service-Area Size (population in thousands)	No. of Public Systems	No. of Private Systems	No. of Total Systems
Under 25,000	7	15	22
25,000 to 50,000	10	9	19
50,001 to 100,000	14	5	19
100,001 to 150,000	9	1	10
150,001 to 400,000	10	0	10
Over 400,0008	1	9	
Total	58	31	89

Source: Data from Canadian Urban Transit Association, 1991.

To place that service delivery pattern in context, consider Table 6, which analyzes ridership patterns by service-area size and system type. Contract operators accounted for 58 percent of the ridership in service areas with a population less than 100,000. Overall, however, almost 90 percent of all riders were served by publicly operated systems.

It is important to consider this skewed service distribution when evaluating the efficiency of public systems because there is a direct relationship between operating cost and system size. Table 7 demonstrates this relationship.[3]

The positive relationship between area size and operating cost highlights a salient fact about the economics of fixed-route bus-transit service. As the size of the service area increases, so do the ridership, the complexity of operation, and the traffic density of the operating environment. All of these add to operating costs. Indeed, the differential between operation in the smallest and largest service areas is 60 percent. Thus, to analyze the potential cost savings of privatization, it is important to carefully control for service area and/or ridership. As these data demonstrate, it is not possible to generalize, as Kitchen's study does,

[3]A subsequent study by the Canadian Urban Transit Association in 1996 found that even when the data are broken out by system type the relationship still holds. For private systems serving municipalities with fewer than 50,000 people, the cost per vehicle revenue hour was $50.90. For private systems operating in municipalities of 50,000 to 150,000 people, the cost was $55.36. Comparable public operation figures were $52.90 and $58.48. There were no larger systems with private operators in this study. For public systems in areas with populations of 150,000 to 400,000 people, the cost per revenue hour was $61.85; for systems in areas with populations greater than 400,000, the cost was $81.96 (Canadian Urban Transit Association 1996, 6a).

Table 6. Service-Area Characteristics: Ridership, 1992 (in thousands)

Service-Area Size (population)	Public Ridership	No. of Public Systems	Contract Ridership	No. of Private Systems	Total Ridership	Total No. of Systems
Under 25,000	994	6	36,124	13	37,118	19
25,000 to 50,000	10,202	9	4,932	9	15,134	18
50,001 to 100,000	22,815	13	6,601	5	29,416	18
100,001 to 150,000	27,142	8	2,666	1	29,808	9
150,001 to 400,000	118,651	10	0	0	118,651	10
Over 400,000	1,004,414	8	128,214	1	1,132,628	9
Total	1,184,218	54	178,537	29	1,362,755	83

Source: Data from Canadian Urban Transit Association, 1991.

Table 7. Operating Costs per Revenue Vehicle Hour by Service-Area Size

Service-Area Size (population)	Operating Cost per Revenue Vehicle Hour
Under 25,000	$45.94
25,001 to 50,000	$48.69
50,001 to 100,000	$54.50
100,001 to 150,000	$56.82
150,001 to 400,000	$61.72
Over 400,000	$73.34
National average	$54.92

Source: Data from Canadian Urban Transit Association, 1991.

about the likely experience of large cities with privatization when much of the reported lower costs result from the operating environment of smaller systems and not the structure of the operation.

Table 8 breaks out the direct operating cost per revenue vehicle hour by service-area size and public and private operation. Although the simple averages bear out Kitchen's (1992) finding and suggest that, among the smaller service areas, private operation is less expensive, the test for statistical significance suggests that differences delineated on that basis may be meaningless. Statistical significance is the term used by statisticians to determine if data sets reflect meaningful underlying differences or are caused merely by chance. In the present case, the finding of statistical insignificance is consistent with the notion that transit productivity is determined largely by factors external to the organization of the transit operation. The data are statistically insignificant not only for the subclasses of service, but for the entire national sample as well.[4]

To understand why this is the case, consider some examples. In the province of Alberta, the Strathcona service area contained 35,500 people in 1990. The Medicine Hat service area contained a slightly larger population of 42,970. Service in Strathcona is provided through private contract. In Medicine Hat, service is publicly provided. The operating cost in Strathcona is $50.60 per revenue vehicle hour. In Medicine Hat, the comparable cost is less: $49.06. In Milton, Ontario, with a service area population of 26,000 the operating cost is $62.64. In Woodstock,

---

[4]A finding of nonsignificance may also mean that the sample size is too small. But in this case, the Canadian "universe," not a sample, was analyzed. With the exception of a few systems that were excluded because of missing data in various categories, the analysis effectively evaluates the entire country.

Table 8. Direct Operating Costs per Revenue Vehicle Hour by Service-Area Size, 1992

Service-Area Size	Public Operation	No. of Public Systems	Private Operation	No. of Contract Systems	Statistical Significance (<10%)
Under 25,000	$53.91	4	$42.74	10	No
25,001 to 50,000	50.87	9	47.36	9	No
50,001 to 100,000	56.16	13	49.09	4	No
100,001 to 150,000	55.66	8	66.15	1	NA
150,001 to 400,000	61.72	10	NA	0	NA
Over 400,000	72.96	8	76.39	1	NA
National average	$58.65	52	$47.70	25	No

Source: Data from Canadian Urban Transit Association, 1991.

Ontario, with a service-area population of 29,029 the publicly provided service costs $41.13. Obviously, there are more instances of the contracted cost being less than the publicly provided cost. However, the larger point is that there is so much overlap in cost among publicly provided and privately contracted systems that it is impossible to conclude that private service is inherently less expensive. The inability to come to a conclusion based on the data is what statistical insignificance means. It is no more correct to conclude that private service is less expensive in smaller systems than it is to conclude that among larger systems the data prove that public service is less costly. The data simply do not permit generalization. A safer conclusion and more accurate case could be made that productivity and cost issues must be examined in an organizationally more complex manner. The data here do not sustain the stereotypical privatization argument that competitive, efficient private service is less expensive than monopolized public service. As with all stereotypes, this bipolar dichotomy is too simplistic to capture the essence of day-to-day operation in urban transportation systems. Moreover, the comparative costs of public and private operation are sufficiently close that the question of savings hinges critically on an analysis of the potential new costs engendered by privatization in comparison to the costs that it would permit public authorities to avoid.

California Dreamin'?

This need to fully address the differential complexity of specific services in specific locations, rather than merely assume that generally private is better than public is ironically and strongly borne out by the methodologically best pro-privatization comparative study. Undertaken in 1984 and sponsored by the Reagan-era U.S. Department of Housing and Urban Development (HUD) (Stevens 1984), this study acted on the administration's philosophical belief that privately contracted service is less expensive than publicly supplied service. HUD commissioned the study with the intention of carefully documenting and validating this observation. The study examined twenty cities of comparable size within metropolitan Los Angeles. In ten of these cities, services were municipally supplied; in the other ten, services were provided by private contractors. Eight services were compared: asphalt overlay construction (street repaving), street cleaning, janitorial services, residential refuse collection, traffic signal maintenance, turf maintenance, street tree

Table 9. Principal Findings of the HUD-Sponsored 1984 Study of Municipal
Service Costs

Service	% of City Budget	% Saved via Contract
Building janitorial service	0.5	73
Turf maintenance	2.0	40
Residential refuse collection	4.2	42
Street tree maintenance	1.3	37
Traffic signal maintenance	0.8	56
Street cleaning	0.9	43
Payroll	0.4	0
Asphalt overlay construction	0.7	96
Total budget impact	10.8	4.9

Source: Data from Stevens 1984.

maintenance, and payroll. Seven of these services were "blue-collar" work, and one (payroll) was "white-collar." Together these services accounted for just over 10 percent of the average municipal budget.

Using a standardized unit of production to compare costs for each service, the HUD study found that the cost of contracting out all the blue-collar services was significantly less than the cost of supplying them directly. The cost of directly providing a service ranged from 37 percent (street tree maintenance) to 96 percent (street repaving) more than the cost of contracting it out (Stevens 1984, 2). Payroll preparation showed no significant difference in costs. Based on these findings, the study predicted that if all these services were privatized, cities in the public subsample could expect to cut their overall expenses by just under 5 percent. Table 9 summarizes these findings.

An interesting fact emerges when we distinguish the first six services listed in Table 9 from the last two. The first six services have three important characteristics in common: (1) All are maintenance services. (2) The tasks involved in at least five of them are not unique to the public sector with traffic-signal maintenance being the exception, although even here both the electrical skills and equipment have many private-sector applications. (3) The skill level required of workers ranges from unskilled for janitorial services and turf maintenance to semiskilled and skilled for the other four. None of the work requires formal education; in every case, on-the-job training suffices. Moreover, the physical capital employed by these six tasks (such as pickup trucks, lawn mowers, mops, ladders, pruning tools, and brooms) is sufficiently general that it can be put to good use elsewhere. Hence, it is relatively easy for government to find competitive contractors who have the labor and equipment necessary to perform the work. Most importantly, contract performance is comparatively easy to monitor because of the physical nature of the tasks themselves. Everyone in the neighborhood immediately knows when the streetlights have been fixed or the trash removed or the lawns mowed.

The HUD study thus shows that privatization for many blue-collar services certainly may be cost effective. The unanswered critical question raised by this study concerns the degree to which this finding can be generalized. With regard to that question, there are two important concerns. First, as Table 9 demonstrates, all these services constitute a small portion of the municipal budget (about 10 percent). If the full range of savings found by this study was captured by every municipality that attempted contracting, the total budgetary impact would still be less than 5 percent. Although any savings are valuable, such a small sum is scarcely sufficient for deeming privatization as a revolutionary way to improve government service. Second, savings is by and large confined to the least costly portion of the public budget, the portion that pays for services delivered by the least-skilled labor. What happens when we focus on services that must be provided by highly educated and formally trained professionals? Because these workers constitute the largest portions of the budget, even relatively small savings can make a significant difference. To understand why the findings of this study might not be easily transferable to these other more complex services, consider the final service: street repaving. HUD found the largest comparative savings (96 percent) for this service.

Street repaving is different from trimming a tree or mopping a floor because the work is highly specialized and almost unique to the public sector. The finding by the HUD study that public repaving costs almost twice what the private sector charges is certainly dramatic and lends credence to the notion that the private sector can be more efficient in more complex services. Are savings of this magnitude generally available or are they unique to small cities in the metropolitan Los Angeles area? What about larger cities where repaving is more routine and occurs almost daily? Or parts of the country where seasonal changes are harsher on road surfaces? Such questions are not trivial. The HUD study pointed out that one of the strengths of its methodology was that "all cities were located in the same geographic area, [hence] it [was] not necessary to control for the impact of varying climates" (Stevens 1984, 20).

In 1989, the comptroller of the City of New York undertook the first of two comparative studies on repaving work that were strikingly similar—but not identical to—the HUD study. These studies carefully compared the costs of contractor repaving with in-house repaving done by the Department of Transportation (DOT) for New York City and came to a far different conclusion than did the HUD study. In the first study, the comptroller's office chose ten study sites (five were repaired by in-house crews, and five were done under contract). The average cost of in-house repaving was $5.65 per square yard. Contractor cost for comparable work was $5.78. This difference is too negligible to be considered significant (City of New York, Office of the Comptroller, Bureau of Management Audits 1989). In 1995, the comptroller revisited the issue of public and private costs for repaving. The second study reached an even more interesting conclusion, namely that it mattered less whether the repairer was public or private; the key determinant of cost was proximity of the job site to the asphalt plant. When the DOT job site was closer to the plant, its costs were lower, but when the private contractor was closest, its costs were lower. The crucial variable was the travel time between the plant and the job site. In every other way, public and private work crews were identical. These two New York studies suggest that the production cost issue is most heavily dependent on factors other than the public or private status of the producer (City of New York, Office of the Comptroller, Bureau of Management Audits 1995).

Although the New York comptroller's studies and the HUD study used different comparative approaches, both are methodologically sound. Thus, we may not easily dismiss the contradiction between the larger conclusions about the inherent comparative advantage of private production. Rather, we are forced to consider the circumstances in which public production might be superior to private production.

Street repaving is a highly capital-intensive undertaking. It uses specialized heavy equipment that has little usefulness outside the construction and reconstruction of public ways. Operators of this equipment are highly skilled and hence well paid. HUD found that the private street-paving contractors paid wages that were 58 percent higher than those in the public sector. Thus, the easy explanation of lower labor costs does not suffice.

Two explanations for the contradiction between the New York and California studies suggest themselves. Large cities may generate a sufficiently large volume of street reconstruction work so that it is efficient for the municipality to invest in its own equipment and maintain a full-time work crew. In the smaller cities examined by HUD, there simply may not be enough streets in need of repair to justify the investment in equipment and crew. Hence, those small California cities that do their own work may be carrying effectively excess capacity. The continual freezing and thawing of road surfaces in New York City and other northern zones during the winter leads to rapid and extensive formation of potholes every spring. Climate then, in addition to city size, contributes to a higher level of demand for ongoing road-repair work in the Northeast. This contrasting example is instructive in two regards. It strongly suggests that, consistent with the ambiguities in the theoretical literature about contracting in the private sector, no easy generalizations are possible about the inherent efficiency of public contracting versus direct public provision per se in these more complex areas of public service. More importantly, as with the postal service anecdote, general conclusions about specific characteristics are not easily drawn, even with a seemingly highly specific service.

The Myth of the Overpaid Public Worker

Proponents of privatization view themselves as champions of a policy change that they confidently believe will lead to a quantum drop in public service costs and, perhaps, even lower taxes (Cox and Love 1990). They contend that this will happen because competitive market economics will be permitted to trump politics. As a result, costs must drop below those of what they label the "monopoly" environment of direct government production. As a result, they contend, it is unfair to label them as either antigovernment conservatives or, more importantly, antiunion antiworker wage-busters. They really do not care about how much workers are paid or if they are members of unions. They merely want costs, including wages, to be set by competitive market standards and not political arrangements. Opponents, especially in the public-sector unions, contend otherwise. Either way, it is impossible to avoid the wage issue. Personnel costs are invariably the largest element of any public-service operating budget. It is impossible to attain meaningful savings without in some way reducing personnel costs. Data generated by HUD suggests that about 71 percent of all direct, municipal, public-service operating costs are labor. Even when the work is contracted out, the combined cost of contract, municipal wages, and fringe benefits still amounts to 61 percent after allowing the same depreciation and over-head exclusion (Stevens 1984, 9).

The strongest case for the efficiency of privatization is a demonstration of skills, compensation, and work quality being the same and output per worker being higher in the private sector. In that case, per unit labor costs would be lower, not because private workers were paid less but because the private workers were producing more. Simply put, the private sector got the job done more efficiently. In the HUD Southern California repaving example, where private-sector compensation exceeded public-sector compensation, the implied case for higher private-sector efficiency was quite strong, although, as demonstrated by the New York City studies, it is far from universal.

Because the comparative data are only rarely as clear cut as the HUD Southern California repaving example, privatization proponents are forced to directly confront the question of public-sector wages. They then argue, in effect, that public employees are significantly overcompensated. To make their case, privatization advocates typically produce studies that compare gross public and private-sector compensation and conclude that rates of increase in public-sector compensation far outstrip its private-sector counterparts. Cox and Brunelli (1992), for example, found that between 1980 and 1989 public-sector compensation, adjusted for inflation, rose 14.6 percent. Private-sector compensation over the same period rose about one-fourth that amount, only 3.4 percent in inflation-adjusted terms. They conclude from this that the public-sector working class is what they call a "protected class." The difficulty with such studies is their failure to adjust for education, skill level, and job tenure. In comparative studies of public and private-sector wages that control for these variables, public-sector employees are paid 4 to 5 percent less than their private-sector counterparts. Whereas approximately 20 percent of private-sector workers have college educations, almost 44 percent of public workers are so educated (Belman and Heywood 1993). In a society in which unskilled labor has become less crucial, such educational differences explain much of the apparent recent rise in public-sector wages relative to those in the private sector. It is only among the lowest skilled and lowest paid occupations that public employees enjoy a significant wage advantage over their private sector counterparts (Gold and Ritchie 1992).

The HUD study found that the two, lowest skilled categories of public workers enjoyed wages and fringe benefits far exceeding those of their private-sector counterparts. Publicly employed janitors enjoyed a compensation package that was almost 70 percent higher than that of their private-sector counterparts. In the case of turf-maintenance workers, the comparable differential was 52 percent.

We cannot generalize to all public workers from the relatively higher rates of compensation at the low end of the pay scale because at the highest levels public compensation lags behind the private sector. Lawyers in the public sector, for example, earn significantly less than their counterparts in private employment. Hence, as the nature of public-service work subjected to privatization becomes more skill- and education-intensive, the utility of private-sector wage differentials as a source of savings diminishes rapidly. Labor-market realities are such that the issue of public workers as a protected class is less the problem than is the challenge of paying enough to attract competent well-educated workers away from private employment. This is especially true in the most costly areas of the public budget such as education and human services.

To the extent that compensation differentials diminish as a rationale for privatization, the money-saving case much more crucially turns on two other factors. These are (1) the degree to which private organizations can create higher *output* per worker and (2) the degree to which private suppliers are compelled to pass productivity gains along to the public purchaser in the form of lower prices. This can occur either because competition from other providers compels it to do so (the central issue of Chapter 4) or because the public agency is able to write a contract that ensures savings are passed along via lower prices (the issue of concern in Chapter 5).

If we want to extend privatization beyond the relatively simple blue-collar tasks analyzed in the HUD study to more complex services such as education and human services, then we need a broader analytic focus. We need to shift our inquiry from a comparatively simple analysis with overcompensation as the key issue to a more sophisticated organizational analysis of the conditions of private supply and public contracting. The intellectual peg on which the privatization case hangs must rapidly move from the public/private wage differential argument to one built around a claim of special expertise or knowledge that private suppliers possess but that public providers cannot access on their own, a far more difficult case to make. It is important to remember that five of the six services for which HUD found savings rely heavily on a high percentage of unskilled and semiskilled labor. Similarly, the one service for which no difference was found (payroll) involved skilled labor performing a more complex task.

Ohio Bridges Standing Up

The combined federal, state, and local governments are the largest consumers of construction services. In addition to buildings, they purchase transportation infrastructure for both mass transit and highways. A highly specialized industry of contractors undertakes virtually all the construction work in the United States. Because the work is complex and involves a series of important judgments that can be made only as the work proceeds, purchasers need to retain a second set of experts to ensure that the construction decisions are made in accordance with their specifications and blueprints. On small projects, it is frequently the architect who performs this intermediary function for the client. On more complex jobs, clients often hire outside construction managers to look after their interests. In state highway departments where highway construction and reconstruction projects are almost continually underway, many maintain a stable of inspectors who continually monitor job sites to ensure that the final product is up to the standards written into the contract. In recent years, under the pressure of privatization advocacy, states have increasingly turned to private inspectors to supervise the work of their other contractors. A survey of contracting practices in eight states concluded "that the cost advantage generally favors in-house, not contracting out transportation service" (Raimondo 1992, v). Included among these services was construction inspection.

A major reason for the lack of cost effectiveness in outside inspection services is the minimal to nonexistent savings on personnel costs. Regardless of who employs them, the engineers who are engaged to supervise construction work are paid at comparable rates. It is the private market for engineers that drives remuneration in this field not public unions or bureaucratic red tape. If savings were to occur, it would mean that private inspectors can be more efficient in some meaningful way than their publicly employed brethren. In 1991 and 1992, the Ohio Department of Transportation (ODOT) contracted out project inspection work on some bridge construction projects. In the past and in other parts of Ohio, state employees did this work. A detailed and exhaustive comparative cost analysis of four of those inspection contracts with the in-house cost of the same work indicated that the in-house costs were, on average, 28 percent less than those of the outside contractors (Vagnier and Sclar 1993). Both the contractors and ODOT used identically trained structural engineers as inspectors with generally similar levels of experience and similar levels of compensation. The cost advantage of ODOT resulted from the fact that small contractors had to charge a price sufficiently high to cover both their direct and overhead costs. ODOT merely had to pay for the additional staff time to complete the work because most of its other costs were fixed in departmental overhead. Had private-sector compensation been significantly less than that of the public sector, it might have been possible for the outside work to cost less.

It could be argued that in some sense this comparison is "unfair" to the private sector. Any accounting of the real cost of highway construction inspection in the public sector must include some allowance for overhead. This is true as a way to capture the big picture but beside the point if savings are our concern. Overhead costs such as bookkeeping and management generally do not diminish regardless of whether the actual work is performed by state employees or outside contractors. From the point of view of the taxpayer who foots the bill, it is the total cost of the job that matters, not the overhead of the contractor. The state must absorb overhead regardless of privatization. The issue for taxpayers is getting the most output for the money that is spent. Therefore, the correct way to compare in-house work with contracted work is on the basis of avoidable costs. That is to say, the comparison must be between the costs that the state truly can reduce (avoid) and those forced on it by the contract.

Bending Cost Curves: The Experience of Transit

Three sets of costs must be considered when deciding between contracting and direct public production: the direct costs of public production, the costs of the outside service contractor, and the internal costs incurred by a contractual arrangement. Public production costs include personnel, equipment, and materials. The costs of outside service are typically the agreed-upon price of the contract. Internal costs include everything related to bidding and letting the contract and supervising the contract work—these are called transaction costs. The comparative

cost analysis of public and private production must include a consideration of the transaction costs regardless of whether the private sector is
more efficient than the public sector at production. What is crucial is
whether the sum of both the contract price and the transaction costs is less
than the cost of direct public provision.

During the 1980s, a spate of comparative cost studies seemed to provide overwhelming support for the notion that privatizing public transit
yields massive savings (Teal 1985, 1988). If true, these findings were of
major consequence. Figuratively, they meant that we could have our
cake and eat it, too. Transit, which is so vital to the functioning of our
great metropolises, could be expanded but budgets held constant or
even cut. The Office of Private Sector Initiatives, a special bureau established by the Reagan administration within the U.S. Department of
Transportation's Urban Mass Transportation Administration (UMTA),
sponsored virtually all these studies. Ralph Stanley, the head of UMTA
during Reagan's tenure, summed up the findings from the commissioned studies as follows:

> We've done a number of policy studies and economic analyses that show
> savings in bus operations ranging from 10 to 50%. . . . We've taken a look
> at the economics of running a bus system, and shown *beyond a shadow of
> a doubt* that it's more efficient to be run privately. (Ryan 1987, 12 and 68;
> emphasis added)

Like most "beyond a shadow of doubt" conclusions, these numbers
are, in fact, too good to be true. Virtually all were generated using an inappropriate accounting methodology—fully allocated cost accounting
(FAC). FAC requires that the direct public-operating costs of transit
routes such as driver compensation and fuel, which would obviously disappear as a result of privatization, be combined with an estimate of the
proportion of fixed system overhead for items such as planning and marketing in arriving at an estimate for the cost of public operation. If overhead was a trivial portion of the total cost, this would not matter much.
But, overhead costs are not trivial. As we saw earlier, overhead ranges
from 16 percent to one-third of total system cost. As a result, the FAC
technique grossly overstates the amount of potential savings via contracting. It, in effect, artificially inflates the estimate of reducible public costs.

The proper way to measure savings resulting from privatization is
through the use of an analytic method called, among other things,

avoidable cost accounting.[5] Both economic and accounting theory are unanimous on this point. This method compares only the additional costs incurred as a result of an action with resulting actual cost reductions or revenue improvements. If the avoided costs exceed the new contract-related costs, savings result. If not, the status quo may be preferable.

The differences between FAC accounting and avoidable-cost accounting may be substantial. Indeed, FAC accounting often demonstrates savings even when an agency loses money as a result of privatization. This is precisely the trap into which the Santa Barbara Metropolitan Transportation District fell during the Reagan years when privatization was vigorously promoted. According to then general manager Gary Gleason:

> We had a private-sector bid a year ago. . . . They bid about $980,000 on this 20 percent segment of our service and our fully allocated costs are within the neighborhood of $1,000,000 so that there was about a $20,000 savings over a year's period to operate this part of Santa Barbara's service. However, in looking at our incremental costs and being able to identify . . . what people in the shop would be laid off, we were able to identify very precisely where a cost reduction would be and as we found out, our cost reduction would, in fact, only be about $380,000 per year. So in order to take advantage of this so-called private-sector situation, it was actually going to cost us an additional $600,000 to participate with the private sector. And right now we are in the process where the sole bidder that we had on the project has protested both to the Washington headquarters of UMTA and the regional headquarters and they have won their protest . . . as the general manager, I'm the one that's responsible every year for writing the checks, and I know, in fact, that if I accepted the bid, that I would have an additional $600,000 . . . cost. (American Public Transportation Association 1988)

Despite the obvious analytic advantages of avoidable cost analysis, the UMTA leadership insisted that FAC accounting be used as the principal determinant in privatization decision making. UMTA wanted to make sure that "subsidies provided to public carriers, including operating subsidies, capital grants, and the use of public facilities" are also "reflected in the cost comparisons" (*Federal Register* 1984, 41312). Mean-

---

[5]The technique is sometimes called marginal or incremental cost accounting. These two terms are typically used by sellers, rather than buyers, to assess their additional costs of providing a given product to a new customer.

while, private bids were not held to such a high standard (*Federal Register* 1989, 15635).

> Only the bids of public agencies and nonprofit agencies must reflect fully allocated costs. UMTA does not intend that a private operator fully allocate its costs or bid this figure in a procurement. The price bid by the private operator is the figure against which a recipient's or a nonprofit agency's fully allocated cost is compared.

This double standard clearly was intended to further the political priority of actively expanding the role of private operators in public transport, rather than to spare taxpayers extra costs.

This political misuse of accounting was flagrant in the experience of Sonoma County Transit (SCT). Using competitive bidding, SCT had a contract with Laidlaw Transit to provide area service. When the contract expired in December 1988, the county sought to award a new three-year contract to a public provider, the Golden Gate Bridge and Transit District. Golden Gate offered to provide the three-year service for a cost of $5.5 million compared with $6.1 million by Laidlaw and $5.9 million by the lowest private bidder, American Transit Corporation (ATC). Based on a protest to UMTA by the California Bus Association, a lobbying and political arm of the private operators, UMTA forced SCT to award the new contract to ATC and not the public operator. UMTA justified its decision on the grounds that the Golden Gate Bridge and Transit District was a public entity and hence publicly subsidized. Because its bid was based on the marginal or additional cost of that service, it was in effect using publicly provided capital to compete "unfairly" against a private enterprise. Yet, as long as the Golden Gate Bridge and Transit District was able to provide service at a price that covered its additional costs, taxpayers would have gotten the greatest value for total public spending.

Consider the case of the Foothill Transit Zone (FTZ), established in 1988 by the Los Angeles County Transportation Commission as a privatization experiment. The FTZ is a quasipublic agency that originally contracted with private providers to run fourteen lines formerly served by the Southern California Rapid Transit District (SCRTD) in the San Gabriel and Pomona valleys. The Los Angeles County Transportation Commission hired Ernst & Young to conduct an FAC analysis of the FTZ. It concluded that the FTZ generated a 43 percent cost savings (Ernst & Young 1991). However, the SCRTD, who lost the service contract, countered with an avoidable cost study conducted by Coopers & Lybrand. It found that in fact SCRTD and FTZ costs differed by less than 1 percent and that when the figures were corrected for cost differences engendered by differences in the ages of the bus fleets of the two operators, the public operator SCRTD was actually 7.6 percent less expensive (Coopers & Lybrand 1991). This conclusion was confirmed by a follow-up study done by the Massachusetts Institute of Technology for the Los Angeles County Transportation Commission (Richmond 1992).

There is general professional consensus that FAC is inappropriate as a basis for analyzing privatization cost savings. In a letter to Jack McCroskey, the former chairman of the board of directors of the Denver, Colorado, Regional Transportation District, Robert Peskin, a senior manager at the consulting firm KPMG Peat Marwick, explained:

> There are convincing arguments that such a fully-allocated approach *is not appropriate* (my emphasis) in the context of *contracting* (Peat Marwick's emphasis) of transit service, as in the case of privatization. (Peskin 1991)

He concluded that "incremental cost (read avoidable cost) analyses yield hard 'out-of-pocket' estimates of savings that are useful in real-world decision-making" (ibid.). Even the staunchly pro-privatization Reason Foundation concurs:

> The use of fully allocated costs is generally inappropriate in estimating the *savings* to be realized by contracting out a target service that is currently being conducted in-house. . . . When attempting to determine the potential cost savings associated with the contracting out of a target service, the appropriate in-house costs to use in the comparison are the "avoidable costs." (Martin 1993, 9–10)

Government audit and fiscal oversight agencies such as the U.S. Office of Management and Budgets and state and local comptrollers and auditors unanimously call for the use of avoidable-cost models to perform the kind of comparative analysis demanded by privatization decisions.[6]

Although it may be argued that FAC accounting can estimate long-term *potential* savings (because as direct public service activity shrinks over time, so too will overhead), the contingent future is a poor basis on

---

[6]See, for example, United States Office of Management and Budget 1990, and Commonwealth of Massachusetts, Office of the State Auditor 1994.

which to defend privatization presently. As a general rule, if a proposed privatization does not demonstrate clear hard-cash savings in the short run, a very detailed analysis explaining exactly how the long-term savings will be generated must be an integral part of the decision process. It is unacceptable to simply assert that in some unspecified way "competitive savings" can be expected. Absent such convincing additional evidence, decision-makers should be wary about embarking on a particular privatization when the avoidable cost analysis produces small to nonexistent savings.

Conclusions

The strongest, but often unspoken, case for privatization has always rested on the nagging suspicion that public-sector employees are overpaid and underworked. Although there are undoubtedly instances in which this is true, this chapter has demonstrated that such conventional wisdom is a poor basis for wide-ranging policy change. A stronger case would rest on the notion that the private sector can add real and measurable value to the public product, not merely duplicate what public employees do for about the same cost. This must be value that the public sector could not obtain on its own. The problem here is that most public work is highly labor-intensive. There are no ways to patent workplace routines. In fields as varied as fire protection and education, state-of-the-art techniques are effectively in the public domain. To the extent that there is patented value to be added, it typically comes via the intellectual property of items such as computer software and hardware. But, these are equally available to public and private purchasers. Consequently, it should not be surprising that comparative cost studies do not yield an unambiguous result one way or the other. The ambiguity of the result is consistent with the fact that publicly supplied services themselves can and are produced as variants by private sellers. Thus, although there are clearly situations in which contracting works well, there are at least as many, if not more, in which the existence of direct public service is a rational economic strategy. The real challenge, then, is not to chase after the unanswerable Hamletesque question, "To privatize or not to privatize?" Instead, we must look at the evolution of technology, the service responsibilities of government, and the existing organization of service delivery and begin to fashion new ways to combine public employees and private suppliers to truly enhance value for the tax dollar. Simple mutually exclusive approaches to the question are inadequate.

4

What's Competition Got to Do with It?

Market Structures and Public Contracting

Competition and Its Constraints

Proponents of privatization often argue that they do not necessarily oppose direct public service—they oppose the waste of money. From their perspective, too many public managers and employees conspire, consciously or unconsciously, to squander taxpayers' money. They successfully do this because public service is insulated from the cost-cutting rigors of the competitive market and suffers from the bureaucratic equivalent of hardening of the arteries; too many public dollars get stuck in the passage between the public treasury and service to citizens. By exposing public services to private-sector discipline and competition, privatization forces public servants to clean up their acts. Either they learn a new ethic of workplace efficiency, or they forfeit their jobs. From this analysis flows the rationale and mantra of privatization: "It's not a matter of public versus private, it's a matter of monopoly versus competition."

Contracting out is seldom so simple because it occurs in a variety of market and public-agency settings that rarely approximate the textbook model of competition. Most public contracting takes place in markets that range from no competition[1] (monopoly) to minimal competition among very few firms (oligopoly). Although oligopoly is preferable to monopoly, it is still far removed from the salutary competition venerated by privatization advocates. In oligopolistic markets, the few sellers are

---

[1]A recent audit of consultant contracts in California found that almost two-thirds of them were let on a sole-source basis (State of California, Office of the State Auditor 1996).

well aware of each other's presence. Even when there is no outright collusion, they frequently submit bids with an eye on the anticipated needs of their ostensible "rivals" as well as needs of their own. Oligopolists recognize that their individual long-term best interests are tightly entwined with the collective, long-term interests of the industry. A peaceably divided market promises greater long-term profitability than that provided by any adversarially won short-term gain. The biggest and best case in point is the ongoing saga of abuse of the public treasury that we euphemistically call "defense contracting." Documented cases of bid rigging, price fixing, revolving-door executive employment,[2] and outright corruption among the handful of oligopolistic corporations that control defense spending are enshrined in U.S. folk history with the oft-told tale of the $600 toilet seat.[3]

When responsible public officials contemplate privatization, it is imperative that they understand the true structure of the market that they are entering. The assumption that the market is competitive is incorrect. Indeed, even when a market initially appears to be competitive, policy makers must remain wary. Public-contract markets, like most markets, change quickly and continually. Often, the very act of creating a public-contracting process sets anticompetitive forces in motion. What begins as apparent competition quickly transforms itself by the second or third round of contracting into monopoly or, more typically, oligopoly.

Wall Street is well aware of this dynamic quality of public contracting, even though privatization advocates often choose to ignore it. Recent market analyses prepared by investment bankers to promote shares in the Wackenhut Correctional Corporation, the second-largest contractor in the new for-profit prison industry, made precisely this point. Reports pointed out that there are "effective barriers to entry for smaller competitors, thus helping the industry leaders grow their market share." Furthermore, "as the private correctional industry consolidates there will be fewer players competing for market share" (Prudential Securities 1996; Lazard Freres & Co. LCC 1996). Such market contraction is commonplace in public service contracting.

---

[2]Revolving-door executive employment is the hiring practice by which defense contractors employ outgoing public officials who have awarded contracts to them in the past.

[3]Good descriptions of this oligopolistic boondoggle can be found in Fallows (1981) and Shaller (1991).

Consider what happened when the government of Fort Lauderdale, Florida, decided to close its municipal pipe-laying department in the early 1990s. Local officials estimated that in the previous year they had paid about $90 per linear foot when they infrequently used outside contractors and assumed that this figure was less than their in-house cost. As word quickly spread through south Florida that all of the pipe-laying work in Fort Lauderdale was about to be privatized, contractors readied bids ranging up to $130 a linear foot. Meanwhile, city engineers prepared a careful, avoidable-cost analysis in anticipation of the upcoming privatization but were surprised to learn that their in-house cost was actually between $68 and $73 per linear foot. At about the same time, department employees had approached city officials via the municipal labor–management conciliation organization with a credible complaint that even this estimate was too high because the work was poorly organized. When the work was reorganized along lines suggested by the employees, in-house cost dropped to $43 per linear foot. When the outside contractors learned that Fort Lauderdale was having second thoughts about its privatization decision, they lowered their bids to the $50 to $60 range. But, by then it was too late. The department remained public but reorganized.

This example is remarkable for two reasons: (1) It illustrates the power of workplace reorganization to save money; this is perhaps the best way to ensure value for the public dollar but is often overlooked in the rush to privatize. (We explore this option more fully in Chapter 6.) (2) More germane is the market behavior of the local contractors. As with the Massachusetts highway-maintenance example, firms that do heavy construction work often comprise a small, regional, and tight-knit community. Frequently bidding against each other for public work, they are keenly aware of the local economic and political conditions under which they all operate. In such instances, market strength vis-à-vis the public agency, instead of cost, often determines product pricing. Perhaps the true private cost of laying pipe in Fort Lauderdale was $90 and the contractors initially thought the city had tilted the bargaining situation in their favor. Perhaps the subsequent lower bids were loss leaders[4] designed to close down the municipal department. We will never know

---

[4]A loss leader is an item that is priced extremely low so as to entice customers to give sellers more business. Supermarkets frequently employ this "bargain" pricing on staple items such as milk to attract shoppers to make larger purchases at higher prices.

for sure. We do know, however, that when sellers have an oligopolistic relationship with one another, pricing behavior reflects market strategy more than the actual cost of production.

Because of the key role played by market structure in determining public-sector advantage, it is important to consider both the current state of the market and the dynamics that are shaping its future when assessing the efficacy of privatization. To better understand these dynamics, this chapter presents three case studies of contracting out public services, first in a monopolistic, and then in an oligopolistic, market.

A Monopoly Market: Fire Fighting in Scottsdale, Arizona

Fire protection often has been cited as an ideal candidate for privatization (Donahue 1989; Osborne and Gaebler 1992; Poole 1980; Savas 1987). It is expensive, sometimes accounting for more than 20 percent of the general funds of a municipality (Osborne and Gaebler 1992, 223). Alternative service-delivery arrangements already exist: not only local volunteer fire departments but also a publicly traded, profit-making corporation, Rural/Metro, that has provided fire protection to Scottsdale, Arizona, since 1948. Nearly every important study advocating or studying the privatization of municipal services refers to Scottsdale, yet few cities have followed its example. Even among those that have, they often drop the practice after a brief experiment because the Scottsdale experience is historically unique. Although it demonstrates that private for-profit fire protection is feasible in the United States, it is an example of a monopoly rather than competitive contracting. Every year, without competitive bidding, Rural/Metro and the City of Scottsdale negotiate a cost-plus-profit contract for fire protection for the next twelve months.

Rural/Metro was founded when Scottsdale was a sparsely populated, unincorporated region beyond the Phoenix city line. After a neighbor's home burned to the ground, Louis Witzeman organized local residents to provide their own voluntary fire protection. But, after Witzeman personally made the down payment on a fire truck, the collective effort dissolved. He completed the purchase and, in a pioneering innovation, created a subscription-supported fire company to recoup his investment. Neighbors were free to subscribe to his newly created "Rural Fire Department." When the City of Scottsdale was incorporated in 1951, rather than create a fire department from scratch or establish a volunteer company, it hired Rural, which by then had three fire stations and several vehicles. The voluntary, individual-subscription service was converted into a municipal master contract for protecting the entire area and financed traditionally by a general tax levy.

The population of Scottsdale at that time was a mere 2,000. As Scottsdale grew to its 1998 population of 179,012, so did the company. The original Rural Fire Department became the modern Rural/Metro Corporation. Historical accident created the long-term relationship between Scottsdale and this company. Today a midsized or large city might be tempted to try a private contractual arrangement if it promised to deliver fire protection that was significantly better and/or cheaper. Available data suggest that the anomalous arrangement in Scottsdale offers neither benefit.

Analysis of three studies conducted over the last two decades reveals an interesting pattern in the comparative costs of private and public fire protection. In the early 1970s, an econometric study that used community characteristics to estimate fire protection costs in Arizona and the state of Washington concluded that the per-capita costs in Scottsdale were about half the expected costs if the system had been municipal (Ahlbrandt 1973a,b). In 1976, the Institute for Local Self-Government compared actual per-capita fire protection costs in Scottsdale and three neighboring communities and found a similar magnitude of differences (Table 10, column 6). During the 1971–75 study period, per-capita costs in Scottsdale averaged 57 percent of those in Mesa, 66 percent of those in Tempe, and 51 percent of those in Glendale. The most recent study of actual per-capita costs (Donovan et al. 1989) found that those in Scottsdale were still lower than those of five other nearby cities, but the gap had narrowed considerably (Table 10, column 5). By 1989, per-capita costs in Scottsdale had risen to 72 percent of those in Mesa and 85 percent of those in Tempe and were virtually identical to costs in Glendale.

In addition to documenting a convergence of costs over time, Table 10 illustrates a clear relationship between population density and per-capita fire protection costs. With 720 people per square mile, the population density of Scottsdale is far less than the regional average. Phoenix is more than three times and Glendale more than five times as densely populated. According to 1996 census data, these figures have remained

Table 10. 1988 Population Density and 1989 and 1971–75 per Capita Fire Protection Costs in Six Arizona Cities

City	1988 Population (Thousands)	Land Area (Sq. Miles)	Density (Pop. per Sq. Mile)	1989 per Capita Fire Protection Costs	1971–75 Avg. per Capita Fire Protection Costs
Phoenix	971	404	2,403	$65.49	NA
Tucson	407	156	2,608	$63.67	NA
Mesa	287	107	2,682	$54.34	$11.43
Tempe	150	38	3,947	$45.88	$10.68
Glendale	143	51	2,803	$39.43	$12.62
Scottsdale	131	182	720	$39.18	$6.48

Source: Data for columns 2, 3, 4, and 5 from Donovan et al. 1989, Appendix A. Data for column 6 reported in Poole 1980, 71.

largely unchanged.[5] Although the number of people living in Scottsdale is comparable to that in midsized cities, the geographical dispersal is much more like that of rural areas where lower-cost volunteer fire departments are usually effective. A comparison of the per-capita, fire-protection costs of Rural/Metro with those for communities of comparable density may demonstrate that the cost of fire protection, like that of asphalt repaving in New York City, is more sensitive to local geography than to the public or private nature of the entity providing the service.

The long-term relationship of Scottsdale with Rural/Metro violates a central tenet of privatization advocacy—that only competition can impose effective permanent discipline on costs and output. The Scottsdale contract is not currently, and could never be, put out for continual competitive rebidding. First, there are not enough alternative suppliers to constitute a competitive market. Even if enough suppliers existed, a new supplier still would have to navigate an enormous local learning curve before it rivaled the quality of service provided by Rural/Metro. Finally, where would the new supplier locate its business? In fire stations used by Rural/Metro? In new ones? Would it bring in a new crew of firefighters or hire employees from Rural/Metro? When local knowledge is critical for contractually providing a complex service, as with fire protection, there are good economic reasons why the threat of competitive replacement is often hollow at best. Once competition is uncoupled from contracting out, determination of the cost-effectiveness of alternative delivery strategies becomes a sophisticated managerial challenge. Competitive market theory provides no guidance.

Given the historic evolution of the institutional relationship between Scottsdale and Rural/Metro, the existing practice of cost-plus-contract negotiations is a reasonable procedure. It only makes sense for the city to pull out and hire a new provider or create a municipal department if the costs of the company grossly exceeded those of surrounding communities. Conversely, it makes little or no sense for a community with an existing municipal system to tear up its institutional history and install the type of private cost plus monopoly employed by Scottsdale. In both situations, the best practical path to sustained, efficient, and effective service is one of continual marginal improvement of existing arrangements.

[5]Scottsdale has 970 people per square mile compared with 2,760 people in Phoenix and 3,490 people in Glendale.

In fire protection, as in every other public service, the difference between public and private costs depends largely on labor costs and productivity. This is especially true when it comes to fire protection, where personnel accounts for more than 70 percent of total costs (Rural/Metro Corporation n.d.). Although the per-capita cost advantage of Scottsdale over its neighbors is fading as the city urbanizes, there is evidence that Rural/Metro still enjoys an edge. This does not, however, reflect an ongoing productivity advantage but highlights qualitative differences in staffing levels, training, and remuneration rates permitted by the more rural density of Scottsdale.

> *Staffing:* Although the norm in public systems is four firefighters to each piece of apparatus, Rural/Metro uses three. The standard firefighter workweek in the Phoenix area is 56 hours in a three-platoon system. Rural/Metro firefighters work 63 hours in a two-platoon system (Hammond 1995).
>
> *Training:* Standard public training requires 564 hours of emergency medical technician (EMT) and paramedic certification. Rural/Metro training takes 80 hours and includes only EMT certification.
>
> *Remuneration:* In 1987, Rural/Metro recruits received $3.50 per hour when local public fire companies paid an annual trainee salary of $21,192. At that time the average annual salary for a trained full-time Rural/Metro firefighter was $22,097 while the local public systems paid an average of $28,121. At higher ranks, the gap narrowed. Rural/Metro captains were paid $34,354 while public system captains earned $38,421 (Porter 1987). Those with longevity, typically higher-ranking officers, also received profit sharing under an employee stock ownership plan (ESOP) (Rural/Metro Corporation 1996).

Rural/Metro readily conceded at that time that it "cannot match, dollar for dollar, the wage rates of surrounding fire departments *and* remain cost effective . . ." (Rural/Metro Corporation 1988, 2).

Lower costs via lower remuneration may create labor quality problems. In a region and occupation where turnover has been almost nil, a city audit estimated a 20 percent turnover rate at Rural/Metro (ibid., 2). At that rate, the entire workforce is completely new every five years. This finding is especially important given the lower level of formal training received by firefighters in the company. A survey of Rural/Metro personnel revealed that many considered their training to be, for all intents and purposes, on-the-job. If turnover is high, the training level of firefighters employed at any moment is significantly compromised. Firefighters in comparable communities are clearly better trained. Thus, to the extent that Rural/Metro enjoys a labor cost advantage, it represents lower-quality labor inputs rather than greater efficiency. Rural/Metro was sufficiently concerned about this problem that it became committed to bringing the wages of its firefighters in line with those of surrounding public companies (Hammond 1995). This commitment to narrowing the labor cost differential helps explain, in part, why the per-capita cost differential between Scottsdale and its neighbors is decreasing.

Because Rural/Metro is a for-profit firm, it has strong market incentives to economize its staffing levels, which it does with an elaborate staffing pattern that involves on-call reserve firefighters as well as volunteers. It can manage in this fashion only so long the population density of Scottsdale remains significantly less than the regional average. As urbanization proceeds, pressure on the company to conform to regional staffing norms becomes irresistible.[6] Given the cost-plus nature of the Scottsdale–Rural/Metro relationship, it is difficult to see how the city can avoid absorbing these added staffing costs. It is easy to envision a time and situation in which an economically booming Scottsdale is transformed from one of the lowest-cost providers in the area into one of the highest.

If It's Such a Good Idea . . .

Arizona is a politically conservative state. If for-profit fire service was clearly more cost-effective than direct municipal service, little would stop neighbors of Scottsdale from following its example. Despite the favorable reviews garnered nationally by Rural/Metro, there is no local groundswell of support to have other cities sign on the dotted line. Indeed, some newer jurisdictions that had contracted with the Scottsdale-based provider have switched to municipal fire protection.

Sun City, Arizona, canceled its Rural/Metro contract and created its own fire company after its fire district board concluded that contract costs had "just gone up, gone up, gone up" (Flash 1988). The feeling among board members was that the company refused to negotiate and simply presented them with a take-it-or-leave-it bid. They calculated that by going it alone they could reduce their $1.3 million annual bill by almost $250,000. These savings included an annual $50,000 management

---

[6]This is in part borne out by the experience of the company in Rye Brook, N.Y., that is illustrated in the next section.

fee, plus the 8.5 percent profit of Rural/Metro on the direct cost of service. Once Sun City made its decision, neighboring Youngtown terminated its Rural/Metro agreement and contracted with the new municipal fire department of Sun City. The Youngtown Common Council estimated that it immediately saved $40,000 and that in future years it would save an average of $17,000 to $18,000 (Sexton 1988, B1). In ensuing years, several other communities also discontinued contract or subscription service with Rural/Metro and replaced it with municipal service.[7] These incidents forcefully demonstrate that at minimum, the local citizens who tried these contractual arrangements did not believe that the privatized fire service that they received was cost-effective. In all cases, cost as well as quality concerns figured in the decision.

The decision to switch from privatized to direct public service probably generated cost savings for the municipalities, although it is difficult to assess uniformly the magnitude of these savings. Accounting systems vary widely, and few municipalities use activity-based cost-accounting systems to accurately compare alternatives. Existing fire-service cost data strongly suggest that almost all cost differences are structural. When the skill level of fire-fighting personnel, equipment, staffing pattern, and area characteristics such as population density are considered, differences between public and private operation become insignificant. When municipalities decide on a given quantity and quality of fire-protection service to be privatized, they essentially buy only outside management. The economics of the make-buy decision boils down to deciding if the cost of added private management buys added public value. Given the strongly monopolistic nature of the local fire-fighting market, the uniformity of the technology, managerial skill required to fight fires, and the universal access to both, not much of a case can be made for significant added value from private for-profit fire-fighting management.

The principal attraction in private contracting, the promise that the profit-seeking contractor more effectively contains costs, is offset by the

---

[7]These were the Laveen Fire District south of Phoenix (1989), the Northwest Fire District near Tucson (1990), the town of Gilbert, Arizona (1989), and the Sun City West Fire District (1994). When Gilbert switched, Rural/Metro funded a referendum drive to overturn the decision by the town council. Gilbert is a conservative, Republican community with a predisposition toward privatization, yet its citizens voted by a better than two-to-one majority to support the decision by the council to create a municipal fire department.

moral hazard[8] inherent in the linkage between cost and profits and the concern in the community about the connection between costs and service quality. Almost invariably, the decision to retain direct control over fire service pivots on the fact that municipalities tend to be risk averse and resolve this dilemma in favor of more protection. That dynamic was clearly illustrated in recent decisions by the village of Rye Brook, New York, over a two-year period.

Rye Brook, New York, is a small, affluent suburban community located about 25 miles northeast of New York City in Westchester County. It abuts the larger working-class city of Port Chester located on Long Island Sound at the Connecticut–New York border. From its incorporation until 1995, Rye Brook contracted with Port Chester for fire service. During the summer of 1995, the two communities engaged in increasingly acrimonious negotiations about the terms of the contract. In December 1995, Rye Brook officials broke off discussions and announced their intention to obtain fire protection service independent of Port Chester. Local officials immediately signed a three-year contract with Rural/Metro to provide the service beginning in February 1996. Money did not appear to be the most pressing concern. The cost of the newly contracted private service was more expensive than the village had been negotiating for the services of Port Chester. Rye Brook agreed to pay $755,600 to Rural/Metro for the first year of the three-year contract. The contested contract fee negotiated with Port Chester was approximately $720,000 (Cascio 1995, 3A; Dublin 1995, 1A). In the context of the acrimonious negotiation situation, the mayor of Port Chester then issued an order that forbade its fire department from participating in any mutual-aid pact with its new for-profit neighbor. All was quiet until December 8, 1997, when a small fire broke out in a single-family residence in Rye Brook. The Rural/Metro firefighters were unable to contain the blaze and requested help from the Westchester County mutual-aid network. Port Chester refused to help. Rye Brook received no help from any other nearby Westchester communities. Eventually Greenwich, Connecticut, sent a company of ten firefighters to extinguish the blaze, but the house was destroyed. Fortunately, no one was injured.

---

[8]In economics literature, a moral hazard arises when the best interests of the provider and the client potentially clash.

The incident, which brought many simmering, unresolved, local political issues to the surface, also helped to illuminate some of the underlying economic dynamics of fire protection in small communities. Personnel expenses for trained firefighters on standby generate the largest proportion of fire protection cost. Because fires break out at any time, this expensive readiness, which permits rapid response time, is the essence of good fire-protection service. To offset the cost of maintaining large numbers of personnel on standby, small communities effectively pool these costs through mutual-aid arrangements. Each locale maintains a small local company with sufficient capacity to suppress small fires of the type that occurred in Rye Brook and provide adequate first-response life-saving capabilities at larger blazes in its community. In these latter instances, it is assumed that local companies from surrounding communities will respond in a prearranged manner. Some will send personnel and equipment directly to suppress the blaze while others will provide backup protection for the community in which the fire occurred. Therefore, the working relationships between local companies are critical to the effectiveness of this arrangement.

An important element of the cost containment strategy of Rural/Metro varies sharply with this local norm of mutual aid. The company keeps its operating costs down by using a minimal number of on-duty firefighters supplemented by the extensive use of reservists, who are not "at the ready." They report for duty when the company calls them and are paid by the hour when they are called. Income from this work is clearly supplemental to that from other jobs, and some reservists are students at local colleges who hope to earn occasional spending money. Rural/Metro introduced this reservist system, developed in its more rural home base of Scottsdale, into suburban New York via its Rye Brook contract. The company established a spare village fire department with three full-time firefighters on duty at all times. That is about half the size of the norm for adequate first response deemed acceptable by surrounding communities. The company maintained that its corps of 25 on-call trained reservists goes beyond offsetting any perceived service deficit.

The local reservists at Rural/Metro were paid $5.50 per hour when called. Note that $5.50 per hour was less than the going rate for teenage baby-sitters in the area. When the December fire broke out, Rural/Metro immediately put out a call for all 25 of its local reservists, but only three responded. The three full-time and three reserve firefighters could not handle the situation. By common local agreement, that size fire should have been handled without outside assistance. For the communities around Rye Brook, the issue was perceived as a "free-rider" problem. "It is not fair to the people in Purchase that we have to strip our district to protect them [Rye Brook]," remarked Chief Peter Decker of the Purchase, New York, fire department (Dublin 1998, 1A).

The immediate response of Rural/Metro to the failure of its reserve system and the regional criticism was to double (to six) the number of full-time on-duty firefighters assigned to Rye Brook.

What became powerfully clear to the citizens in the region was that their individual fire protection equaled more than the product of their local fire departments and depended heavily on the ability of individual companies to mutually support one another in an integrated regional network. When the Westchester County Association of Fire Chiefs, the organization that oversees the mutual aid system, met in January 1998 to discuss its future relationship with Rye Brook, the issue of clashing organizational missions was a paramount concern. According to the president of the association, Bill Nethercott, "some members [were] uneasy about helping a corporation that must balance fire protection against the need for profits" (ibid., 2A). This moral-hazard problem also weighed heavily on the risk-averse citizens of Rye Brook. In March 1998, the village canceled its contract with Rural/Metro. In the March elections, citizens turned out the mayor and village trustees who had hired the Scottsdale-based firm. The village has since recontracted with Port Chester. As part of the new arrangement, Rye Brook constructed, equipped, and bears the costs of a fire substation in the village. Port Chester supplies personnel. This improves response time and gives Rye Brook more control over its fire service. Costs are higher than those with the previous contract arrangement, but the entire incident made the residents of Rye Brook aware of just how risk-averse they actually were. Within reason, they prefer additional costs to additional risk. The new Port Chester contract gives them the advantages of a local fire company and unquestioned legitimate access to broader regional backup. There is no longer an open question of conflicting organizational goals.

The Rye Brook experience is not necessarily an argument against the ability of a for-profit provider to step in and do a good job. It is instead an argument in favor of the need to fully understand the nature of the service before a decision is made. In a large, self-contained municipality where mutual aid is not as crucial, clashing goals and personnel standards among constituent providers are not as serious an impediment. But, in a smaller community where many independent companies must cooperate, the ability to mesh smoothly within the mutual-aid network figures significantly.

Even in the Scottsdale home base of Rural/Metro, ongoing undercurrents of criticism that are rooted in concerns about moral hazard repeatedly raise the possibility of municipalization. As in metropolitan New York and Phoenix, the key to good fire protection is response time. The standard among the municipal fire departments of Phoenix, Tempe, and Glendale is a first-unit arrival at the scene of a fire within four minutes in 90 percent of the instances. The Scottsdale response averages six minutes—50 percent higher. To some extent, this lower standard could be defended because Scottsdale is less densely populated than these other communities. But, it also reflects the mixed motives and incentives of a for-profit operation. Although Scottsdale is the major client of Rural/Metro in the Phoenix area, it is not the only client. In addition to its master contract with the city, the company offers subscription-based fire protection to properties in unincorporated areas beyond the borders of Scottsdale. Rural/Metro provides this protection with equipment and personnel assigned to primary service in Scottsdale. On one hand, such subscription revenue presumably helps lower fire protection costs in Scottsdale. On the other hand, it also creates a moral hazard. According to an outside advisory panel convened by Scottsdale to evaluate its fire service, "fire station location philosophy needs to be examined in light of the best interests of the City of Scottsdale." The report stated that "stations appear to be located too close to city boundaries" (Fire Advisory Panel 1989). Although this may have facilitated service to other clients, it detracted from response time in Scottsdale.

This may not matter at all unless a major disaster occurs. Moral hazards usually remain theoretical until a ValuJet crashes. But, they are commonplace, if inconspicuous, in municipal-service contracting. When the service is complex and is in a category where it is difficult to judge product quality, profit-seeking behavior can easily jeopardize the interests of a client. In Rye Brook, New York, it took an actual fire to move this concern from the abstract to the concrete in the local decision-making process.

Lessons Learned from Fire Protection

Among the general lessons to be learned from private fire-fighting experience, two in particular stand out.

1. *Markets for complex public services are easily monopolized.* Fire protection is not a homogeneous product that can be uniformly provided; every jurisdiction is idiosyncratic. The service must be custom-fitted to local requirements, which makes it difficult to change providers with sufficient frequency to sustain effective competition while maintaining product quality. The local learning curve for new providers is too steep and declines too gradually. Moreover, because the service entails deploying expensive and highly specialized structures and apparatuses at strategic locations staffed by highly trained personnel, privatizing the service frequently amounts to little more than changing managers. It is impractical to move personnel and equipment continually in and out of town in the name of competition. Arizona localities that discontinued Rural/Metro fire-protection service often retained their employees but shifted them from the corporate to the municipal payroll.

Even if the bidding process to select the first provider of a complex public service at first appears to be competitive, often pressures from the buyer push the relationship toward long-term cost-plus-contracting along the lines of the fire-protection arrangement in Scottsdale.

Is that better than direct public provision? There is no single answer. Much depends on the characteristics of the participants in that particular system. The important point here is that initial competition guarantees nothing and can just as easily degrade the product as improve it. Success in privatization depends on how much the service in question lends itself to competitive versus noncompetitive market structures. Most complex and costly public services fall into the latter category.

2. *As the experience of municipalities around Scottsdale that rejected privatization in favor of municipalization implies, cost-plus contracting often exceeds the expense of supplying a public service directly.* Without an effective proprietary technology or managerial technique, the private sector does not enjoy an inherent advantage in providing complex public services. The lack of sustainable competitive contracting is not always, by itself, enough to make privatization less attractive than direct public provision. If monopolistic or oligopolistic private providers control managerial techniques or proprietary technology unavailable elsewhere, privatization still may be a viable option. However, in public-service provision managerial expertise tends to run in the other direction. Privatization advocates implicitly believe that the private sector has more people with superior managerial expertise. That belief must never be taken at face

value but always carefully examined. It is important to remember that privatization intends to bring private firms into the provision of public service, where they, by definition, have little or no prior experience. In such cases, most of the hands-on expertise resides with public managers. It is virtually standard privatization bidding practice for private firms seeking public business to bolster the case for their offer by demonstrating competence via the employment of former public-sector managers. This allays anxiety that the contractor might not have the requisite expertise to fulfill the contract. Private managers are believed to have more expertise, specifically in cost containment in a competitive environment. But, to the extent that the nature of complex public service exists in a noncompetitive environment, the substantive experience of the public managers becomes crucial to cost-effective service delivery. There is nothing a private fire-protection manager or private-school headmaster knows that a public manager or public school principal does not (or cannot) also know. Conversely, the private fire-protection manager and private-school headmaster could learn much from their public-sector counterparts that would help them to run public systems.

The issue is often more difficult. Privatizing complex services does not typically result in competition or monopoly but often ends up somewhere in between, creating a market of a few sellers—an oligopoly. What happens to municipal services in such oligopolistic markets?

Two Examples of Oligopoly in Action

Public Transit in Denver

In 1988, the Colorado legislature passed a law requiring that, beginning in mid-1989, 20 percent of fixed-route public bus operations in metropolitan Denver had to be provided by private contractors. This was the first of only two instances[9] in which a major urban transit system shifted a portion of its existing fixed-route service directly from public to private operation. In most other instances of public transit privatization, the introduction of new services such as express runs or demand-responsive paratransit services accomplished this task. In a handful of cases in smaller cities or semirural communities entire public operations have

[9]On January 19, 1997, the Harris County Metropolitan Transportation Authority privatized about 15 percent of its existing operations in Houston, Texas.

been privatized. From the point of view of major urban transportation systems, the almost decade-long experience with privatized public transit in Denver provides an exceptional opportunity to analyze the long-term feasibility of this approach to an important urban public service. The experience demonstrates how a seemingly competitive public-contracting opportunity evolves into an oligopolistic market structure.

The Denver privatization experience is particularly noteworthy because of the effort expended by its architects to try to ensure that the contracting remained competitive. Its advocates regarded privatizing 20 percent of the fixed bus routes in Denver as the first step in an orderly transition to competitive privatization of the entire system, and they took several measures to make the trial run a fair test of the viability of competitive contracting.[10]

The routes to be contracted out were carefully chosen to represent the best and the worst in the system. Thus, no one could accuse public officials or private contractors of "skimming the cream"—permitting the private sector to run low-cost and/or high-revenue routes while leaving the public system with poorly performing routes. To avoid this, desirable and undesirable routes were bundled into three independent bid "packages."

To discourage the development of a new, private monopoly, the privatization statute prohibited any single contractor from winning more than half of all contracted business. After four years, the packages were to be rebid to create an ongoing system of competitive rebidding in which the Regional Transportation District (RTD), the public agency charged with providing transit service in the metropolitan Denver region, would always be able to purchase the needed service from the lowest-priced, acceptable provider in a continuing cast of several potential contractors. This intention relied on what proved to be an untenable assumption—that a market with a sufficient number of qualified sellers could somehow be sustained.

Eighteen companies, some of them local charter operations and cab companies, attended the initial meeting of bidders. The turnout gratified privatization advocates in Colorado, who, like advocates of privatization elsewhere, based their hopes on the materialization of a large competitive market from the dozens of small transportation companies

---

[10]In 1999, the Colorado legislature passed a law mandating that privatization be expanded to 35 percent of service.

listed in the yellow pages of any metropolitan area. However, upon close inspection of the actual market for privatized urban transit, it turns out that a handful of national firms consistently win the major contracts. These firms have the resources to write expert proposals that respond directly to a request by an agency and have easy access to the requisite bonding and insurance and, hence, to the financing necessary to fulfill any commitments. This is no small consideration for the public boards responsible for public funds. Consequently, the effective contract-transit market has never consisted of the many small suppliers listed in telephone directories but comprises the few large ones found side-by-side in exhibition booths at national transportation conferences.

Denver's RTD ultimately received eight bids and awarded three contracts. All went to national companies: Mayflower, Laidlaw, and ATC/Vancom. Typically, the strategy of such large firms is to capture a new market quickly and drive out small competitors by submitting an extremely low initial bid. Sure enough, Mayflower offered an exceedingly low price of $28.26 per vehicle revenue hour on the first contract. (A vehicle revenue hour is the cost of operating a bus for one hour in passenger service.) This bid price was below the cost determined by KPMG Peat Marwick, the privatization consultant retained by the RTD, to be necessary to break even (KPMG Peat Marwick 1991). Even if smaller local firms could have cleared the hurdles of proposal writing and fiscal security, they lacked the cash reserves to take a loss on an initial contract. KPMG Peat Marwick warned the RTD that the initial charges were strategically motivated and did not reflect the actual cost of the service.[11] By 1993, the price charged by Mayflower had risen to $54.65 per hour, almost double the initial price but far more realistic. The 1996–97 rates ranged from $62.74 to $64.51 per revenue hour, which was about the same cost as public operation (Sclar 1997).

Once the Denver market became established, there was scarcely a whiff of competition. Mayflower and Laidlaw merged in 1995. Under the terms of the 1988 privatization law, this should have triggered a search for new competitors for the next round of contracting. However,

---

[11]"Without knowledge of the overall strategy of each contractor, which is subject to change, the financial performance of individual units of larger businesses may not give any indication of the future price strategy of each contractor" (KPMG Peat Marwick 1991, 2).

the consolidated operation successfully lobbied the Colorado legislature to modify the law, effectively legitimating its de facto market dominance (State of Colorado, House of Representatives 1996).

The original privatization bill had been sold to the legislature with the argument that the efficiency engendered by competitive privatization would reduce operating costs by 40 percent if enacted system-wide. It had been sold a bill of goods (*Rocky Mountain News* 1988, 12). In 1988, when the legislation was enacted, the RTD had an annual operating budget of approximately $100 million. By the end of 1990, the first full year of privatization, operating costs had jumped more than 12 percent to $112.3 million.[12] This sharp increase was particularly troubling because when privatization was initiated, the RTD was one of the most tightly run transit operations in the United States. Between 1986 and 1988, it had actually reduced operating expenses by about 4 percent. Between 1990 and 1995, the cost of contracted service swelled from approximately $14 million to almost $29 million—an increase of more than 100 percent. Meanwhile, the cost of directly provided service increased by just a little more than 11 percent. In six years, privatization cost the RTD more than $9.2 million over the course of public operation (Denver RTD 1996).

In 1997, two providers controlled the private-transit market in Denver, and their oligopolistic interdependence was apparent. A recent round of bidding resembled a game of musical chairs. There were only three bidders in 1997 for four newly configured packages of routes, and ATC/Vancom made the winning bid for all of them. (The second, higher-priced bid came from an "outsider," Grosvenor Bus Lines.) This turn of events may seem surprising because Laidlaw had previously controlled the lion's share of operations. But, this time around, Laidlaw bid on only one of the bundles. In early 1997, Laidlaw purchased ATC/Vancom's national school bus business so that ATC/Vancom could concentrate on public transit. And Laidlaw? Perhaps it bowed out of the bidding in Denver because it preferred to concentrate on the school-bus market. But, that did not deter the company from lobbying the Colorado legislature during its spring 1997 session to expand privatization

[12]Unless otherwise specified, all the financial data in this report are taken from the Comprehensive Annual Financial Reports of the Regional Transportation District. A national certified public accounting firm audits them all.

to 50 percent of the RTD's service. The campaign failed.[13] Whatever the motivation of Laidlaw, the fact that it engaged in business with ATC/Vancom outside the Denver market suggests that the relationship between the two ostensibly independent competitors may have been closer than arm's length.[14]

The cost and efficiency considerations that are the alpha and omega of competitive contracting are now beside the point. Contracting decisions in Denver are driven by the strategic considerations of the contractors in control of the Denver market. Once a regional leader in public transportation, RTD's management has been reduced to that of merely a passive broker attempting to mediate the often conflicting claims of the riding public, taxpayers, labor unions, and the politically astute contractors whose lobbyists regularly patrol the halls of the Colorado legislature. The situation is aggravated by the fact that the RTD board of directors is elected, not appointed, as in other major systems. As a result, an ideologically charged issue such as privatization is able to split the board and further paralyze the ability of management to use internal reform and contracting to control the operation. The general manager of RTD serves at the discretion of the board.

Something similar happened in the United Kingdom, where bus privatization has been under way for a longer time and implemented more extensively. Competitive bidding quickly turned, in one observer's words, "away from 'on the road' competition to 'boardroom' deals" (Pickup 1991, 237). Where initially there had been many small competitors, only a handful of large, consolidated firms now provide service. Fares are up, and ridership is down about 30 percent (Cormier 1996).

On the other side of the Atlantic, suburban Westchester County, New York, privatized its entire bus service in 1975. In the beginning, sixteen companies operated routes with none of them carrying more than a third of the passengers in the county. Within a decade, the number of

[13]A subsequent campaign was attempted in early 1998 but also failed.

[14] In 1999, the RTD did attempt to introduce a new lower-cost provider on thirty routes. TCT Transit Services, a Tennessee-based national provider, offered an extremely low price to get a foot in the door of the Denver market. It began operation there in September 1999. TCT was never able to secure a sufficient number of qualified drivers at the low wages it needed to pay to meet its contract price. As a result, by mutual agreement with the RTD, TCT gave up its contract about ninety days after it began, in November 1999. Once more, this left only Laidlaw and ATC/Vancom, the two firms that entered the market at the beginning, and continued control of Denver's transit privatization.

contractors was cut by half, and the largest remaining company was collecting 93 percent of the fares (D'Adamo 1985). By 1997, the largest operator controlled 97 percent of the operation. Costs were above those of comparably sized systems.

School Busing in New York City

With more than one million students, New York City is the largest school district in the United States. It also has the most expensive municipal school-busing system in the country (Myers 1995). It is so expensive mainly because it is privatized but not competitively contracted. It is not competitively contracted because it is too immense and complex to permit the kind of continual churning of service providers required by competition. Although the initial intention of creators of the system was to foster competitive contracting, disrupted school schedules and risks to child safety that could happen with frequent changes of providers proved unacceptable in a system of 3,800 routes. The key to reliability and safety is the continuity of the personnel who transport the children. The personal familiarity of drivers, dispatchers, and bus monitors with their charges year-in and year-out is crucial for knowing where children are during transit between home and school. Continually changing drivers, bus monitors, and dispatchers creates confusion and unacceptable risk to children.

The system had become a de facto system of franchises by 1979 when a bitter strike put to rest any lingering pretense of competitive bidding. To ensure labor peace and reliable service, the school board agreed to pay its contractors sufficiently so they could peg their wages to whatever settlement arrived at by the New York City Transit Authority (NYCTA) with its bus operators. Since public-transit wages are far higher than those typically paid to private school-bus drivers, costs ballooned.

For twenty years the school board has awarded contracts for the same routes to the same companies. Prices are determined by underlying costs plus a profit for the contractor. By all accounts, the system runs smoothly. High wages ensure low labor turnover and, therefore, a good safety record. The contractors have no incentive to keep a lid on salaries because they are paid what amounts to a management fee that is proportionate to operating costs. The higher the costs, the higher the fee. Thus, everything in this arrangement conspires to drive up its costs.

As part of his campaign to reduce municipal spending, Mayor Rudolph Giuliani decided in the spring of 1995 to take on school busing. He wanted to return to competitive contracting. Because owners, employees, and even parents had no reason to favor such a change, he had to impose it from the top. However, the size and complexity of operation made his threat to open the contracts to new bidders an empty one. There was no effective, outside, private competition and no public school buses or drivers to whom he could turn to challenge the entrenched system. Every viable operator in the area already had a piece of the action. As a result, the mayor suffered one of his first political setbacks. He obtained a substantial cut in the costs of the next contract and persuaded the vendors and their unions to uncouple their wages from those of the NYCTA, but the noncompetitive structure of the market remained in place. Even if competition could have been reinstituted, given the nature of the service, the market would more than likely evolve once again in exactly the same manner.

An alternative would be for the city to begin to create its own school bus fleet. Given the cost and inevitably fierce opposition from contractors, this alternative is difficult to imagine. Had it been a public system all along, the mayor would have had enormous leverage for controlling its costs. The workers would be public employees, and as such, they would not have a right to strike. The city could redeploy its own vehicles and routes as necessary without negotiating with outside contractors, a far more efficient management tool.

"Fixing" Market-Structure Problems with Contract Terms

Thus far we have not delved into the question of contract details. The market structure analysis was presented implicitly in the simplest terms: situations in which public agencies contracted to purchase public services from outside providers. In fact, the relationship between Scottsdale and Rural/Metro is more complex in terms of asset ownership, as is also the case with the RTD and its contractors. It is fair to ask what might occur if the service for which the public agency sought an outside supplier might be structured in a manner that made it easier for outside providers to behave competitively. If, for example, all fire equipment and all transit equipment were always publicly owned, would there not be more suppliers prepared to provide personnel and management? The short answer is unequivocally yes in the immediate period but probably no in the long run. The problem continually boils down to one of information sufficiency about an unknown future.

The alternative of public-asset ownership and private personnel and management is actually just one arrangement along a continuum of options for structuring privatization contracts. At one end is the situation in which the contractor is merely an outside manager, but all resources are publicly supplied, including personnel, equipment, and consumable supplies. At the other extreme, the public sector buys a finished product but supplies nothing. It merely writes a check for services rendered. The contractor provides the inputs and delivers output.

It is occasionally argued that the closer the contract can be structured to the pure management pole, the easier it is to maintain a competitive contract market. This argument rests on the presumption that there are many more potential suppliers of general managerial skill than there are providers capable of fulfilling the highly specialized requirements of very specific public services.

Although abstract logic on this point is powerful, in practice it changes little. The issue always comes back to the quality of the information held by public decision-makers when deciding on contractors and judging their work. Absent strong information, the time, money, and experiential costs of using the market option to discipline outside providers become too expensive and risky to use in all but the most extreme cases of malfeasance. The notion of incurring public displeasure for the disruptions of hiring and firing suppliers in situations of perhaps only marginal or nonexistent improvement or no improvement at all leads to erosion of competition regardless of the details of contract structure.

In the final analysis, the principal determinant of the contract-market structure remains the degree to which product quality can be monitored at low administrative cost. Typically, the products that meet this standard are products for which there is a preexisting private market. For products that are unique to the public sector, contract structure matters less than the trust built into the relationship between the provider and public agency. But, this has little to do with the nature of the market option. It has everything to do with the institutional environment in which the parties operate. This environment provides the context for both market and nonmarket options. If we are to use contracting more extensively in public service, we must better understand the relationship between these factors and interorganizational relationships. We turn our attention to these matters in Chapter 5.

Conclusions

In privatization debates, beneficial competition is treated as analogous to a common and hardy lawn weed that sprouts wherever its seeds touch the earth. A more accurate analogy would be a rare orchid, whose beauty is undoubtable but only blossoms under very special conditions. For policy purposes, it is far more realistic to think of the beneficent contracting competition described by privatization proponents as merely one of many structural forms taken by the contract relationship between public agency and private providers. More importantly, it must be understood that this structure is far from the most common one. Once a contract is put in place, buyers often find the costs of changing suppliers sufficiently daunting that they exercise the option in only the most extreme circumstances. Sellers, for their part, find that mergers and acquisitions that squeeze out excess capacity and push up profit margins become increasingly attractive as the contract market settles into place. Resultant forces on both sides of the market thus conspire to create situations of oligopoly and monopoly. This is a far cry from the imagined ideal of competitive market governance pitched by privatization advocates.

Even when competition exists, it is a double-edged sword. Its potential for harm may equal its potential for good. Much depends on the setting in which competition occurs. Economic history abounds with important lessons in this regard. The contemporary policy debate over health care provides interesting illustrations. How many hospitals are needed by a region? Hospitals are expensive to construct and staff. Competition in this case means supporting overcapacity relative to population size. While managed care companies competitively vie with one another in pursuit of market share, the supply of medical care remains the same. Hence, competition essentially means moving large numbers of people in and out of different administrative organizations every year when large employers hold open enrollment periods or when small ones shop for alternatives. We pay a steep price for this competition. In the United States, about 25 cents of every health-care dollar is spent on administration and profits. In Canada, which has national health insurance, the comparable overhead figure is 15 cents (Woolhandler and Himmelstein 1991).

The problem that confronts public officials who seek to privatize the public sector through contracting out "by the book" is the requirement of shouldering two costly burdens: (1) costs associated with trying to establish a stable, ongoing, and beneficial competitive market in which to buy the goods and services they seek and (2) costs associated with being both participants in and guarantors of that market. The costs associated with this double burden tend to be so large that they effectively are ignored most of the time. As a result, the more typical contracting situation confronting public decision makers is one in which the types of problems identified in this chapter are commonplace. Such situations involve trying to secure the best possible deal for the public sector in the context of a market in which the few sellers, even if they do not collude, do work somewhat in tandem with one another and in which the information available to the public decision maker is both imperfect and uncertain.

In that context, the examples reviewed in this chapter were intended to illustrate aspects of the real-world play of markets and politics that confront efforts to privatize services. They demonstrate the ubiquitous and imperfect structural complexity of the marketplace in which privatization contracts must be written. In Chapter 5, we more formally consider the dynamics of contracting.

5

All in the System

Organizational Theories and Public Contracting

Although the push for privatization is fueled more by an ideological desire to shrink government than a wish to enhance public service, the latter remains important. Public contracting is the principal vehicle in this political drive because it offers the possibility of linking the two. But, as the preceding chapters have demonstrated, it is a problematic course at best. The challenge from the standpoint of pragmatic reform is to uncouple the two goals. For those of us primarily concerned with the improvement of public service, it is necessary to shift the emphasis. We must seek to delineate the *economic* conditions under which public contracting can be an effective managerial tool.

From a political standpoint, it is easy to understand why proponents of less government link the goals. It permits the establishment of a broader political base in the service of their primary agenda. It also helps to explain why the intellectual linch-pin in the argument is the standard market model. The model is the ultimate justification for laissez-faire public policy. Although politically linking the case for extensive public contracting with laissez-faire economic theory may have short-term political appeal (we can have our cake and eat it, too), it obscures real reform opportunities. Worse, it exacerbates the risks that accompany any process of public-sector reform. Practically speaking, expanded reliance on contracting only works when it is part of a comprehensive reform strategy that simultaneously strengthens, not diminishes, public-agency performance. Such enhancement means that agencies can regulate more effectively and deliver services better. Ideological privatization proponents seek the polar opposite of this outcome: diminished capacity to regulate.

Nonetheless, the conservative drive to promote privatization and deregulation has political momentum that cannot be ignored. Although this overly simplified approach to such an important arena of public policy is lamentable, it creates an opportunity for substantive improvement in public-sector performance by forcing us to question our assumptions about the inviolability of existing organizational forms and the boundaries between so-called public and private activity. It is neither politically possible nor economically desirable to re-create the public bureaucracies that, on the one hand, successfully carried forward the visionary impulses of the Progressive Era and New Deal and, on the other, mossed over such impulses. For those of us who believe that a responsive and efficient public sector is the lifeblood of a progressive democracy, there is now only one way to move forward; we must embrace the opportunity afforded to us by new organizational forms. Our goal should be to reconstitute and improve how public agencies serve the public. Value for the public dollar should be a progressive, not conservative, watchword.

If we are to reach this goal, we need to anchor our analysis of contractual relations and organizational behavior in a theoretical context that realistically accounts for the behavior of contracting parties as they *are* rather than as we wish them *to be*. Under what types of organizational and institutional conditions is it preferable to displace bureaucratic forms of coordination with market mechanisms (contracting)? How may we recast bureaucratic organizations as more responsive organizations? In recent years, extensive literature has appeared that addresses such related questions of intra- and inter-organizational behavior. We draw on this literature to develop a sophisticated conceptual framework within which to analyze reform alternatives.

The standard market model is essentially a comprehensive and highly formal theory of exchange. It is not a theory of continuing relational behavior between individuals or organizations. Privatization proponents attempt to avoid this reality. They argue that there is little to differentiate the static conception of arm's length exchange relationships, which characterize the model's implicit "spot market," from the longer-term dynamic interactions between parties that characterize contracting. To analyze these complex differences, we need theories that more fully explain the dynamics of interpersonal, intraorganizational, and interorganizational behavior. With no firmer conceptual basis available, we are trapped debating the relative charms of two very unattractive straw men—red tape as far as the eye can see versus shady deals between politicians and contractors. To move on, we need to develop a fuller understanding of the limits and possibilities for cooperative long-term inter- and intraorganizational relationships.

Fortunately, literature on the economics of organizational and interorganizational behavior is rich and extensive. It can greatly improve the discussion. This literature predates the time when privatization became a fashionable buzzword. It is well beyond the scope of this book to provide an in-depth and comprehensive exposition of this literature. But, it is important that we understand and adapt its main insights, especially in relation to privatization. In Chapters 6 and 7, these insights are employed to suggest ways to improve internal organizational operations as well as relationships between public agencies and outside service providers.

Transaction-Cost Economics

If the world worked as smoothly as depicted in the standard market model, questions of organizational structure and contractual relations would be meaningless. If all parties to an exchange possess equal and adequate information with which to make decisions about the bargain they are striking, then, as the model implies, the world could be construed effectively as a collection of independent contractors continually making market deals with one another to accomplish their goals. Mistakes are rectified painlessly in the next round of deal making. But, if information is chronically inadequate and unequally distributed, then market-based transactions impose costs. As a result, when people decide to use markets to accomplish certain ends, organizations incur significant time and money costs to obtain the information necessary for using the market wisely. Because the decision to use a market is not "free," organizations face choices. They can either invest resources to use the market (contract out) or organize labor and capital to directly produce the desired output. In general, when the bureaucratic costs of an organization exceed the transaction costs of markets, rational decision makers opt for smaller organizations and more market-based interorganizational contracting. When the calculus is reversed, so is the decision. In the latter case, rational executives opt for larger organizations and less reliance on contract markets (Coase 1937). This important insight has led to the development of the larger field of organizational inquiry called transaction-cost economics (Williamson 1996).

Transaction-cost economics moves beyond the standard market model in two crucial ways: (1) its assumptions about the extent of rationality as a guide for economic action and (2) the substitution of transaction for price as an essential unit of analysis. These are explained below.

Rationality as a Basis for Action

Although it shares the neoclassical assumption that individuals and organizations behave rationally in pursuit of their goals, it holds that this rationality is bounded—limited by the availability of information and ability to properly process it. In contrast, the standard market model assumes hyper-rationality. Hyper-rationality implies that not only is all relevant information available to all parties, but they also know how to use it to their own best advantage. The less heroic notion of a limited rationality based on constrained information better describes the reality of day-to-day decision making. Economic actors frequently have some, but not all, of the pertinent facts when they make decisions. Consequently, even when they undertake a string of rationally defensible actions in pursuit of their goals, they often may end up in a worse position because of inadequate information. Moreover, it is wrong to presume that they all know how to best use the information they do possess.

Rationality and Guile

A corollary notion is that market participants act with not only bounded rationality, but also self-interested guile when dealing with others. In a world in which existing information, regardless of its adequacy, is not uniformly distributed, individuals and organizations with differential access to superior information are in a position to act opportunistically and frequently at the expense of the other, less-informed party to the contract. This situation is called information asymmetry. As a result of information asymmetry, we must concern ourselves with the transaction costs imposed by contracting in the form of opportunistic actions by one party or the other during the life of the contract. These actions undermine the contractual relationship and impose additional transaction costs on the market option relative to bureaucratic action.[1]

[1]Please note the terms *self-interested guile* and *opportunism* do not necessarily imply illegal behavior. Parties to an agreement often are hurt by actions of the other party that are perfectly legal under the terms of the contract because they occur in a situation not foreseen when the contract was drawn. Moreover, because interpretation of terms and conditions in contracts may be ambiguous, parties to a contract often behave in ways detrimental to the other party's interest yet not beyond the legal bounds of the written terms.

Transaction as the Unit of Analysis

Whereas the central analytic focus in the standard market model pertains to understanding the adjustment in the level of output relative to a change in price, in transaction cost economics the analytic focus is on the organizational processes through which the output is created (Williamson 1988).

Given the behavioral assumptions of bounded rationality and guile, contracting efficacy typically boils down to three factors: the frequency or volume of transactions engendered by the relationship, the degree of uncertainty in the contract situation (particularly with respect to quality of the output), and the need to make asset-specific investments to carry out the agreement. The more frequently the parties to an agreement must transact business with one another, the more cost effective it becomes to integrate the two operations organizationally.[2] The higher the degree of uncertainty about output quality and/or work process, the more expensive transaction costs are as related to thwarting opportunistic behavior; hence the less attractive is the contracting option. Finally, the more asset-specific investment that is required to foster the relationship, the higher the costs are for responding to a display of opportunism by one of the parties via exit from the relationship. The exiting party risks losing the relationship-specific investments. Opportunism becomes a problem especially when the external environment changes in an unforeseen manner and one of the parties stands to benefit by undermining the contractual relationship. As a result of the presence of such asset specificity, in a context of uncertainty it is often more rational to expand organizational size to accomplish the needed task. Similarly, the lower the volume of transactions, the easier it is to judge the quality of the output; and the lower the asset specificity of the needed investments, the easier it is to use market-based contracting relative to larger organizations. These conclusions of transaction-cost economics flow directly from the behavioral assumptions of the analysis: individuals operate from conditions of bounded rationality and with self-interested guile.

---

[2]This is not always the case. Holstrom and Roberts (1998) argue that the choices faced by firms are not simply dichotomous—integration of the operations versus contracting. There is, in fact, a wide spectrum of network-like accommodations in between. In Chapters 6 and 7, we explore the implications of these options for the public sector.

The New Institutional Economics

All economic activities occur in the context of the formal laws, informal rules, and norms that govern social behavior known as social institutions. They are critical to the efficient operation of markets in general and contract markets in particular. But, the standard market model pays scant attention to them. According to the standard market model, social institutions are passive, reactive, and hence largely irrelevant, analytically speaking. They occasionally may be important in the short run if they impede market efficiency, but in the long run, it is assumed that they passively adapt themselves to the requirements of market efficiency. Social institutions, in this view, are effectively a collection of learned and evolved behavior patterns. Their evolution is guided by concerns of economic rationality. Behavior patterns of contracting parties are presumed to be the most rational in light of the situation of the contracting parties. Analysis presumes that the contracting parties choose these patterns as a rational response to recurrent exchange experiences (Ménard 1995).

The problem here is that this explanation assumes hyper-rationality (i.e., the parties know all there is to know and they continue to improve market efficiency as a result of that knowledge). If that assumption is replaced with one of bounded rationality, then evaluation of the role of social institutions becomes more complex. Because social institutions embody both formal and informal rules by which society conducts its business, organizational form cannot be considered apart from the institutional structure in which it is embedded (North 1984). In practice, social institutions are the embodiment of values other than the rational pursuit of individual wealth, and they do not passively adapt to market strictures. They actively constrain how the market can operate. The Mutual Aid Pact (see Chapter 4) among Westchester fire companies is a prime example of this phenomenon. Therefore, two substitutions must be added to our analytical frame of reference. We need to replace the belief in institutional malleability with one that grants more enduring power to social institutions.[3] And, consistent with transaction-cost economics, we substitute the assumption of bounded rationality for the stronger one of hyper-rationality. Together these two more realistic assumptions give us basis for a reasonable, if conceptually less precise,

[3]"Enduring" power does not imply unchanging and unbending but means slowly changing. However, the change is not always favorable to market efficiency.

standard against which to judge the alternative means of enhancing agency operation. Using this analytic scheme, a contract can be considered efficient if it represents the best possible among institutionally *feasible* alternatives (Williamson 1996).

The key expression is "institutionally feasible." Such feasibility makes no claims for Pareto optimality (no one's situation can improve unless someone else's is diminished) (see Chapter 1). Feasibility recognizes that society often values social constraints on market outcomes. Pareto optimality puts less value on social institutions that are deemed impediments to market rationality. The social theory implicit in the standard market model effectively assumes that such "irrational" social institutions are forced to adapt to the pressures of the market. Russian transition to a market economy makes painfully clear on a very large scale that we must learn to settle for the more constrained outcome of institutional feasibility even though market optimality always appears within reach and more attractive. Recall that when the Russian transition first began, neoclassical economists with a base of theory rooted in the standard market model predicted that a strong dose of market deregulation would quickly "shock" the social institutions of Russian society into accommodating themselves to the requirements of a competitive market. The economists were wrong. It is the market that is adapting (some say distorting) itself to accommodate the social institutions of Russian society. The Russian "market society" that has emerged is a far cry from the one embodied in the standard market model. Perhaps if the process of policy advocacy and change began with a better appreciation of the constraints of social institutions, actual reform would have moved a lot farther and a lot faster than it has as of 2000.

The new institutional economics,[4] which connects the rationality concerns of transaction-cost economics with the formal and informal rules that social institutions impose on the behavior of individuals and organizations, creates a more robust but less specific context in which to evaluate contractual and organizational behavior. That synthesis is important because it permits us to legitimately introduce directly into our

---

[4]The new institutional economics breaks with neoclassical economics by making institutional analysis an important part of the analysis. It differs from the older school of institutional economics associated with Thorstein Veblen, John Commons, among others, which was indifferent if not outright hostile to the rationality concerns of neoclassical economics. The new institutional economics seeks to build an analytic bridge between the broader concerns of social institutional analysis and the rigor of neoclassical theory.

analysis concerns about larger institutional factors such as the political context of public organizations and the role of labor unions. The standard market model tends to treat such factors as essentially unwarranted and illegitimate intrusions to be dispatched as quickly and cleverly as possible. In essence, this synthesis gives us a theoretical framework that allows us to work with the reality of public contracting as it is rather than as we wish it to be.

Contracts in Theory and Practice

The Classic or Complete Contract

Contracting commonly is viewed as being static, a set of legally enforceable provisions written up in a document that defines the reciprocal obligations of two parties. However, the reality of contractual relationships is often more fluid. In privatization we must consider long-term interorganizational commitments as the basis for public-service delivery. To do that effectively, we need to work with a more encompassing concept of the possibilities for a contractual relationship. The contract needs to be construed less as a tangible object—a written document—and more as an evolving process of interorganizational relationships. In this light, the concept of contracting becomes a tool for evaluating alternative approaches to public-service delivery that is far more powerful and nuanced than the rigid and unrealistic assumptions of the standard market model. Contractual relationships can be broken down into three general types: (1) classical or complete contracts, (2) incomplete contracts, and (3) relational or network contracts (Macneil 1974, 1978). Each corresponds to a different situation in terms of the elements of transaction cost economics—transaction volume, asset specificity, and situational uncertainty.

The most straightforward contract that comes to mind when the term "contract" is mentioned, is a *classical* or complete contract. It involves an arm's-length[5] and largely legalistically defined relationship between the parties. It is typically drawn up for the creation of highly specific deliverable output in a tightly specified time frame. The relationship between buyer and seller is shaped and disciplined by the marketplace. If the seller performs in a less than satisfactory manner, the buyer may opt to seek another supplier. To the extent that there is a

[5]An "arm's-length" relationship is one in which the economic contract between the parties is in no way tainted by elements of favoritism, such as nepotism or political graft.

conflict that cannot be settled by this mechanism of market governance, the parties may resort to the courts in a situation in which the points of law are usually settled, and the courts are asked to make a determination based on the facts. In terms of transaction-cost economics, the relevant characteristics of a classical contracting situation are a low frequency of contracting transactions, a low level of asset specificity, and little uncertainty about the work to be undertaken. Contracts that fit this situation are usually for a brief, specific duration. Such contracts are characterized as complete because generally the contract terms effectively capture all present and future rights and obligations between the parties. Concerns about the impact of changes in the broader business environment on relationship terms vary from none to very little because of the time-limited nature of the contract. The provided product typically precludes a strong likelihood for repeat business. Hence, the contract is not complicated by a significant risk for loss of future goodwill if one of the parties undermines the terms of the contract through exercising opportunism.

Public contracting situations that fit this model are contracts for periodic projects such as putting a new roof on the town hall or designing new software for the computer system in the state department of motor vehicles. The work is discrete, involving easily evaluated deliverable products, and repeat business is so far in the future that neither party reasonably expects that the same firm will get the business next time. In the case of public contracts that fit this classical model, firms do have some reputational concerns in terms of future business with other public customers. These concerns, however, only condition contract performance to the extent that contractors believe news of poor performance is widely disseminated and relevant to other decisions.[6]

The Incomplete Contract

Situations of *incomplete* contracting are characterized by a high frequency of transactions, uncertainty about product and/or process, and

---

[6]Although this occurs to some extent, such information exchange is often more haphazard than commonly believed. In 1996, Suburban Carting Corporation was found guilty on federal racketeering charges related to some of its public contracts in Westchester County, New York. The day after the verdict, the State University of New York at Purchase—located in the county—awarded a contract to the firm for its trash hauling. The campus spokesman said that they were unaware of the issue. It would have been a factor in the decision process if the university had known. In Chapter 7, we suggest ways to make contract markets more efficient via the enhanced sharing of such pertinent information.

significant relation-specific asset investments. Typically, the contract is written for an extended period of time, and the contractor desires to capture future business. Because of the longer, and often indeterminate, time horizon and the intensity of the relationship between the parties, the expressed contract terms do not realistically specify behavior in all contingent future situations. It is no longer possible to easily exit the contract arrangement (market governance) to discipline opportunism on the part of the contractor because the length of the contract limits the ability of the agency to simply fire the contractor without compensation for asset-specific investments or other penalty clauses.

In situations of incomplete contracting, the parties typically recognize at the outset that the contract is incomplete by necessity. It is often impossible to specify all the future situations intended to be covered by the contract. Typically, one way around the creation of an overly expensive and unwieldy contract is an agreement by the parties to use it as a vehicle for planning future contingencies by other means. This is expressed through the deployment of contractual clauses for situations of hardship and arbitration for dispute resolution. Williamson (1996) calls such provisions "trilateral governance" because explicit provision is made for a third party to help settle differences.

It is essentially within this realm of incomplete contracting that several problems deriving from information asymmetry appear. Commonly, but not exclusively, this asymmetry favors sellers. They are always "in the market," whereas buyers enter the market sporadically. Sellers are more apt than buyers to be aware of the implications of different future scenarios on contract performance. The three most important forms of information scarcity in incomplete contracting situations are principal–agent problems, adverse selection, and moral hazards. Although these may be conceived as distinct situations, they are essentially variations on the single theme of information inadequacy. For purposes of exposition here, we present instances of actual contract failure as examples of these forms. However, it is important for readers to understand that in practice any instance typically incorporates manifestations of all three.

Principal–Agent Problems Principal–agent problems typically arise when one party (the principal) hires another (the agent) to carry out an assignment, but the agent is able to serve its own interest at the apparent expense of the principal because of information asymmetry. When consultants to the city of Scottsdale concluded that the decision to locate fire stations closer to the city border rather than the center better served the interests of Rural/Metro than those of the city, they raised a concern that a principal–agent problem had occurred (Fire Advisory Panel 1989). Rural/Metro, the agent in this case, had individual fire-service contracts in areas bordering Scottsdale, the principal. More peripheral locations for fire stations made it possible to capture subscription business and fulfill its contractual obligations to Scottsdale. The consultant's evaluation suggested that this pattern of location might better serve the interests of the agent than the principal.

In the early 1990s, Westchester, New York, county executive Andrew O'Rourke proposed what he saw as a model public–private partnership at the county medical center. Instead of the then publicly owned medical center directly operating its own parking facility, an outside professional operator, APCOA of Cleveland, Ohio, received a contract. Without any public money, the private operator financed, built, and operated a new parking garage as well as ran the existing nineteen lots in this sprawling suburban complex. APCOA built the new parking facility at an estimated cost of $11 million and opened it to the public in 1994. Before APCOA took over, the cost of using the hospital lots was $1.10 per hour. When the new facility opened, rates jumped to $1.75 per hour. By the spring of 1997, rates had risen another 26 percent to $2.20 per hour. The contract, intended to run through the year 2014, gave the private contractor (the agent) the right to set parking rates. The medical center's chief executive officer, Edward Stolzenberg, decried the situation in 1997 saying that "(t)he existing prices are a detriment to the hospital and an unfair imposition on people who use the hospital." The burden on patient families was sometimes difficult. One 79-year-old woman with limited income, who had a son dying of cancer at the hospital, strictly monitored her stays so that she did not inadvertently park for more than two hours when the rate jumped to another fee range (Wilson 1997b, 2A).

The problem here relates directly to mission conflict between agent and principal. The agent, APCOA, is in the parking lot business to make as much profit as possible. The principal, the county medical center, regards parking as an ancillary service to its patients and their families and would like to run the operation as close as possible to breaking even. But, the deal as struck left the principal with no room to maneuver. In hindsight, it is easy to see how a more informed negotiating position on the part of the county could have given it more control over a crucial, asset-specific investment in the transaction and hence a better outcome.

But, APCOA is in the parking-lot business all the time; Westchester County is not. APCOA had a far better understanding of the profits and pitfalls of its contract-negotiating stance. The principals in this case, the medical-center trustees, apparently underestimated the full implications of ceding control of parking rates before experiencing the problem. The agent, of course, always understood its need to protect revenue sources. This problem points out one of the manifestations of the operation of bounded rationality.

In early 1999, with a political change in county leadership to an ideologically moderate county executive, the medical center moved to extricate itself from the oppressive and skyrocketing parking rates for patients and visitors. The Westchester Medical Center purchased the complex from the contractor at a price of $14.2 million—30 percent over the costs of construction. "I don't care if we lose money on this," said Stolzenberg. "It's one of those things we need to do. When you are charging so much to park, the person is mad before they even walk in the door" (Kohn 1999, B1).

The dénouement of this venture into privatization and reintegration[7] is instructive in two regards. First, it illustrates the problem of "holdups" when one party gains control of asset-specific investments. When this occurs, one party can force the other to pay a premium to get out of an increasingly bad deal (Klein 1993). The taxpayers of Westchester County and patients of the medical center, in one way or another, absorb the costs of this takeover. Moreover, had the county built the facility in the first place, it would have been able to use tax-exempt financing to pay construction costs, which would have been far less than the costs incurred by allowing a private firm to build the facility at conventional financing rates.

The second lesson is even harsher. The original deal was revealed as put together by the leading Republican power broker in the county, Albert Pirro.[8] Mr. Pirro is an influential Republican Party fundraiser who is connected to many of the major, public real-estate deals in Westchester County. As part of the original agreement, APCOA paid him a "consulting fee" of between 10 and 20 percent of the project's gross revenues

---

[7]Between the privatization of the garage and its repurchase, the medical center itself was spun off as a not-for-profit public benefit corporation and was therefore no longer a unit of county government. Hence, the repurchase is more accurately seen as "reintegration" rather than "governmentalization" of a private function.

[8]At the time of this writing, Mr. Pirro is under indictment for federal income tax evasion.

(Wilson 1999, A2). Hence, between 22 and 44 cents of each hourly parking fee went directly to Mr. Pirro. He likely received around $500,000 from the sale. It is often extremely difficult for the public to learn about such political side arrangements when public contracting takes place. Every effort is made to keep them from the public record. The fine line between guile in negotiation and outright corruption is too often quite thin and permeable. Therefore, it is important that public contracting, especially if it is to be expanded in the name of privatization, explicitly recognize incidents such as this as an ongoing part of the institutional political reality of public contracting rather than as an anomaly. Privatization must be placed under exceedingly strict supervision. This is one of the topics discussed in Chapter 7.

The poor performance by Westchester County in contract negotiation points out an inherent problem in incomplete contracting situations. In situations of classical contracting, the interests of the agent and principal typically align easily. Easy enforcement of the contract by law serves to ensure in an overarching sense that the agent carries out the principal's wishes. More importantly, the quality and/or work process is sufficiently transparent that the principal understands exactly what the agent is supposed to do and whether or not it was actually done. If the principal's wishes have not been fulfilled, he or she may withhold payment until the work is completed in a satisfactory manner.

When we shift to the longer-term situations of incomplete contracting, product transparency often fades. Even a product as a priori straightforward as parking services may take on very different qualities in the context of an incomplete contract having many other factors. In such situations, the purchased goods and services are not easy to evaluate before the contract is executed. They are what economists describe as "experience" goods. This distinguishes them from "search" goods. Search goods are like the family car; the quality of the product is well understood by the buyer before the purchase. The buyer invests time to find the best buy—an exercise well suited to classical contracting. Experience goods—the stuff of incomplete contracting—are impossible to evaluate before the purchase. It is only in the process of using the good that the buyer learns the qualitative attributes of the purchase that he or she values. This is exactly what occurred in Westchester County Medical Center's parking contract.

To offset information asymmetry when making a contracting decision, public agencies or private firms that find themselves disadvantaged in incomplete contracting situations often hire third-party consultants to advise them on contract provisions. The city of Scottsdale did this when it sought an outside evaluation of its contracted fire-protection service. Westchester County could have followed a wiser course by getting such help when it was negotiating its privatization agreement. But, it is important to note that it took Scottsdale about four decades to decide to bring in a consultant. The Westchester experience was complicated by the fact that powerful political players in the county had a stake in the outcome, making such neutral advice harder to purchase. Moreover, outside consultancy can be expensive and is not a sure cure for the problem. The principal–agent problem is both inherent and ongoing whenever seeking a service whose quality is not readily apparent.

Moreover, it is important to understand that the problem of bounded rationality can be even more complex than merely one of information adequacy. It also involves the value scale applied by individual decision makers to the information they do receive. In the case of Westchester, the evidence from many other experiences there is that county government was a more than eager victim. The county executive, Andrew O'Rourke, who oversaw negotiations about the parking agreement was considered to be a zealous—indeed overzealous—advocate of privatization. Consequently, positive information about the public–private partnership was more highly valued by public negotiators than negative information.

Adverse Selection   Adverse selection is a situation in which the party with inferior information about the market situation acts first in seeking to establish a contractual relationship (Salanié 1998). The notion originally derives from the experience of insurance companies. Insurance companies are aware that if they offer a product at a price that suffices in an average situation, there is a high probability that they will sustain a loss. The loss occurs because individual buyers are more aware than the company about the true state of their individual condition. People most likely to sustain a loss will seek insurance while those with the least risk will not. Hence, the average situation does not reflect the potential market for the insurance product. This situation is called adverse selection.

To remain profitable, insurers seek to counter this adverse selection of their product. They do this by setting the premium higher than the average cost. But, when they raise premiums, they drive even more low-risk individuals out of the market. They may sustain the added costs of an aggressive marketing campaign to convince a broader group to use this product or impose conditions on the transaction that are intended to even out the disadvantageous informational asymmetry between themselves and potential customers. If allowed to do so, terminally ill people would buy large amounts of life insurance just prior to their deaths. If insurance companies knew their potential customers were terminally ill, then they could refuse to sell insurance to them. It makes no sense to collect, say, a $1,000 premium this month and then pay out $250,000 within the ensuing months. To avoid problems caused by adverse selection, life insurers require potential customers to have a physical examination prior to issuing a policy.

In the context of public contracting, especially in situations of privatization, adverse selection is often a serious problem. It occurs because the public buyer is faced with a need to select a contractor from a universe of inexperienced sellers. Although privatization advocates argue that via a "yellow pages" test public purchasers can learn quickly and inexpensively about the existence of qualified sellers, as we have seen, publicly supplied services are often similar to, but not the same as, ostensibly analogous private products. The adverse-selection problem arises because often the less-qualified contractors offer the best prices. Since privatization is ostensibly about a quest for lower costs, this poses a serious dilemma.

Contracting is always a future-oriented activity. Contractors are asked in the present to specify their price for a product that they will deliver in the future. The future is always unknowable, so contracting is always an uncertain venture—even complete contracting. But, the problem is even worse in privatization situations for longer-term contracts. The longer the term of the contract, the more likely it is that more relevant factors are likely to change. To protect themselves in such situations, contractors can and do build some allowance into their offer price to cushion themselves against unforeseeable contingencies. The more competitive the market and experienced the bidders are with a product, the smaller is the contingency built into their offer prices. In classical contracting, contingency is usually not a serious problem because the degree of uncertainty is typically small.[9] The ground trodden by bidders

[9]At the limit when knowledge is perfect, contingency payments are zero. The theoretical case for contracting over direct production is unassailable. In the presence of uncertainty and hence contingency payments, the theoretical case for the superiority of contracting over direct production dissolves. See Sappington and Stiglitz 1987.

and the customer in such situations is familiar to all. Information asymmetry is, at best, a minor problem in these situations.

In the incomplete context that typically characterizes privatization situations, the story is different. The actual size of the contingency that any bidder builds into a contract varies, not just with the pressure of competition and the level of uncertainty, but also with the ability of the bidder to tolerate risk. Bidders with a high degree of risk tolerance build a lower contingency payment into their offer price than do those who are more risk averse. From a public vantage point, the challenge is to create a contract in which payment is rendered for service received and not to offset perceived contractor risk. Indeed, one of the main reasons for privatization is to shift risk from the public sector to the seller. If the public sector is willing to assume risk, then sellers have significantly less incentive to act efficiently.

In actual practice, bid prices in incomplete contracting situations related to privatization vary less on how relatively efficiently the bidders do the actual work and more on how they differentially perceive and price the uncertainty in the situation. That most likely occurred in the bids that MassHighway received for its Essex County highway maintenance privatization, although without knowing the internal workings of each of the bidders, it is impossible to say for sure. Submitted bid prices differed by almost 120 percent, from $3.7 million to $8.1 million. Given the straightforward, simple, and standard nature of the bulk of the tasks, such as lawn mowing, it is difficult to imagine that such large price differences reflect differences in relative firm efficiency. The more likely explanation is that these differences reflect differences in perception of contract risk and risk tolerance among the bidders.

How can a public agency know if the low bid that it receives reflects more efficient work or merely a higher degree of risk tolerance? Phrased slightly differently, how can a public agency know if the lowest bidder is the most competent or merely the most risk tolerant firm?[10] Too often, risk tolerance is akin to a well-known source of bliss: ignorance. That is, the least knowledgeable bidders often bid the lowest price. Or, the lowest bidder may be aware of the risk but is most desperate to get the work. This dilemma confronts any buyer who seeks a contractor but is worse in public-contracting situations because public agencies are usually bound

---

[10]In the terms of an economist, we seek to separate elements of "economic rent" from true costs of production.

by law to accept the lowest bid from a qualified bidder. Rules on qualification of necessity must be written in such a way that they reflect obvious and measurable qualities of potential contractors. This is necessary because unsuccessful bidders often challenge contract awards both administratively and legally. Yet, intangible qualities such as risk tolerance and ability to work well with the public customer are often critical for efficiency and effectiveness. These qualities, so important to private buyers, always fly under such rigid regulatory radar screens.

This interconnected problem of systematic risk tolerance and adverse selection has cropped up frequently in recent years in the provision of paratransit services. Paratransit services are publicly provided door-to-door transportation services that are typically used to meet the mobility needs of disabled and elderly populations. Paratransit is provided on the basis of prearrangement between the user and the provider. The user calls the provider and makes an appointment to be picked up, taken to, and brought back from a destination. Think of the service as existing between individual taxi service and scheduled and routed bus service. Paratransit often involves the use of small buses and vans equipped with wheelchair lifts and other devices for transporting the disabled. Typically, each run carries several passengers. The 1992 Americans with Disabilities Act (ADA) required that regional public-transportation agencies expand available paratransit service. Because paratransit entered urban transit as an unfunded mandate via the ADA, the initial reaction was to keep the service at a distance. In practice, this meant attempting to provide as little of it as legally possible and at the lowest level of cost and acceptable safety. Most agencies responded to this mandate by contracting for service with outside suppliers.

The "yellow page" contractors who most easily fit the bill for this work were local taxi companies and small, contract school-bus operators. These firms were especially appealing to the larger regional public agencies for three reasons: (1) They have experience with door-to-door service, a hallmark of paratransit and thus appear to comprise a highly competitive market. Taxi operation, with its low cost of market entry when not constrained by regulation, easily fits this requirement. (2) School-bus operation is a bit more complex, but to the extent that a contract in hand can finance rolling stock, it tends to permit small firms to operate, too. (3) These firms have a history of being low-cost providers because they tended to hire their workforce on a contingent or as needed basis. As a result, labor costs, and by implication overall costs, are low in these industry segments. Together, these characteristics made the initial costs of privatizing paratransit appear to be remarkably low, especially when agencies contracted with small operators. The contrast is especially sharp in relation to the costs of fixed-route public transit operations.

One problem with low costs generated by low wages is that they directly correlate with an inordinately high rate of labor turnover. The impact of that on training costs, accident rates, and low-quality service becomes a serious problem when the public agency is politically responsible for a high-quality service standard and is, to some extent, legally liable for damages. According to the Southeastern Pennsylvania Transportation Authority (SEPTA), in the mid-1990s the driver turnover rate among its contracted operators was between 20 and 30 percent per month,[11] which meant that in one year the entire operator labor force of the typical contractor turned over, on average, between 2.4 and 3.6 times. Not surprisingly, this led to a high rate of passenger complaints— one measure of service quality. Contractor complaint rates ranged from 9.4 per ten thousand up to 46.3 per ten thousand passengers. By comparison, complaints on the portion of paratransit service provided by the better compensated employees at SEPTA was 7.9 per ten thousand, about 20 percent below the best of the other contractors.

The use of small providers may be "beautiful" in theory, but in practice competition among small providers can be a costly lesson in the pitfalls of risk tolerance and adverse selection. Small is often synonymous with undercapitalized. The market, to which regional transportation agencies like SEPTA turned for competitive paratransit operators (although it does have some large well-managed providers) is filled with many undercapitalized small competitors whose resources were not up to the challenge that the higher-quality and more complex modern paratransit service brought into existence with the 1992 ADA legislation demands. Nonetheless, these small providers were prepared to represent themselves as capable of delivering a service that they were in fact unsuited to deliver—this is the adverse selection problem.

One of the main characteristics of undercapitalization is the tendency of such firms to have chronic cash-flow problems. They eagerly seek new business to mitigate this cash crisis. The problem of taking on more business than the organization can realistically absorb becomes

[11]This is a SEPTA response to a query from Allstate Transportation concerning the desire of SEPTA to impose a minimum hourly operator compensation rate requirement on outside contractors (SEPTA 1997c).

manifest in poor service. When the possibility of winning public contracts for ferrying the disabled and elderly appeared, these poorly capitalized small operators severely underestimated the true internal cost of the contract. The exact reason for the decision of any particular firm to bid on work always results from a complex mixture of facts. But, for the small firms that won so many of the contracts and then abandoned service or went bankrupt, in all likelihood the decision was driven by some combination of risk tolerance born of ignorance and pressing cash-flow considerations. These unqualified companies undoubtedly hoped that if they could convince the agency to award the contract to them, they would be able to move down the learning curve and weather their cash-flow problems simultaneously. Without full-blown access to the books and thinking of the small entrepreneurs who operate these firms, it is impossible to know the exact mix of factors in any particular case. But, from the vantage point of observable behavior, it is clear that the outcome is consistent with a situation of adverse selection. The least *effectively* qualified providers offered the best prices.

The low, attractive, initial prices offered to the public-transit agencies by these small, ill-equipped firms proved irresistible, but inadequacy quickly became apparent in missed appointments, traffic fatalities, unqualified drivers, and poor vehicle maintenance. Moreover, the vehicles they were now required to maintain were new and more expensive than the ones used in the past. At the same time, they had to contend with the fallout of their low wage–high labor turnover milieu in both operations and maintenance. This led to situations in which many providers either abandoned the service or filed for bankruptcy, the situation in which the Walsh Cab Company, doing business as Access Transit, found itself when it filed for Chapter 11 bankruptcy in October 1996. It is not unique in this regard.[12] The filing for bankruptcy by the firm put the matter both bluntly and correctly: "the bids which stood as the basis for the contracts were not high enough to allow [the company] to *profitably* (emphasis

---

[12]A similar situation occurred in Toronto, when the cab company providing paratransit service also went into bankruptcy. The Toronto Transit Commission (TTC) established Wheel-Trans to continue the service. However after establishing an outside task force to examine the issue on its merits, the TTC concluded that it was preferable in terms of service quality, cost, and system integration to continue to provide the service directly rather than return to the instability of outside contracting. The same problem also occurred in Baltimore when the operator abandoned the service suddenly and the agency and its union were forced to develop a way to continue the work.

added) perform under the contracts" (Walsh Cab Company 1996, paragraph 4). This collapse, in turn, compelled SEPTA and its operating union, TWU Local 234, to step in and temporarily establish an in-house paratransit operation, Freedom Transit.

The dilemma confronted by agencies that are committed to returning the work to outside providers for reasons of ideology or politics is one of avoiding future adverse selection problems. Due diligence to guard against adverse selection repeating itself among a universe of ever-changing small competitive providers is costly in terms of time *and* money. Instead, these agencies move to what is essentially a form of managed competition in which they work with a selected group of higher-cost private providers. In addition, public agencies, out of necessity borne by their legal mandate, become more involved in the day-to-day operations of their contractors. To improve service reliability, SEPTA to a large extent now micromanages its providers by mandating the wage levels paid by its paratransit contractors to drivers and taking control of the dispatch system. Recognizing that risk tolerance and undercapitalization have caused prices to fall below the costs of production, SEPTA has also adjusted contracts upward from the initial competitively bid prices of the undercapitalized firms to ensure that their providers stay in business (South Eastern Pennsylvania Transit Authority [SEPTA] Board 1997). Although stabilizing the service and keeping it "privatized," this practice also removes any incentives from contractors to behave in a cost-efficient manner. Once the virtues of competitive market-based risk sharing have been set aside in the name of defense against the fall out of adverse selection, there is no special virtue in contracting rather than providing the service in-house. Much of the decision to privatize hinges on the nature of local conditions. In the case of SEPTA, there was a good in-house alternative in Freedom Transit.

In fact, the experience of SEPTA with directly provided paratransit service had been extremely positive. In late April 1997, just prior to the reprivatization of the operation, the in-house paratransit operation ran at an operating cost that was almost 17 percent below the amount SEPTA initially budgeted for that operation when it was performed by Access.[13] Nonetheless, SEPTA disbanded Freedom Transit and awarded

---

[13]The year-to-date net budget amount for the service had been $10.9 million as contract work. In house, the actual net budget has been $9.1 million or a savings of $1.8 million (South Eastern Pennsylvania Transit Authority [SEPTA] 1997b).

the work to a new vendor, Atlantic Express, that is not a small undercapitalized provider. It is a large multistate operator with a unionized and dependable workforce that can provide a reliable high-quality product. But, real cost savings via contracting are no longer possible. Estimates prepared by TWU Local 234 indicated that the costs of continued in-house operation would have been approximately $3 million less than the $10.7 million contract price awarded to Atlantic Express.[14] Although SEPTA rejected these estimates, it conceded that the difference between in-house costs ($33.03) and contract costs ($32.95) were virtually nonexistent: $0.08 per vehicle revenue hour (South Eastern Pennsylvania Transit Authority [SEPTA] 1997a). In this instance, the issue of privatization at SEPTA is a matter less of economic rationality and more of the institutional constraints of ideology and politics.

In a larger sense, the example demonstrates the powerful dilemma created by the presence of adverse selection for the process of public contracting in even the most competitive of circumstances. It is possible to have a large market of small competitive sellers, but the costs of avoiding adverse selection or mitigating its damage can be unacceptably high. Or, an agency can create a less competitive but more carefully managed bidding process among a small number of larger firms. This prevents the adverse selection problem, but then the prices paid likely will be higher. It also means that in such situations, public agencies are well advised to take a fresh look at direct service provision. We consider all of this in Chapter 6.

Moral Hazards Moral hazards refer to potential problems of reduced incentives on the part of the agent to fulfill the goals of the principal. In the early 1980s, Reagan administration transportation officials were so sure of the ultimate economic simplicity and superiority of privately contracted transit operation that they decided to sponsor a controlled experiment in which private and public buses ran simultaneously. They assumed that the experiment would prove beyond a shadow of a doubt that private operation was superior. The Metro-Dade Transit Agency (MDTA) that serves the Miami region of Florida was bus-starved. The administration gave the MDTA a grant of $7.5 million to acquire 80 new buses at a cost of $93,750 each on the condition that they be used in a Private Enterprise Participation (PEP) demonstration. The buses were

---

[14]Comparative cost analysis prepared by TWU Local 234 from SEPTA provided data.

to be run on ten carefully matched routes. Half were run by the MDTA and the other half by Greyhound Lines Inc. under a three-year service contract. Greyhound won the right to run these buses by submitting the lowest competitive bid for the work. Given its core business as an inter-city bus line, there was presumably little question about the competence of Greyhound to operate rolling stock over fixed routes. At that time there was also little doubt that Greyhound was adequately capitalized to carry out the work. Adverse selection did not appear to be a problem.

The demonstration was intended to provide carefully monitored evidence of the superiority of private operation. Price Waterhouse was hired to monitor the experiment (Price Waterhouse 1990). Although reported operating costs were lower on the Greyhound routes, the "savings" came at a steep price. The contract failed to specify any perform-ance standards for ridership and, more importantly as it turned out, equipment maintenance. The level of complaints on Greyhound routes rose by more than 100 percent. These routes experienced an 18 percent loss in ridership in the first six months and an additional 13 percent loss in the next six months. By comparison, the routes run by MDTA had significantly lower complaint levels and maintained their ridership. The results were so dismal that the experiment was abandoned after eigh-teen months. The alleged savings also came at the cost of improper equipment maintenance. The buses, which were owned by the MDTA and not Greyhound, were so poorly cared for that only ten of the forty new buses could be put back into service after eighteen months. Buses such as the ones used in this demonstration are expected to last twelve years with normal use. In essence, after correcting for eighteen months of depreciation, $3.3 million of the original $7.5 million—as well as a major share of the public transit ridership in the region—had to be writ-ten off as a total loss.

The problem in this situation was the federal government's exclusive focus on cost. Given the ideological predilection of the decision makers, they merely assumed that the contractors would take responsibility for the ridership and equipment. As a result, the MDTA, under federal di-rection, fashioned a contract in which low cost was the deciding factor. It created incentives for the winning low bidder to achieve its goal at the cost of the central mission of the agency—the provision of public trans-portation. The combined presence of information asymmetry and the lack of any contractual incentive to care for either the customer base (the system's ridership) or the equipment created a moral hazard. This moral hazard could have been avoided by inserting clauses in the contract that specified penalties or liquidated damages for such breaches as lost ridership and required the buses to be periodically inspected by the MDTA—a qualitatively different and more costly contracting process. Even if the terms called for tighter control, questions of effective enforcement could still render it uncertain.

Effective enforcement as a solution for problems of moral hazards is often easier and less expensive to advocate than it is to implement. For example, principals often hire agents to perform motor-vehicle repair work and the agent almost always controls the relevant information. However, there is a great deal of difference when the contracting decision is made by an individual motorist and when it is made on behalf of a public fleet. First, individual automobile owners have strong obvious incentives to perform due diligence to safeguard both their vehicles and their checkbooks. Public contracting automatically creates a moral hazard because the vehicles are public property. The experience of the City of Albany, New York, with overcoming the expense of moral hazards in privatization of its motor-vehicle maintenance illustrates the problem.

In January 1992, the Department of Public Works (DPW) in Albany privatized its entire in-house motor-vehicle maintenance operation by turning the work over to local repair shops. An investigative study undertaken by the American Federation of State County and Municipal Employees District Council 61 and Blue Collar Workers Union Local 1961, the local union that represented the displaced mechanics and helpers initially exposed the moral hazard. Among their more egregious findings are the following:

> One contractor charged the city $80 to check all the lights on a sanitation vehicle and replace broken marker lights. Two weeks later, after traveling only five miles, the same repairs were once more performed by the same contractor on the same vehicle at a cost of $128.
>
> Another sanitation vehicle was brought to a local shop to have a hydraulic leak repaired. The necessary work was done. In addition, the hydraulic oil was checked, the brakes adjusted, all lights checked, bad bulbs and bad marker lights replaced, and necessary wiring repairs performed for $183. Three weeks later, the vehicle returned to the same shop. This time the hydraulic oil was topped off, the brakes were adjusted again, and all the lights and wiring were once again judiciously repaired. This time the city was charged $203.
>
> A police car was brought into a local dealership with faulty parking lights. In order to solve this problem, the dealership mechanic examined the entire wiring system before locating a pinched wire behind the back

seat. The former municipal mechanics charge that this was an inefficient approach to the problem. But the city was forced to pay $489.07 for this repair. The cost broke down as $9.07 for parts and $480.00 for labor.

Prompted by such revelations, City Comptroller Nancy Burton undertook an independent evaluation of vehicle maintenance contracts for the DPW. In April 1995, she announced that as a result of her investigation the City of Albany reduced its 1994 vehicle-maintenance spending by $240,295 in the Public Works and Police departments, the two departments for which the privatization effort was created. That amount represented an 18 percent drop from that spent a year earlier. The magnitude of actual savings announced by the city comptroller is consistent with the estimate of an independent outside evaluation by a management consultant expert hired by the city to examine its municipal vehicle fleet maintenance program. The consultant estimated that Albany was overspending by 20 percent (David M. Griffiths & Associates 1995).

The bulk of the savings found by the comptroller came from more aggressive supervision of bills submitted by contractors and more careful monitoring of the work. But, such savings came at a high price in terms of added transaction costs. Comptroller Burton pointed out that the necessary close auditing of contracts and services required the city to "re-engineer" its voucher and data-processing system. This meant that added computers and audit personnel were needed to track the contractual transactions. Although the red tape associated with more extensive and expensive audit procedures helps to mitigate the temptation to turn moral hazard into actual abuse, it is not enough to optimize the vehicle-maintenance program of the city. Auditors only question the validity of bills; expert mechanics must judge the need for and quality of the work. Retrospective auditing is an inefficient and expensive way to manage an ongoing operation such as vehicle fleet maintenance over time. For an agency to be effective, the cost control mechanism must be internal and prospective regarding its day-to-day operations. Damage control is workable but often not terribly efficient. Given the cost of mitigating moral hazard, muncipalization may prove to be a more cost-effective alternative. In Chapter 6, I consider that alternative when reviewing the experience of Indianapolis, Indiana, with its internal reorganization of vehicle fleet maintenance.

Privatization advocates acknowledge the prevalence of these types of overlapping problems of information asymmetry but contend that these problems can be fixed by a stronger dose of market incentives in the form of contract clauses that provide incentives and penalties to align the interests of the agent with those of the principal. Although the argument is superficially appealing, it never works well in practice for two reasons: (1) Because we are typically dealing with "experience" goods, improvement is largely a process of Monday morning quarterbacking. It is comparatively easy to diagnose how the contract *should* have been structured after the problems appear. But, it is also expensive to correct a problem that is ensconced in a legally binding agreement, as the experience of Westchester County illustrates. There is a certain irony in this because the contract—ostensibly the product of the discipline of the free market—was supposed to avoid the problem in the first place. (2) More importantly, it is a process that presumes more unbounded rationality and more ability to crunch experiential information than most organizations and decision makers possess.

Despite these drawbacks, it is via such a "muddling through" contracting style that much privatization sustains itself. Many public-service privatizations, which occur within the incomplete contracting context, are characterized by incomplete but serviceable public contracts. The fact that such contracting can be workable is scarcely an argument that it represents an improvement over the original status quo.

A Final Word on Asset Specificity   Although personnel costs account for the largest portion of spending on publicly supplied services, plant and equipment expenditures (capital) remain significant. Frequently the handling of these capital assets is the critical factor in the success or failure of privatization. It was the inability of the Westchester County Medical Center to keep effective control over the parking structure that turned what appeared to be an ideal public–private partnership into a serious loss for the county. In 1996, the wealthy suburban county had a population of almost 900,000 people living in about 330,000 households with an average household income of $118,500. Westchester County was capable of absorbing the loss imposed by this privatization incident and chalked up the whole episode to "experience." What happens when such a costly loss of asset control hits a small and poor jurisdiction?

Problems in a less affluent area can be devastating, which is what occurred in Washington County, New York, a small, poor county nestled between the Hudson River and the Vermont border. Its 1996 population was about 60,000 and declining. Average income for its 22,000 households was $45,600, about 40 percent of the Westchester average. As with all local governments, the county and its constituent townships long have been faced with the ongoing environmental problem of solid-waste disposal. In late 1984, the largest trash hauler in the region approached the Board of Supervisors of Kingsbury, the largest of the seventeen townships in the county, with a proposal for a private incinerator that could serve all of Washington County plus the neighboring counties of Warren and Essex. In addition to burning trash from the three counties, Essex, the most northern and least-populated of the three, would supply a landfill site for the toxic ash.

The initial proposal (demonstrated by subsequent events to be too good to be true) and the contract that ultimately resulted from the proposal illustrate just how crucial knowledgeable asset control can be in public–private partnerships. The plant, which was ultimately built in the village of Hudson Falls within the town of Kingsbury, was first pitched to local officials as an entirely privately funded venture with a price tag of $31 million. The tipping fee (the price charged to those seeking to dispose of solid waste at the incinerator) was projected to be only $8 per ton. When the initial proposal came before the town board, the most prominent local law firm in the area, Miller, Mannix, Lemery, and Pratt (Miller/Mannix) supported it. Smith, Barney, Upham, and Harris (Smith Barney), the Wall Street investment banker, was confident that the private financing for this project could be obtained easily. In the politically conservative precincts of upstate New York, there was little reason to doubt that the private sector could solve a large, public-sector problem cheaply. Moreover, given the leading local and distant names associated with the project, it would have been difficult for local officials to be skeptical. Indeed, given the project as proposed, there was a good chance that a sow's ear could be transformed into a silk purse. Washington County stood to share in the revenues to be generated from the electricity created by the burn plant. Spurred on by the lure of a low-cost way out of a high-cost problem, Washington County, Kingsbury township, and Hudson Falls officials moved quickly to complete the venture.

The international boiler builder Foster-Wheeler was selected as the preferred vendor to build and operate the plant. Miller/Mannix became the environmental attorneys for the county for the project. Smith Barney became the underwriters, and an engineering firm recommended by Smith Barney prepared the technical analysis. The local Industrial Development Agency (IDA) proposed to aid Washington County in securing tax-exempt public financing to subsidize the project. The project would continue as a privately built and operated, but publicly owned, venture. Under New York State law, tax-exempt financing requires competitive project bidding. But, there was already a high-powered consortium in place. It was argued that competitive bidding would only slow down the project and add no value to it. Area legislators hurried a bill through the state legislature to exempt this project from the state competitive bidding requirement. Within four months of the initial proposal, Washington County had issued $50 million in bonds, an amount equal to the entire annual operating budget for the county. This was the first long-term debt in its history.

Everything then began to unravel. Unfortunately, the technology that was supposed to make the incinerator project happen was unproved. A sister incineration plant also built by Foster-Wheeler in Binghamton, New York, failed to get a state building permit. More ominously, a similar plant built by another operator in nearby Rutland, Vermont, declared bankruptcy less than a year after it opened. Local political support in Kingsbury and the village of Hudson Falls began to dissolve quickly. Politicians associated with the plant were turned out of office, including the mayor of Hudson Falls. Essex County, after an independent review of the project, pulled out as both a customer and landfill provider. There were lawsuits and countersuits. Nonetheless, the local backers of the plant maintained their political hold at the county level and prevailed. In 1991, the Hudson Falls incinerator began burning trash.

But, a few things had changed. The final plant cost was $87 million, not $31 million. Because it was now a public works project, the county was forced to foot the bill for the difference. Because Foster-Wheeler was the builder, not the owner, they had to be paid for the overruns. Although the county owned the plant, the contract gave operating control to Foster-Wheeler for the full twenty-year life of the plant. The company thus has the best of two worlds. It reaped the gains but was not liable for any loss. Instead of an $8 tipping fee, the actual fee was $91. Under the terms of the contract, Washington County also had to ensure that either enough trash was delivered to keep the plant operating at full capacity or pay Foster-Wheeler for any shortfall. However, even with the trash from Warren County, there was not enough solid waste to fulfill one-third of the required capacity. In 1992, Foster-Wheeler began to bill Washington County almost $880,000 per month to cover the shortfall. This was an impossible burden for a county with only 20,000 largely low-income property taxpayers. Moreover, loans to the county have nearly doubled. Commencing in 1990, a messy series of suits and countersuits began to fill the docket of the state and federal courts stemming from

this privatization. Citizens groups and local residents sued the local government; the local government turned around and instituted countersuits against its people. Some key decision-makers were indicted, tried,
and acquitted on criminal charges stemming from this privatization.
The county governments in Warren and Washington counties were
suing the plant operator in an attempt to break the contract. As of the
end of 1999, the legal situation is far from solved.

Regardless of how this situation resolves itself, the important point
here is that by ceding asset control to the contractor, the county now
finds itself in an extremely weak financial and legal position. Clearly
much could have and should have been done differently at many points
along the way. It could be argued that this problem occurred because
the plant is such a central asset in the process and because the technology was flawed. But, many well understood the evidence that this was a
problematic venture when the deal was moving ahead in the late 1980s.
Unfortunately, there was never a "smoking gun" to prove that the idea
was bad, and, instead, it fell into that large gray area of uncertainty
where so much of life is lived. Crucial to the decision by local officials to
proceed in the face of this doubt was the judgment of the conflicted "experts" who advised the county. Most obviously, the advisors or consultants who guide local officials in such matters should not be permitted to
have a financial stake in the outcome of the project. They should be paid
a flat consulting fee for advice given and demonstrate that they have no
ties to the parties carrying out the project.

Although some local residents suspect some elements of plain old
vanilla flavored corruption, this is besides the point here. Even the most
conscientious public officials are almost always systemically on the short
end of information asymmetry inequality. This is especially true when
venturing into areas of new technologies and services that are at the
heart of the business relationship. When a public–private partnership is
based on the operation of highly specific public assets for which the public sector retains responsibility, the degree of scrutiny must be extraordi-
narily high, but scrutiny is expensive in time and money. Reputation
provides no short cut to due diligence (Higby 1995, 14).

Relational Contracting

When privatization efforts fail, that failure invariably results from the in-
determinacy and high information costs built into incomplete contracting situations. The typical reaction to the concept of privatization is the

attempt to modify the arrangement to work more like a classical contract. However, classical contracting situations are only appropriate in a small number of cases. Clearly, another alternative is needed. Experience in both the public and private sectors demonstrates that this is not the only option, even in the presence of the chronic problems of interorganizational information asymmetry. A very different mindset about the nature and possibilities for both intra- and interorganizational relationship is required. In place of the competitive notion of arm's-length relationships among somewhat adversarial parties, we need to fashion a concept of a relationship based on sources of cooperation. Without this "third way," the alternatives are unattractive. In a worst-case scenario after a privatization failure, there is reversion to the status quo, which most likely was far from ideal. Or, the privatization muddles on without the efficiency discipline of market competition. Instead, service provision occurs under an ever more involved cost-plus-profit reimbursement scheme embedded in a contract laden with penalty clauses for poor performance, incentive clauses for acceptable performance, ever more detailed cost and product definition clauses, and finally arbitration clauses for dispute resolution over the meaning of the other clauses.

The evolving situation in the field of privatized prisons is a textbook example of this contract-fattening process. After each prison malfunction, such as escapes, brutality, or deaths among prisoners, public officials step in to write a lengthier contract. The intention is to avoid repetition of the specific abuse that caused public embarrassment in the first place. Of course, each time more information and performance standards are demanded, the cost of the contract increases. The fictionalized belief that this is a competitive market-based solution then is extended one more time. At best, the arrangement buys time to build public prisons, which is far more cost effective in the long run. No one involved in this field seriously argues that private prisons run to public standards save money. The public-policy question pertains to how political momentum can be changed given the growing power of for-profit prison contractors (for more information see Bates 1999, 22; Belluck 1999, A1; and *The Atlanta Constitution* 1999, A12).

The experience of SEPTA with the evolution of de facto managed competition and contractor micromanagement provides another example of this privatization netherworld. The agency failed to reap the benefit of real cost savings and now has the added burden of additional direct day-to-day oversight of the operations by its contractors.

Although in-between solutions such as these obviously are workable, they provide neither enhanced efficiency in the public sector nor benefits of market competition. To overcome the "lesser of two evils" approaches to public services, we need to transform the notion of contracting from a market-based arrangement to one rooted in interorganizational trust. But, such a notion wreaks havoc with a public contracting process rooted for years in the belief that the competitive market can finally be made to govern the relationship "if only. . . ." We turn our attention to how this might be accomplished in Chapters 6 and 7. In this chapter, we look at the conceptual nature of such *relational* contracting, which involves moving beyond the traditional boundaries of organizations and beginning to think about forms of "bilateral" governance such as joint ventures and how these can be fostered in the public sector. Such alternatives hold much promise for enhancing public-sector efficiency. This category of interorganizational relationship is at times referred to in the literature as a "hybrid" organization or a network relationship (Williamson 1985; Powell 1990; Holstrom and Roberts 1998).

Relational contracting occurs in situations similar to those of incomplete contracting—situations characterized by a high degree of uncertainty, a great deal of relation-specific investment, and a large volume of ongoing transactions. Whereas in the case of incomplete contracting there are attempts to use devices such as "managed competition" to sustain the notion of market governance, relational contracting begins with recognition among the parties that for all intents and purposes they depend on one another. In such situations, the formal contract or agreement is less important as a reference point for dispute resolution than is the quality of trust between the organizations. This concept is very powerful because it applies to both interorganizational relations between agencies and outside contractor and to intraorganizational relations between agency management and employees. Hence, it provides a basis for simultaneously improving both the internal workings of public agencies and their external relationships.

Relational contracting typically occurs because the parties to the arrangement, for one reason or another, come to realize that they do not have a feasible potential alternative to working cooperatively. The concerns about artfully structuring contractual incentives to overcome principal–agent problems, the hallmark of incomplete contracting, are recognized as irrelevant. It is in the parties' self interest to adjust flexibly to one another's concerns, regardless of the formal stipulations of the legal contract that frames their ongoing relationship. The types of clauses, such as hardship provisions and provisions for liquidated damages, are usually too rigid. Instead, the organizations evolve an informal, but often highly effective give-and-take, process of dispute resolution between themselves (Deakin and Michie 1997, 12).

This type of tight interdependence occurs far more frequently in both the private and public sectors than is commonly recognized. One of the best everyday examples of relational contracting is the alliance, which characterizes home remodelers. Typically, one craftsman establishes a customer network through word of mouth or as a result of work with local architects. When they bid jobs, they draw on a network of other specialists to put together an estimate. The general contractor may be a carpenter, and the subcontractors may be plumbers, electricians, and masons. Trust, far more than price, is important for these networks to work well. The general contractor does not bid each of the subcontracts. Instead, each member of the network submits an estimate of costs for his part of the work, and the general contractor submits a total bid to the homeowner or the architect. Timing, cooperation, and reliable quality work are the keys to profitability in this industry. Contractors simply cannot afford the time, money, and experience costs of the marketplace, but they do not have the capital to retain a stable of skilled craftspeople in an industry where cash flow is so unpredictable. Instead of classical contracting or large organizations, they turn to a variant of relational contracting. Trust makes the entire operation work.

Harrison (1994) described how an up-to-the-minute fashion marketer—Benetton—contracts with many small local producers in small shops in one of the industrial districts in northern Italy. These are longstanding relationships. When market demand shifts in its retail shops worldwide, the information is used to reorient the output of these small flexible manufacturers. Once more, it is a long-term relationship built on trust and experience. Another company that uses relational contracting effectively is the athletic footwear and apparel giant Nike. Nike is famous for building a business in which all manufacturing is done through worldwide network partners. This outsourcing has evolved into a separate branch of partnership known as supply chain management, where the basic goal is to improve timing and costs in manufacturing through strong vendor relationships (Wines 1996, 32). Competitive market-based contracting would be a far more cumbersome way in which to get the work done. Womack, Jones, and Roos (1990) told a similar tale about the just-in-time manufacturing relationships pioneered by Japanese automakers. Good examples of this are situations of new and rapidly changing technology, as in the early stages of biotechnology in San Diego and computer development in Silicon Valley in northern California, where networked relationships among small-scale specialists created state-of-the-art technological products while keeping their overhead low (Aries 1996). Typically, as the pace of technological change in an industry stabilizes, some network relations give way via mergers and acquisitions to larger organizational forms. The added costs of overhead in such situations are more than offset by scale economies in production or more market share. Relational contracting works so well in so many situations because the information costs of the market are too high relative to the gains in a context of uncertainty—the nature of rapidly changing situations. Unless clear scale economies are present, there is little incentive to take on the high overhead costs of larger organizations. Trust less expensively glues together organizations than does the market with its high information costs.

Such networking is also quite common in the public sector. The relationship between public funders and human-service providers especially has been characterized by a long history of relational contracting. Historically, private not-for-profit agencies established human services in response to the harsh conditions of the industrial city in the late nineteenth century. When government became an active participant in the provision of human services in the Progressive and New Deal eras, service provision was typically accomplished via contracting with these existing agencies. In places where these voluntary providers did not exist as extensively, government direct service provision occurred. Thus human services in the United States have grown as a dual system in which both contracted and direct service provision often operate side by side. Contracting is not employed in the competitive market, but the public agency and its providers view themselves as locked into a cooperative long-term relationship (Hanlon 1999).

Not surprisingly, given the lack of certainty in product specification, a "stable networks model," the type of relationship that characterizes these public–private partnerships, tends to emerge in human services (Miles and Snow 1992). The stable network is essentially a core organization with long-term relationships with a fixed set of service providers. Unlike a traditional market-based contract in which bidders set prices for specified outputs, input measures weigh far more heavily in cost determination. Typically, the funding level is set by the size of the agency and an estimate of its caseload. The funder and the agency tend to have a general shared goal in terms of serving the vulnerable populations for which they have a mandate and/or mission statement. The core network organization eschews growth through increased size. Instead, it seeks to accommodate itself to change through its alliances.

Each participant in this stable network exercises a fair amount of power in determining the outcomes. The service providers translate legislated intentions and public implementation rules into effective services. They inform the funders about the limits of possibilities. Both the funders and agencies constantly scrutinize the broader profession to determine if the level of best practice has changed. If they find examples of improved practice, they work collaboratively to alter the ongoing relationships within the constraints of the existing legal and social structure. The process is never as neat, clean, and quick as the standard market model suggests the competitive market could operate. Instead, drawing on the new institutional economics, it accounts for the formal and informal rules of a complex social structure. The legislature continually receives input from the providers, agencies, outside public advocates, and lobbyists. In response, it adjusts the legislative requirements for program as well as funding allocations. At best, this is a very imperfect process with room for change. As we gain a better understanding of relational contracting, it has far more promise of improving the performance of the public sector than does the quick and simple "revolution" of so-called "competitive contracting."

Because of the complexities of the services themselves and the inherent uncertainty as to their effect, a key to the stability and effectiveness of these networks is the level of interorganizational trust. The characteristic not-for-profit providers and the public agencies with whom they network share the same goals in terms of effective services. The present drive for expanded privatization often takes the form of introducing profit-seeking service providers into this matrix. Although "new blood" always has the potential to shake up old assumptions about how things might be done in positive ways, new blood can also be problematic. There is a learning curve to be negotiated that is often quite costly to master. The need for a profit adds another goal to the list of what is to be accomplished through the collaboration. The danger in this is that what is profitable for the contractor and what is effective for the public agency may diverge sharply; a classic principal–agent problem. Another way to put this is to say that it effectively introduces the problems of incomplete contracting into a situation of relational contracting. Thus, instead of improving the situation, it runs a high risk of making matter worse. A far more promising avenue of development is the creation of networks of older providers who can help newer ones take part in the process. If not a zero-sum game, this type of networking can be very promising. For example, "old line" social service providers can work as mentors to grassroots organizations to improve services. One does not have to replace the other as suggested by the current competition-based models of service delivery.

When managed-care organizations first came onto the health-care scene, the hope was that they would bring new efficiency to a medical practice based on fee-for-service with its inherent bias to service overutilization. But, it created another problem by providing incentives to increase profits through undertreatment. The current drive in Congress and state legislatures to more tightly regulate the managed-care industry reflects a desire to offset this new form of information asymmetry. Given the inability to know with certainty the outcome of many medical procedures, employees of these profit-seeking providers confront a moral hazard. They find themselves under enormous investor pressure to choose cost control over the risk of overtreatment. That is the type of danger inherent in a helter-skelter rush to bring more profit-seeking providers into the networks that provide human services. This is not to say that it is impossible; instead, I argue that it is problematic at best. More importantly, the move occurs without any appreciation of the intertwined issues of service quality or network stability.

For purposes of privatization, especially in service areas that directly impact the well-being of individuals, focusing on structures of cooperation is important. The concept of well-being, although understandable in the abstract, becomes quite squishy when we try to pin it down. As a result of this large information void, it becomes especially important that we consider the role of organizational goals in establishing networks. The alternative to such a deliberative process is to continue this movement towards market-based privatization in the human services but to honestly recognize that it requires preparation by public agencies to spend significantly more money on administration and supervision as the process moves forward. That means establishing stringent specification of intake levels, case mix, levels of service, training for service workers, and the creation of measures, however crude, of the expected outcomes. The danger in this last effort is that given the lack of consensus about well being, agencies should be extremely careful about what they seek from their contractors in the way of performance measures. If the agencies are effective, they stand a good chance of getting precisely what they sought regardless of whether it is what the situation truly warrants.

Conclusions

Rather than remaining stuck between the alternatives of an unresponsive bureaucracy on one side and ever-more complexly regulated privatized markets on the other, it is possible to realistically envision a third more robust and practical approach to cooperative public-sector restructuring built around the idea that two sets of concerns must shape our decision process. On one side are the concerns of transaction-cost economics: transaction frequency, uncertainty, and asset specificity. On the other side are organizational alternatives: market (classical contracting), hierarchy (in-house production), and hybrid (relational contracting). The challenge for restructuring is the development of a good understanding of the service in question and matching it more closely to the format in which it will most productively operate, given the constraints of political and social institutions.

Within the context of the social and political institutions that define public life, extensive reliance on contracting to get around the problems of public-sector operation does not work. However, thanks to the ideological pedigree of the term "privatization" that is attached to this approach to change, it certainly does go a long way towards polarizing and stymieing debate on real reform. If we are committed to a process of meaningful and positive transformation in the public sector, we need to move away from a narrow concept of contracting toward one that can accommodate itself to existing social and political realities. According to the new institutional economics and contrary to the standard market model, these realities are not always roadblocks. They are often important signposts that direct us toward our destination. Recognition of public agencies as historically evolved and institutionally complex in social, political, and economic terms is necessary, and we must also recognize that a one-size-fits-all approach to the concept of a contract has no basis in reality in either the private or the public sector.

The problem with the take-no-prisoners push for contracting, which is the hallmark of many privatization campaigns, is typically the placement of the public sector in the worst contracting situation—the middle range of incomplete contracting. That is an unstable long-term environment for the private sector, which only gets worse for the public sector. Because enhanced contracting may contribute to improving operation of the public sector, it must be successfully embedded in a relational format. For that method to work, public agencies need to move forward on two tracks: internal relational reform and the establishment of stable and long-term external networks, the antithesis of competitive contracting.

By taking a comprehensive view of contracting, we do not produce proposals for change that are as intellectually clean and satisfying as those promised by free-market privatizers, but we greatly enhance the chance of actually effecting meaningful change.

6

Restructuring Work
The Relational Contract

In April 1996, the 84 employees of the Indianapolis Fleet Service (IFS) took part in an unusual ceremony. Their boss, Mayor Stephen Goldsmith, came to their workplace and handed out bonus checks totaling over $75,000, which represented one-quarter of the money saved by the unit over the departmental budget for the previous eight months. The bonuses were the first installment of a broad, innovative incentive developed between these public employees and their employer, the City of Indianapolis. In the private sector, such an arrangement would not appear to be so extraordinary. In the public sector where it is not easy to envision an efficient arrangement to effectively link employee compensation to the value of the work performed, it is often a different story. The IFS employees, along with the Goldsmith administration, are part of a seeming revolution in public work.

By initially forging an alliance between the rank-and-file workers and direct-line managers in the unit, the IFS was able to successfully convince the mayor that not only was workplace innovation viable in the public sector, but it could be a superior alternative to privatization. The public employees—managers and line workers—and elected officials in Indianapolis transformed their relationship from one characterized by adversarial uncertainty and contractual inflexibility to one in which informal and more positive arrangements define the decision-making process and the workplace. As a result of the trust created by this arrangement, the IFS achieved documented and significant improvements in its performance and savings for Indianapolis taxpayers.

What makes this change noteworthy is its accomplishment within an environment that initially was polarized between a staunchly pro-privatization city government and an angry and discontented municipal workforce. Even as many of the incomplete contracting problems described in previous chapters characterize various outsourcing initiatives of "successful" privatization efforts by the Goldsmith administration, this reorganization is proving to be a harbinger of a more enduring approach to public-sector reform. In this chapter, I examine the history of this restructuring effort to cull important lessons about the broader potential for public-service reform.

Too often, cooperation arises only after the two sides of a conflict exhaust themselves by futilely attempting to vanquish one another. From a rationalist perspective, vanquishing a foe is an inefficient way to achieve a better result. The saga of how the employees of the IFS and the Goldsmith administration arrived at cooperation sooner thus becomes important and illustrates how a healthy dose of pragmatism, on both sides, can achieve quicker public reform to a better result. The historic narrative in this case is unique in terms of dates, times, places, and political and governmental constraints but is universal in terms of the underlying labor–management dynamic, beliefs about public work, and the organizational economics contained therein.

It is important to stress that this is not the only instance in which public employees and political leaders have found a way to forge an alliance for positive change in public agency operation (U.S. Secretary of Labor's Task Force on Excellence in State and Local Government Through Labor-Management Cooperation 1996). This case should be regarded as one of a genre of labor–management cooperation success stories. However, the cooperative approach to public management implicit in these cases is not treated by privatization advocates as evidence of a potentially better way to improve public work. Instead, just as with cases of privatization failure, they are treated as a collection of anomalies. In both instances, this is so because the results are contrary to the predictions of a conventional wisdom formed by an ideological belief in the market as the only standard of efficiency and, in a similar belief, the inherent and chronic venality of public employees, both managers and workers. But the cases are not anomalies. Instead, they reflect a consistent set of qualities that are found in both public and private organizations and work well.

If we are to successfully improve the operation and responsiveness of public agencies, then we need to learn how to encourage these cooperative qualities within the larger ethos of public work. The alternatives of stalemate, polarization, and continual organizational churning serve the long-term interests of no one. Although we shall see how contracting can play a part in change, markets are not universal engines of reform. Contracting is at best an element of change. The only effective driving force is qualitative improvement in the labor–management relationships within public agencies. Phrased slightly differently: Why would an agency that could not competently manage itself automatically be able to competently manage outside contractors? Markets are driven by profits, not morality. Why would a market necessarily produce desirable contractor behavior? Or, why would an agency left to its own devices more likely reward positive behavior than negative behavior, given the pressures of the market? How well markets serve us depends mightily on the context in which we choose to use them.

The Indianapolis Fleet Service: A Description

The IFS is responsible for the maintenance of the entire motor vehicle fleet for the city of Indianapolis, approximately 2,700 vehicles. These vehicles range from administrative sedans to fire-fighting apparatus. As a full-service maintenance department, the IFS is responsible for all motor vehicle–related needs of the city, which include procuring, managing, maintaining, fueling, keeping records for, and disposing of vehicles owned, leased, and operated by the various departments and agencies of city government. Maintenance and repair services include preventive maintenance, remedial repairs (including auto body repair), mobile service, tire service, towing, welding and fabrication, preparation of new vehicles, fuel site management, motor pool management, and any other services to assure the effective and economical operation of the motorized fleet of the city (David M. Griffith & Associates 1994). The IFS also performs contract fleet maintenance work for the privatized municipal advanced wastewater treatment facility and some of the small municipalities in Marion County and surrounding environs.

The Roots of the IFS: Setting the Stage

Until its 1993 name change, the IFS was known as the Central Equipment Management Department (CEMD). The CEMD had one of the worst, if not *the* worst, reputations for performance within the municipal government. It was created in 1978 from the independent fleet service of the operating departments of the city. By centralizing the vehicle-maintenance facilities of the police, the public works, parks and recreation, and fire departments—the major municipal consumers of motor-vehicle services—the city hoped to reduce costs through the scale economies of centralization. Beyond the belief that consolidation could create sizable savings, little thought was given to the practical problems of managing this reorganization. The predictable result of this poor planning was a poorly run and costly agency.

Because each department had a different operational mission, each had a distinctive approach toward vehicle fleet maintenance. When consolidation via executive mandate arrived, interorganizational clashes were inevitable. Each department had not only a staff of vehicle maintenance personnel but also a cadre of supervisors, some of whom had been appointed because they were competent, but others for political reasons. There was no immediately apparent way to separate the two. With reorganization, this entire staff was thrown together as the nucleus of the new department.

The predictably poor vehicle service made the CEMD the scapegoat for all the shortcomings in the performance of the individual operating departments. If trash was not collected on time, the problem was poorly performing packers. If parks were not maintained, motor-equipment failure was a reasonable source of the problem. Whether such faults were lain fairly at the feet of the CEMD was almost beside the point. Perception is what counts. To remedy this situation, in 1980 the city hired a professional outside public fleet maintenance manager to transform chaos into order. This municipal manager came of age in an era of expanding government spending and tended to view the operating budget as a ratcheted document. Cost could go up, but never down. Any organizational problem could be corrected with the infusion of more resources. He was universally characterized as disliking unionized workers far more than the average. In a typical year, more than 100 grievances were filed in his unit. In contrast, by mid-1996 there had been only one filed grievance. Because labor is the principal component of vehicle maintenance, as in most all public service, any meaningful internal restructuring must involve the active cooperation of the work force. In a unionized shop, attaining this cooperation means forging a positive working relationship with the union. This was not the unit manager's strong suit.

Funding for the CEMD was based on the amount of work it performed. Under the Indianapolis budget process, vehicle-maintenance funds were initially placed in the budgets of operating departments. Later, CEMD drew down these operating accounts as work was performed. However, given that the notion of fiscal accountability was more an idea than reality, the CEMD made no attempt to explain the costs contained in the charges that it levied against the operating departments. Because it was a conglomerate unit with a surplus of supervisors, it had high overhead costs that found their way into departmental bills. Even the simplest oil change appeared outrageously expensive to the operating departments. Department heads began grumbling that they could get the work done far less expensively and far more quickly if they could be permitted to take their vehicles to local repair shops. (This impulse is identical to the one that led to the complete privatization of vehicle maintenance in Albany, New York.)

The 1991 Mayoral Election: A Changing of the Guard

As a result of internal labor–management tensions, high overhead, and perceived poor service, CEMD was everyone's favorite example of everything that was wrong with public service. When Stephen Goldsmith launched his pro-privatization campaign for mayor, he often cited the CEMD as the prime example of his case. The assertion did have superficial commonsense appeal. After all, there are vehicle repair shops all over Marion County. Why did the city and county need to duplicate services that could be purchased easily from the private sector?

One unanticipated result of Goldsmith's electoral victory was that it also set a process of change in motion within the CEMD. Goldsmith's election became the impetus for the embattled CEMD administrator to announce his retirement, and his deputy, John McCorkhill, took over. McCorkhill proved to be the right man at the right time for the challenge faced by the agency. He was a manager with a strong background in accounting and finance who was interested in the costs and efficiencies of his operation. This goal-oriented approach was complemented by a personnel management style built around conciliation and negotiation, not confrontation. He moved quickly to convince line workers that a new day in labor–management relations was at hand.

If every cloud has a silver lining, then the one positive outcome for the CEMD staff in the 1980s was the siege mentality that they developed to survive both the internal strife with their boss and the interdepartmental criticism they endured from fellow municipal employees. These pressures taught them to stick together, and their cohesion proved important as they faced down the emerging threat to their livelihood from Goldsmith's drive for privatization. Unlike the previous widespread but imprecise criticism from department heads and municipal coworkers, the mayor's opinion rightly or wrongly bore directly on their future. Although they understood much of the criticism leveled at their agency by their coworkers in other city departments, given the poor relationship with their supervisor, they felt that their hands had been tied in terms of improving the situation. They were convinced that not only could they do a far more cost-effective job if only they were given a chance, but they also believed that they could do better than just meeting the prices set in the private sector. The political opening created by the new official privatization policy could not have been better from their perspective, but they had to act quickly.

One of Mayor Goldsmith's first official decisions drove home the idea that time was of the essence. In the first month of his administration, January 1992, Goldsmith telegraphed his intention to shut down the maintenance operation. He placed a 30-day delay on the ongoing construction of a new vehicle-maintenance facility. He told the *Indianapolis News* that "I don't want to be in this business. We can't afford the garage. There is plenty of capacity in private industry" (see Langosa 1992a). If their new workplace disappeared, the drive toward privatization would become inexorable. Fortunately, the bonding obligations related to construction of the facility made cancellation too costly. Said Mayor Goldsmith, "If I didn't have the bonds and related legal matter to the bonds to worry about, I'd just walk away and leave it" (ibid.). Within a month, the construction halt was ended (Smith 1992). The mayor said that although he intended to proceed with construction, the CEMD was not out of the woods: "it doesn't guarantee that we won't do some of the work outside or even let someone like Ryder run the whole facility" (for further detail, see Langosa 1992b). Alternatively, it was his intention to make the CEMD compete against private vendors for heavy-equipment maintenance work (Morrison 1992, 1–2).

In light of these moves, McCorkhill and then union president Dominic Mangine began their own campaign to force the new administration to give them a real chance to restructure fleet maintenance. They knew that time was working against the department. If a decision to privatize was made, it would be even more of an uphill fight. Typically, a privatization decision is a strong implicit, if not explicit, vote of no confidence in the present line management and workforce. At that point having meaningful input into the decision process becomes more difficult, if not impossible. Even the best arguments and evidence are then discounted as self-serving by those who now have a vested interest in implementing the decision to privatize.

Thus, when Mayor Goldsmith appeared before an Indianapolis Press Club luncheon in early 1992, and once more asserted that privatization of vehicle maintenance would be a cost savings move (Schuckel 1992), Mangine immediately questioned the plan. It was important that no allegation go unanswered. He requested that the mayor visit the garage and talk with workers. He pointed to the existence of seven consultant reports that supported the cost effectiveness of the centralized garage operation. He challenged the mayor to release any data supporting his claim that the city should not be in the equipment management business (ibid.). McCorkhill pointed out that there were 40 percent fewer employees servicing 36 percent more vehicles than when the CEMD was established in 1979. In 1979, there were 187 employees in the newly consolidated department (ibid.). McCorkhill said that 75 percent of repairs are completed in less than two hours compared with private services that close for the day between 4:00 and 6:00 P.M., the CEMD is a 24-hour-a-day, seven-day-a-week operation (McCorkhill 1992). Mangine argued that city workers can be more competitive because their hourly wages don't increase in the evenings or on weekends. Mangine argued that workers were not afraid to compete with private companies as long as the competition was fair.

If such arguments were not to fall on deaf ears, then the larger adversarial atmosphere between the new top management in the city and the municipal labor force had to be markedly dampened at both the departmental and city levels. The first step was to establish a good working relationship with the new administration. Mangine held a meeting in late January with interim deputy mayor Robert Wood and a second meeting the last day of the month with Charles "Skip" Stett, then director of asset management (Schuckel 1992). McCorkhill followed up with his own invitation to Stett, who was by then director of enterprise development for the new administration, to visit the fleet maintenance operation. Stett's role as a mayoral advisor was far more powerful than suggested by his titles. Stett went on to become the senior deputy mayor. In the meeting between Stett and his staff and Mangine, McCorkhill, and their staff, a careful cost analysis was presented to make a case for the continued in-house operation of vehicle maintenance. It was well recognized on all sides that the major impediment to being competitive with outside maintenance operations was the high overhead of the unit. The first step was to seek political backing from the Goldsmith administration to take control of that high-cost overhead.

The meeting could not have gone better. According to Stett, regardless of how things turned out, the administration fully intended to ask the unit to bid on the work for several reasons. The Goldsmith administration was well aware that contract-monitoring costs were substantial because motor-vehicle maintenance is difficult to measure. Stett viewed the employees of the CEMD as among the most highly trained line employees in the city. Finally, the private market for the type of comprehensive service that CEMD performed did not exist. Thus, there was always a high probability that the work would stay in-house. But, something else happened at that meeting. The employees convinced Stett to work actively with them in transforming their agency. Stett said that he was "struck by their sincerity in terms of the seriousness with which they took public service and their willingness to take any necessary steps" (Stett 1996).

Although the internal one-to-one relationship between the unit and the administration was critical to the outcome, external context was also important. District Council (DC) 62 of the American Federation of State, County, and Municipal Employees (AFSCME), the umbrella organization that includes Local 3131, the union that represents the fleet maintenance employees, made it clear that they were prepared to fight any and all privatization efforts in the city to the bitter end. The importance of this political backdrop in shaping the atmosphere in which the IFS restructuring occurred should not be underestimated. From the perspective of AFSCME, if Goldsmith was permitted to implement all of his proposed privatization, the death knell would have rung for public-sector unions in that city. According to Stephen Fantauzzo, the executive director of DC 62, "you do not have to be a nuclear physicist to figure out that nearly one half of the union's members faced job loss within the first year of the Goldsmith administration" (Fantauzzo n.d.). The union response was to fight hard. First, the union virtually ran the campaign of the mayor's opponent. After the change in administration, they fought each and every initiative. When the garage construction moratorium was announced, DC 62 geared up a massive media campaign to make the public aware of the stiff financial penalties faced by the city if it pulled out. DC 62 took the city to court over the privatization of the advanced wastewater treatment plant. The hostility continued at a fever pitch for the first four to six months of the new administration. After a particularly bitter round of contract negotiations, Department of Transportation Director Mitchell Roob approached Fantauzzo and proposed a more conciliatory path of negotiations on privatization matters. He proposed a genuine "level playing field" for city teams to compete against private vendors. While the unions always thought they could win in such a context, they were also nervous about the implications of yielding ground on their notion that privatization was philosophically wrong. After much internal discussion, AFSCME agreed to go forward but set five conditions on this participation (ibid.):

- The right to participate from the very beginning of the process and to name the employee team members;
- Advanced training for those participating provided by the city and the opportunity to submit several practice proposals prior to actually bidding;
- The right to look not only at personnel but also all aspects of a job and redesign it as the team saw fit;
- The administration's assistance in freeing up union members from the bureaucracies that stymied the ability to provide services competitively;
- The ability to discuss overhead and have it eliminated where appropriate.

Fantauzzo summed up why the union believed it could do a more cost-effective job than the private sector.

> The key element for us was overhead. We knew that our wages were competitive. We believed that if we didn't make a profit; were not paying taxes; could purchase our fuels, equipment, and materials cheaper; could borrow capital at a better rate, we should be able to not only compete, but win. If not we had a problem with the service delivery system or we were carrying too much overhead. (ibid.)

It was within the context of these changes in citywide labor–management relations that Local 3131 and McCorkhill proposed their own three-step effort. First, they asked that the administration help them downsize in terms of midlevel managerial and clerical positions. They then asked that the city trust them on their own plans for reorganization, which would take time. Third, they asked that they not be forced to bid for the work until the third year when they felt that they would be fully competitive. Because of the support they had gained by winning Stitt's trust, he helped remove internal barriers that impeded the reform efforts of CEMD. In addition to helping remove patronage employees, which went a long way toward gaining the trust of the rank-and-file workers, he also helped to streamline monopolistic procurement procedures, which led to overpriced parts and, at times, inferior contractors (ibid.). By the time formal bidding for the fleet-maintenance contract was undertaken in January 1995, the CEMD had shrunk itself, with full support from the Goldsmith administration, from 119 to 84 people. All the shrinkage took place in middle management and among clerical workers. Beyond attrition, no jobs were lost on the shop floor. The local union presently represents 62 of the 84 workers in the shop. There are now four foremen; when the process began, there were eighteen. In 1993, the CEMD changed its name to the Indianapolis Fleet Service (IFS) as part of its new image.

The Bidding and the Aftermath

The process leading up to the release of the request for proposals (RFP), the evaluation of the proposals, and the awarding of the contract to provide fleet service in Indianapolis was exemplary. A consulting firm with a national reputation in the area of fleet-services management, David M. Griffith & Associates, was retained to write the actual RFP. A citywide team of two union members, one administrator, one representative of the city legal department, one representative of the purchasing department, one customer (in this case the DPW), and Deputy Mayor Stett, representing the administration, oversaw preparation of the RFP. McCorkhill, as the IFS administrator and the individual who would administer the contract, regardless of who was selected, also worked on the proposal. I must make clear, however, that IFS did *not* craft the proposal—that would have given IFS an unfair advantage. The citywide team set the scope, and David M. Griffith & Associates did the drafting and technical work. To further ensure that the internal proposal preparation was aboveboard, as soon as the RFP was drafted, McCorkhill left town for an extended vacation until all the proposals were received by the city. Mangine's local and McCorkhill's deputy, Stephen James, were left on their own to write the IFS proposal in response to the RFP. Also in the interest of fairness, Stitt removed himself from the final decision-making process. The RFP was released on November 2, 1994, and was mailed to thirty-three firms. All proposals had to be received by January 13, 1995. The preferred provider was selected in February, and the contract was to commence on May 1, 1995.

Four entities ultimately bid on the contract: MLS/Ryder, Johnson Controls, Tecom, and the IFS employees. The proposals were judged first on the basis of technical quality and then on the basis of cost. The IFS was presumed to have high technical quality. Given the inevitable transition costs, the review group felt that if IFS was within 5 percent of the lowest bidder in terms of price, they would get the contract as the lowest-cost provider. There was not, however, complete consensus on this point, even at the end.

As it turned out, IFS was actually *the* lowest-cost bidder; it was $78,000 below MLS/Ryder for the three-year term. From the point of view of IFS, not only was it the low bidder, but the process confirmed that IFS knew how to run the operation. Its proposed staffing of 84 employees was almost identical to the staffing proposals made by the outside competitors: MLS/Ryder proposed running the operation with 85 employees; Tecom proposed a 79-employee staffing pattern; and Johnson Controls proposed 86. The IFS proposed running the operation for three years at a cost of $16.312 million. The second-lowest proposal was $16.391 million. Tecom proposed $16.5 million, and Johnson Controls bid $20.2 million (McCorkhill 1995). Under the terms of the proposal, IFS employees agreed to forego a previously negotiated 3 percent pay increase. In exchange, they were granted 25 percent of any first-year savings below the proposal price and 30 percent of any savings in the second and third years of the contract. These incentives were in addition to their next regularly scheduled pay increases. The $75,000 that they received in the spring of 1996 was their savings incentive for the first eight months.

It was estimated that by the end of the new contract in 1997, the municipal garage operation saved the city $8.4 million since the beginning of the Goldsmith administration (see Gelarden n.d.), which represents $3.4 million in actual in-house savings since 1992 as a result of the employee-led reorganization carried out to prepare for the contract, plus the projected savings of $4.6 million under the contract itself, and more than $400,000 saved below the contract price in the first eight months.

Although cost savings are important, an even more important part of this story is the way in which the work relationships within IFS have changed. John McCorkhill talks about the degree to which his job is shifting from being a line administrator to a contract administrator. The body shop now runs without any foremen. Each worker is trained to use the computer to look up parts, estimate the cost of work, and provide a

Table 11. Indianapolis Fleet Services: Comparative Budgets, 1991–96

	1996	1995	1994	1993	1992	1991
Unadjusted budget (thousands)	$12,578	$12,192	$12,561	$13,997	$13,854	$13,688
Less new costs since 1991						
Belmont garage	(1,147)	(1,242)	(1,230)	(1,232)	(342)	(233)
Fire department as customer	(1,133)	(1,062)	(1,058)	(1,121)	(209)	(209)
Added cost of IPD take home	(862)	(610)	0	0	0	0
Total adjustments	(3,142)	(2,915)	(2,288)	(2,352)	(551)	(442)
Adjusted budgeted costs	$9,437	$9,278	$10,273	$11,645	$13,302	$13,246

Source: Data from Indianapolis Fleet Services.

cost estimate for the work to the operating departments. Workers with minor injuries no longer automatically take sick leave or file for worker's compensation. If they can undertake limited duty, they report for work and work is found for them until they fully heal. One foreman told me that his instructions to mechanics pertaining to repair versus disposal decisions is simple. Mechanics should make the same decision they would make if it were their own car: is it worth fixing or should we recommend disposal? Everyone is more entrepreneurial. The staff is ever vigilant for other local area government work, such as school-bus maintenance, which the IFS could do. Sending work out that could be done less expensively by a private specialist is no longer a problem since everyone shares in the savings.

Performance by the Numbers

Just as the proof of the pudding is in the eating, so is the success of this restructuring assessed by its outcomes. Let us begin by considering cost. The data in Table 11 are IFS budget comparisons for 1991–96. Because the agency took on three costly new functions in that time period, three adjustments are necessary to make the starting and ending data comparable. In 1991, the Belmont facility of IFS was still under construction, and its operation was not yet a full part of overall costs. Similarly, until the opening of that facility in 1993, the fire department was still servicing a significant portion of its fleet. Finally, beginning in 1995, the police

Table 12. Indianapolis Fleet Services Performance Indicators, 1990–95

	1995	1994	1993	1992	1991	1990
Fleet size	2,202	2,104	1,967	1,969	2,043	2,153
No. of employees	81	84	93	109	119	113
Written complaints	7	5	6	24	30	149
Customer meetings	165	192	156	139	81	NA
% under 8 hr. turnaround	80%	72%	72%	70%	71%	71%
Indirect labor as % of cost	33%[a]	31%	35%	38%	40%	40%
Lost hrs.—workers' comp.	1,119	4,062	2,619	3,903	6,040	4,933
Miles driven (000)	25,388.7	20,991.9	18,534.8	NA	NA	NA
Miles driven/vehicle	11,530	9,977	9,423	NA	NA	NA
Tire expense (000)	$640	$684.8	$637.3	$830	$787	$728.7
Net auction proceeds (000)	$1,300	$1,113.5	$1,378.9	$826.1	$1,432.2	$315.6

Source: Data from Indianapolis Fleet Services.

[a] Increase due to use of union group leaders instead of mechanics and managers or contractual janitorial firm to perform cleaning services.

department instituted a take-home program for police vehicles that increased maintenance costs. The impact of these three changes on costs is documented in Table 11.

Total unadjusted costs between 1991 and 1996 fell about $1.1 million or about 8 percent. When budget costs are adjusted to reflect added activity, the underlying costs fell $3.8 million, or about 29 percent. These figures are not inflation-corrected.

The drop in costs was not accomplished at the expense of quality. Furthermore, it reflects improvement in the quality of the work environment, which is demonstrated by the data in Table 12.

Although most rows in this table are self-explanatory, four need some additional comment. Customer meetings refer to a proactive policy that has become a strong part of the IFS service program. In 1991, after assuming leadership of the agency, John McCorkhill instituted a series of regular meetings with the operating departments that are IFS customers. These meetings are supposed to obtain customer feedback on service-related issues. Starting at just less than two meetings per week in 1991, these meetings averaged out to over three per week in 1995 and constitute an important link in the ongoing quality circle instituted by IFS. Notably, in the first year of restructured operation, turnaround time of less than eight hours improved by almost 10 percent from about 72 percent to 80 percent. The marked decline in hours lost to worker's compensation is perhaps one of the strongest indicators of changed perceptions among rank-and-file employees about the nature of the work. It is also important to note that the city is getting more service from each of its vehicles at a lower cost per vehicle, a fact reflected in both the decline in the cost of tires despite an increase in the number of miles driven per vehicle and the increased miles driven per vehicle even as overall operating costs of the IFS have been decreasing (see Table 11).

Conclusions

If we asked Mayor Goldsmith to characterize this experience, he would undoubtedly cite it as an example of the salutary effect of competition on the public sector. He would be correct only in that his insistence that fleet service be subject to competitive outside bidding played a role in the restructuring of the IFS around budget incentives. However, if we focus solely on this aspect, we miss the far more important contribution to change made by Goldsmith's administration: its role in changing the substantive relationship between city hall and the IFS.

Although we can (and did) measure success here by the numbers, we run the risk of confusing cause with effect if we do no more than this. Measurable real change is a result of the substantial transformation in working relations within the IFS and between the IFS and the rest of city government. IFS won the bid because it had shrunk itself from 129 to 84 employees by the time the RFP "hit the street." Internally initiated change of that magnitude could not occur in a public agency if the relationship between itself and city hall was antagonistic and suspicious. All the measures of lower cost and improved quality listed above occurred before competitive bidding and result from the informal but powerful way in which the contractual employment relationship between the city and its employees was transformed from one exhibiting all the worst features of an incomplete contract into a relational one. Several people in different roles told me about the knock-down screaming matches between the president of the union and the former agency administrator. One such incident that was recounted to me involved the two of them standing in close quarters and shouting provisions from the master collective bargaining agreement into each other's face.

The substantive contribution of Mayor Goldsmith and his administration to the transformation was not the language of competition that they brought to their work, but rather their ability to exhibit a genuine willingness to take the unit's employees seriously. Goldsmith, in effect, officially sanctioned the IFS to go ahead with changes that the employees had wanted for more than a decade. His display of political courage in helping them to remove their excess management, which they carried as a small part of "the last bastion of Republican machine politics in urban America" went a long way in building trust among those workers to carry out their own internal reforms. It is this trust between city hall and the municipal garage that is at the heart of all the positive changes in costs and quality. The formal contract with its incentive bonuses is an outgrowth of this, not vice versa.

IFS employees knew exactly how to organize their service for efficiency and quality. The shop workers understood the direct work process, and McCorkhill and his staff understood the important elements of the relationship between the agency and its customers. Both management and labor were able to quickly learn to translate their informal understanding into an operating business plan in an atmosphere of trust and cooperation. The IFS employees knew virtually everything about the operation of a municipal fleet service and needed an organizational form that would permit putting their knowledge to productive use. A private outside manager could add no value to that situation.

A key element in this transformation was the good accounting system of the IFS that was in place from the beginning. The IFS was able to cost out all its work with great accuracy and in an easily understood manner. Each employee has a barcode number, as does each part in inventory and each vehicle, which means that all the parts and labor on every job were traceable with a remarkable degree of accuracy at comparatively low cost. (This is usually not the case.) As we learned earlier, activity-based cost accounting is a crucial step regardless of whether the work is privatized or reorganized.

Politicians like Goldsmith are important for another reason. Although there was a great deal of dissatisfaction with the operation in the years before his election, this dissatisfaction was much like the weather: everyone talked about it, but nobody did anything. Clearly, the mayor was a catalytic agent in changing public "business as usual." His lasting contribution was a willingness to respond pragmatically to the proposals that came from the managers and staff of the old CEMD.

The simultaneous desire for improvement and feeling of powerlessness is not uncommon among public employees. But, Goldsmith proved to be an uncommon politician. When I visited Boston to research the MassHighway case, I met with the leadership of the Service Employees International Union–Local 285, the collective bargaining agent for many of the state-highway employees. The union leaders proudly described the changes that they instituted or recommended to save money for the commonwealth. I suggested that if Governor Weld was in the room with us at that moment he would have argued that the only reason they were now talking about change and productivity was because he challenged them with privatization. Their response was to turn around and open a file cabinet with letters and memos going back to 1972. These documents were written to successive commissioners and other officials urging changes to make the department more efficient. What privatization meant in both cases was a chance to share their ideas with a leadership that would, hopefully, finally listen to them seriously. In Indianapolis, the workers were given a genuine hearing. In Boston, they were largely ignored.

The core of the privatization argument is that the pressure of external competition forces internal reorganization. However, market-based competition has little to do with most of the work that most people do everyday. They work more or less productively depending on how well their immediate work environment is structured. The IFS employees who are doing an outstanding job today are the same ones who were the scapegoats of the old CEMD. The substantive changes for them were the replacement of a divisive leader with a conciliatory one and the transformation of the larger, indifferent, municipal environment into one in which both their work and opinions were appreciated. The threat of contracting was stressful, but their desire to do a good job antedated privatization. If their old boss had stayed, they would not have been able to organize and restructure their work.

At best, competition amounts to the use of a bidding process to select the service agent. It is a sporadic and costly event to stage. Once a contractor is selected, although the terms of the contract define the outer limits of the relationship, as we learned in Chapter 5, those terms have little to do with the practical ongoing relationship needed to get the work done. Unless there is an egregious problem with a particular contractor, the transaction cost of reinstituting further competitive bidding to change agents is simply too high to be considered a credible threat. Instead, processes of persuasion and negotiation are initiated. If these processes fail, existing trilateral governance procedures are then employed. As a result, it is the quality of public management not competition that determines effectiveness of the day-to-day operation, whether it is contracted or directly supplied.

Thus, the question of municipal-service reform really resolves into one of making a choice between taking on the challenges of contract management versus the challenges of personnel management. For ongoing municipal services, such as vehicle maintenance, both transaction-cost economics and the Indianapolis experience make a strong case for the notion that the costs of directly managing municipal workers are less than the costs of managing outside contractors. Indeed, as Deputy Mayor Stett pointed out, the notion of in-house service maintenance was always the best possibility because of all the problems with competitive markets and information asymmetry. The innovation here was to convert an adversarial relationship into a trusting relationship.

Although the turnaround at the IFS engineered in part by its employees is a particularly stellar example, it is, like the Fort Lauderdale example, one of many instances around the country in which broadened worker participation in the design and execution of public work has led to large savings and dramatically improved service (see U.S. Secretary of Labor's Task Force on Excellence in State and Local Government Through Labor–Management Cooperation 1996). We should heed these lessons at least as well as we heed the calls to consider privatization.

The complex nature of so much public service does not make it an easy candidate for privatization because it too often falls beyond the bounds of classical contracting. Attempts to create situations that look like classical contracts only put the public sector into the informational asymmetric bind of incomplete contracting. Forming a working relationship based on trust is often the most efficient way to resolve the dilemma but may seem daunting because the pressures that create support for privatization are typically derived from a long history of mistrust between the parties. It can be difficult to imagine cooperative relationships with people you regard as adversaries. But it is difficult to imagine worse initial acrimony than that in Indianapolis before the CEMD became the IFS.

Avoiding the larger relational atmospherics and simply turning towards contracting as the solution often worsens the situation. Consider the contrasting experience of Albany, New York, where full-scale privatization of motor-vehicle fleet maintenance proceeded in the manner initially envisioned by Mayor Goldsmith. That city now has the worst of all worlds: higher costs and an inability to do the work itself. What makes the two cases noteworthy is that both efforts proceeded at about the same time in the early 1990s.

One important outcome of the Indianapolis restructuring was that it permitted the IFS to resort to contracting in an organizationally integral manner. The auto-body shop at the IFS only does about 25 percent of all the body work on the municipal fleet. When I questioned the body-shop staff about this, I was told that they estimated their in-house costs for body work and concluded that it cost them about $33 per hour but outside contractors charged only $26 per hour. They intended to take some of the work back in-house as soon as they could better control their costs. One could argue that they behave this way because they receive incentive bonuses for coming in under budget, but that is only true because of the nature of the trust relationship between the IFS staff and the city administration. The more important issue is that they feel secure in their jobs and empowered in their roles as decision makers. The body shop works with no foremen. Incentive pay is, in a sense, icing on the cake for them. Contracting out in this context is no longer a zero-sum game (if they win, we lose). Instead, it helps to create both effective internal working arrangements and effective outsourcing.

The issue that follows from this review of the Indianapolis experience is assessment of the degree to which it is an isolated instance unique to its time and place and the extent to which it is a replicable model. The short answer is that, yes, much is owed to the individuals and the timing of events. However, many of the characteristics of the situation are replicable and worthy of imitation.

The strongest element of uniqueness in this case stems from the pragmatism exhibited by all the principal parties. The mayor came into office with a strong ideological bias towards privatization with the idiom of private markets and competition very much the currency of policy talk around city hall. At the same time, the mayor and his top associates exhibited a strong willingness to learn from experience.

Pragmatism also characterized the actions of the leadership of both Local 3131 and AFSCME Council 62. They, too, took a risk by deciding to work through this restructuring with municipal officials who were then known for their strong desire to privatize public service. The risk for the unions was that by going along with the rules of the bid process they could be viewed as implicitly legitimating privatization. Adding insult to injury, it could still have resulted in a major loss of jobs and foregone pay raises. On one hand, the Goldsmith administration gave every indication that it would play fair with the bid process, but it made no promises about the outcome. On the other hand, the union knew even better than anyone else that the IFS needed to change and that the union had to be central to that change for it to be an effective one.

Finally, the fact that the IFS administrator, John McCorkhill, was also a pragmatist is no small factor in the success of the entire operation. He was the man in the middle who needed to retain the trust of both the rank-and-file workers and the Goldsmith administration. His ability as a skillful conciliator and negotiator contributed in no small way to the success of this restructuring.

Although a cast of reasonable and sophisticated actors was essential for this pioneering effort, the Indianapolis case also demonstrates how the nature of the product lends itself to a more cooperative approach. As we saw vividly in Albany, there is a great deal of information asymmetry in vehicle-fleet maintenance and repair, which lends itself strongly to in-house operation. The only real question is whether the operation is well organized or poorly organized. In that regard, two lessons from the Indianapolis experience are especially important to note: change takes time, and reform must involve everyone. The CEMD did not become the IFS overnight. Three years passed before agency personnel felt competent enough to manage themselves, but importantly, this was simultaneously both a bottom-up and top-down restructuring.

Too often in the present United States, ideologically driven political leaders grudgingly let workers "bid" on jobs, as was the case in Massachusetts. Such an approach never leads to the type of fundamental and innovative change that can make for more responsive and flexible public work. Workers need the help of their superiors if they are to truly learn how to take charge. By the same token, those at the top have to realize that very competent people are in their employ at both the middle-management level and on the line who need a meaningful chance to work together to make the type of great changes that redound to everyone's credit. Public employees do not go to work every day to do a bad job. The extent of their failure almost always reflects on the structures in which they operate and is not a blot on their moral character. Although complete change takes time, savings begin to occur quickly. In the case of the IFS, $3.4 million was saved between 1992 and 1995 when the actual restructuring was completed.

As pioneering pragmatism transforms itself into stable institutionalized behavior, another important issue to be considered is the degree to which it is an economically sustainable model. There is a lower limit to the amount of savings to be found because workers still need raises to stay even with the cost of living even as gains in their productivity level off. Similarly, the cost of contracted services and parts rises with the general level of inflation. In such a situation, long-term viability of the model rests on how future budgets are constructed. Future negotiated budgets should be set at levels that realistically cover costs. At the same time, to ensure that they do not become simple cost-plus arrangements, they should be set at levels that workers can undershoot. In this way, both cost of living and gain-sharing incentive pay to keep the agency efficient and effective and can be fashioned into an ongoing relationship.

Thinking about these future issues is important because too often the first blush of innovative efficiency disappears as organizations slip back into older habits and forms. Such behavior is known in the management literature as the "Hawthorne effect," which refers to experiments in industrial organization conducted at the General Electric Company's Hawthorne plant in the 1920s. The initial results of any change in workplace organization led to an immediate spike in productivity. However, without any long-term prodding to reinforce the new behavior, productivity lapsed quickly as older habits reappeared. The innovative budgeting process put in place by Indianapolis labor and management can become an important device to ensure that the Hawthorne effect does not overtake this important public-sector innovation. But, even more importantly, all parties need to work to retain relationships of trust and cooperation. Good working relationships are not set in concrete, and good public management in the end is the ability to lead people through trust rather than fear.

The unanswered question remains: To what extent is the threat of privatization needed to stimulate change? I conclude that although it may be appropriate at times, in most instances the threat is overused. A change process can be facilitated without ideological pyrotechnics. The past problem was ironically the willingness of the more liberal political leadership to live with the inefficiencies and unresponsiveness of public bureaucracy so that it could concentrate on what it viewed as its larger and more important goals. Contemporary conservative leadership seizes upon these same shortcomings as a way to achieve its larger goals. In a sense, neither liberals nor conservatives are terribly interested in the conditions of public operation. But as demonstrated by the IFS experience, leadership committed to pragmatic improvement, regardless of political values, can effectively open a window for innovative middle managers and rank-and-file employees to do their best work in the public interest.

7 The Privatization of Public Service

Economic Limits of the Contract State

Newark, March 21—Jackie R. Mattison, the former chief of staff for Mayor Sharpe James of Newark, New Jersey, was found guilty today of taking bribes from an insurance broker in exchange for lucrative contracts (Smothers 1997, 25).

The More Things Change . . .

The old New York County Courthouse opened for business in 1872. Located in lower Manhattan and faced in an exterior of fine Massachusetts-quarried marble but forlorn and boarded up now, it is an exemplar of mid-nineteenth century public architecture in the United States. The interior contains a soaring rotunda that encases an elegant spiral staircase leading from the street-level entrance up to its second-floor courtrooms. Although the mundane process of dispensing justice to scruffy local miscreants has long been removed to other precincts, popular interest in the restoration of this relic abides.

Some aspects of the courthouse are far from aesthetic. The courthouse was commissioned in 1858 by the New York Board of Supervisors, and the project began with an initial appropriation of $250,000. By the time the edifice was completed, fourteen years later, the final cost had ballooned at least fiftyfold—historians estimate between $12 and $15 million. Bear in mind that these are late nineteenth-century prices, uncorrected for more than a century of inflation. Adjusting cost estimates in a roughly contemporary situation results in a public project with an initial price tag of about $40 million that ends end up with a final tab of more than $2 billion. Although there is architectural justification for restoration, the claim of the courthouse on history has even greater merit as a physical memorial to the power of corrupt public contracting. Never before had so few pocketed so much public money at such a sustained and rapid pace.

Standing on Chambers Street, at the foot of the Brooklyn Bridge just behind city hall, and gazing at this partial ruin heightens appreciation for the exquisite art of contractual plunder when it is undertaken by masters. The notorious Tweed Ring that supervised creation of this cathedral of criminality was perhaps the best known of the late nineteenth-century political machines. The courthouse project is to ordinary public contract abuse what high art is to street-level graffiti. Boss William Marcy Tweed and his band of Tammany Hall rogues were not unique. Every city of significant size had its own version of them. Although beaten back by a generation of dedicated reformers, the epidemic abated even though the underlying disease will never be fully eradicated.

Among Boss Tweed's contemporary progeny are the well-tailored, coiffed, and compensated corporate executives who routinely stand side by side before the bar of justice with their less sartorially splendid or amply compensated public-sector partners to have their public–private wrists ceremonially slapped for exposed transgressions. Looking appropriately contrite, these officials typically and routinely plead no contest to the charges of bribery and price-fixing that are by now an all too ordinary and ingrained part of the day-to-day practice of public contracting. Fines, occasional "community service," and some sternly and judicially uttered "tsk tsks" are viewed by all the participants as merely the downside risks in one of the oldest professions in the United States. With the collapse of the Cold War, perhaps $600 toilet seats are no longer vital for national security, but the same corporate "skills" and creative energy that crafted those deals are now focused like a laser on state and local officials who are empowered to create highly remunerative contracts for the privatization of other public responsibilities.

Some recent forays by the Lockheed Corporation, the largest defense contractor in the nation, into privatization in the largest U.S. city are textbook lessons about the incidence and prevalence of moral hazard and influence peddling in the practice of public contracting. Lockheed has a particularly checkered international reputation in terms of bribery of public officials, price-fixing, and the art of defiantly pleading no contest to such charges when they become public. Twice during the

1980s, Lockheed was caught in a major political scandal over its use of undue and perhaps illegal influence to convince key high-level New York City officials to privatize their parking enforcement activities via a contract to the company (for the official account, see City of New York, Department of Investigation 1993; for historic background see Barrett 1993). Repercussions of the two separate incidents were sufficiently severe that they contributed to the downfall of two mayors: Edward Koch and David Dinkins. Rudolph Giuliani, who succeeded Dinkins as mayor, was a U.S. attorney at the time of the first scandal. He was well aware of the *modus operandi* of the company when it pursued public contracts. As one of his first official acts, Mayor Giuliani barred Lockheed from any business dealings with the city for four years. Despite that ban, Lockheed secured a contract to work in the city via its ability to influence contracting decisions at the state level. To pursue a contract to privatize the management information system of public transportation in the city, Lockheed worked through the regional transportation agency, the Metropolitan Transportation Authority (MTA). Lockheed hired Douglas Rutnik, an individual with no previous lobbying experience, as a state lobbyist at a cost of $10,000 per month. Rutnik was, however, the companion of Zenia Mucha, one of Governor George Pataki's closest advisors (see Bernstein 1997). Lockheed maintained that its pursuit of a privatization contract and the hiring of Rutnik as a state legislative lobbyist were unrelated. Regardless of the details, this episode points out the unavoidable ties among influence peddling, the awarding of public contracts, and privatization. These linkages are especially apparent for companies such as Lockheed, which have built the vast portion of their corporate wealth on contracting with the public sector.

Although the specific links between influence peddling and contracting have changed stylistically since the time of Boss Tweed, the substance of the situation has not changed. For the generation of muckraking national, state, and local political reformers who came to power in reaction to the abuses of the Tweed Ring and its brethren elsewhere, the reality of the immutability of the problem was clear: the nation needed a cadre of public employees not indebted to political power brokers to carry out the people's business. Although public contracting was needed, that necessary evil had to be contained and limited.

In many ways, the contemporary debate about contracting replays the debate that took place more than 100 years ago. In a recent, important, historic paper, economist Moshe Adler investigated the on again,

off again privatization history of the approach by New York City to cleaning its streets (Adler 1999). Adler found a deeply ambivalent common
council (the forerunner of the modern city council) that could never
quite make a decision between public provision and private contracting.
Between the 1820s and the 1890s, common councilors would first conclude that contracted private street cleaning was less expensive. But,
they soon concluded that the streets were not being cleaned and
brought it back as a public service. Then they decided that, even though
it was effective, public street cleaning was too expensive. The city then
once more sought to contract out the work. Shortly thereafter, they
again brought it back in-house because of contractual nonperformance.
Each time they revisited the issue of contracting out, they asserted that
this time they really knew how to write a foolproof contract, but they
never really did. Adler found that every single contemporary argument
pro and con in the debate about privatization was used in the past. Every
single trick to overcome principal–agent problems has been tried. But,
then as now, no one found a way *not* to pay the contractors when the
work was shoddy or nonexistent. The New York debate was similar to debates that raged in other major cities during that same time period. Finally, in the 1890s at the dawn of the Progressive Era, a strong national
consensus developed that professional municipal service was the better
answer. The head of the Chicago Board of Health declared in 1892
"[t]here are few if any redeeming qualities attached [to the contract sys-
tem]. No matter what guards are placed around it, the system remains
vicious" (Adler 1999, 88). In 1895, Mayor Pingree of Detroit observed
that "[m]ost of our troubles can be traced to the temptations which are
offered to city officials when franchises are sought by wealthy corporations, or contracts are to be let for public works" (ibid., 88).

Since then we have learned much about how to contain the worst
overt abuses of public contracting or at least dampen their visibility. But,
we have not been able to solve the inherent fundamental accountability
problem. Because public money is "everyone's" money, in practice it is
always up for grabs by "anyone" with the quickest hands. Almost as soon
as one egregious abusive crack in the edifice of public accountability is
exposed and patched over by a new layer of regulatory red tape, another
invariably appears. But, red tape is always easy to slice through if the
stakes are sufficiently tempting, as was the case in Washington County,
New York. When the requirement for competitive bidding appeared to

hinder the money grab, the state legislature obliged the privateers with a waiver. Ditto for the competitive contracting requirement in the Colorado bus privatization legislation. Almost every day, at least one newspaper article appearing in the country reports on the loss of public money or degraded public service resulting from public contracting. Invariably the story ends with a report of an intention to file either criminal or civil charges against the contractor and/or the public official who awarded the contract. Almost as invariably, the charges peter out to virtually nothing in the way of penalties.

The bottom line is that public contracting continues to be a cumbersome and expensive instrument for the delivery of public service. There is an ongoing cost trade-off between the inherent risk of moral hazard and the cost of effective oversight. Furthermore, because the moral hazard is almost invariably compounded by an information imbalance that favors contractors over public officials, it becomes easy to see why, as a matter of economics and not politics, direct public service continues. It is often less expensive than contracting, despite its own set of problems. Although once a contracting scandal erupts it becomes a political fact of life, it is important to remember that it was the economic incentives that brought it to life in the first place. In the final analysis, Americans are conservative people. Anything that the private sector can do better than the public sector is, in all likelihood, already being done privately. We have so little privatization despite two decades of an ideological full-court press for change because Americans are also pragmatists. The public sector in all its complexity abides because it is simply too expensive to underwrite *effective* private contracting to replace it. Ultimately, the existing distribution of public activity between contracted work and direct service is far more understandable as a matter of economic rationality than of politics.

Public Management by Remote Control

Despite the well-documented and rich history of the serious systemic moral hazards and informational asymmetries in public contracting, since at least 1980 a strong continuing conservative political consensus asserts that the extensive use of contracts to provide public service is "the key to better government" (Savas 1987). Proponents of this view either ignore the transaction costs or essentially argue that the last generation of reformers did not know how to write a good contract. They in essence hold that it is not only possible but also easy to write an almost self-enforcing public contract for services. Relabeled privatization, this new push for expanded public contracting is touted as the ultimate public-management tool. Privatization advocates dismiss the notion that it is possible to improve the organizational flaws of direct public service.

Viewed in light of the textbook theory of perfect competition, privatization is effectively advocated as a process of wholesale remote-control organizational change. Without getting into the messy issues of either the politics of contracting or the gritty service and personnel problems of effective public-sector leadership, proponents of this view of privatization promise a quick, easy, and almost dreamlike solution to all that ails public service. They exhibit a fundamentalist faith in the imminent arrival of a level of competition that always proves to be just beyond reach. They believe it will compel the lazy and/or devious individuals in public jobs to either figure out on their own how to mend their ways efficiently or forfeit their livelihoods to more energetic and wholesome private providers. Lost in this crusade is any substantial understanding of the systemic, and largely economic, forces that shape contemporary public work and limit the effectiveness of public contracting.

The experiences recounted here are just that, experiences. The very nature of case analysis as a research method means that cases themselves can neither prove nor disprove anything. They do, however, powerfully illuminate the otherwise unseen organizational dynamics of contractual relationships and hence the several pitfalls to be fully considered if privatization were to be adopted as routine and widespread public policy. At the most general level, these experiences question whether the accountability problems of public contracting can be easily or inexpensively solved. It is important to remember three things: (1) Most contracting occurs with a high degree of uncertainty about both product and process. (2) All the players act with bounded rationality. (3) Most act with a sense of opportunistic guile. The almost childlike faith in an invisible hand that will somehow guide contractors to pursue the best interests of the public even as the contractors pursue their own interests pales in the harsh light of these realities.

There is no competitive remote-control technique to make the challenge of good public management magically disappear. A self-enforcing and competitively renewable contract to perform work for the public sector is similar to the perfectly competitive market: an ideal. The reality of public work is that much of it is complex to perform, complex to administer, and complex to evaluate. Although contracting always has an important role to play in public service, the wisdom of the older government reform movement (to focus energy on the improved operation of public agencies as they exist) and the insights from contemporary privatization experiences converge on one conclusion. The role of contracting in public-service production must be balanced with a major investment of resources in the development of good public management. There is no easy, market-tested method for ensuring that citizens cost-effectively get the public services that they want.

The lesson of the privatization experiences recounted here is especially powerful. All these experiences are drawn from the class of blue-collar services thought to be the easiest to privatize because they are the easiest to visually inspect. Yet, problems of accountability and control persist. These findings do not augur well for calls to privatize larger, more complex, and less easily evaluated services such as public safety, education, corrections, health, human services, and welfare, although these services comprise the bulk of the public budget.

Conclusions: Eight Rules for Improving the Public Sector

About half of all public money is dispensed via contracts. This practice is unlikely to change. Consequently, even if the ideological calls for privatization disappeared tomorrow, public contracting would still loom large in day-to-day operation of government. If our goal is to improve the functioning of the public sector rather than ride one of the "either/or" horses in a political race, we need to move forward on two tracks: improvement of the environment of public service and improvement of the public contracting process. The issue is not what to privatize and what to keep public. The real issue is how we reorganize the agencies that provide public service and, within that context, improve the use of contracting. To that end, I conclude by proposing the following eight guidelines for a process of public-sector reform.

Carefully Delineate the Output of Any Public Service Considered for Reorganization

A public service, especially if it is a publicly supplied service rather than a pure public good (e.g., the lighthouse in Chapter 2), is almost invariably a far more complex product than is the private-sector counterpart with which it is compared. As the comparison of postal service and private package delivery service in Chapter 2 illustrated, public services almost always have both equity and direct service outputs implicit in their mission. Unless this complete service mission is fully understood, a hasty plunge into contracting stands a large risk of creating the wrong product. Local post offices fulfill community service functions as well as mail delivery. Although the former may be implicit and the latter overt, both are highly prized by the general public. The maintenance of low-cost and high-quality first-class mail service is still a vital social function. In an age of television and internet service, that role perhaps has changed, but it has not disappeared. It is noteworthy that the Tory government in Great Britain was forced to back away quickly from its proposal to privatize the British postal service. The popular reaction was both swift and unequivocal. Much of this had to do with the high value placed on the informal parts of the agency mission by most citizens.

Process and product often cannot be separated. Albany, New York, came to grief because it failed to recognize vehicle maintenance as part of a larger public-service delivery system. Indianapolis, Indiana, understood this. Municipalities maintain varied fleets of motorized vehicles that include everything from sedans for city officials to heavy packers for waste collection. The exact size and configuration of any fleet are determined by the size of the municipality and the functions for which the fleet is responsible. Regardless of fleet size and composition, the economics of fleet maintenance are straightforward. Maintenance cost varies directly with the average age of the fleet; older vehicles require more maintenance and repair to provide effective service. Cost also varies directly with the intensity of use. The more miles a particular vehicle is driven, the more frequently are repairs needed. If a city elects to run one vehicle 36,000 miles in a year rather than use two at 18,000 miles each, its capital costs are lower but its maintenance costs are higher, all else being equal. The point at which a municipality decides to invest in new equipment rather than pay more for maintenance depends on the relative time and monetary costs of the alternative. Alternatives reflect the costs of borrowing for capital versus the costs of sustaining higher maintenance levels. Sometimes it is more economical to fund new equipment through the sale of bonds. At other times it is less expensive to sustain older vehicles with more maintenance. Finally, the efficiency of the maintenance effort is also related to the vehicle acquisition and disposition program. Cities that carefully control purchases to ensure consistency in terms of makes and models with the existing fleet find the predictability of repair problems and the stocking of spare parts more predictable and hence less costly.

Because these functions are so intertwined with the core service mission of government, in-house fleet maintenance is typically the norm. But, there are many ways to organize the work. A centralized facility can provide the work, as in Indianapolis, or smaller facilities within each operating department can do it, as was the case in Albany before privatization. Facilities can be comprehensive or partial. Should all the maintenance work be done by the in-house staff, or should specialized work, such as body work, be contracted out to local shops? There are no readily apparent answers to these questions. Much depends upon the relative costs of the various alternatives. But, isolating the vehicle-maintenance function from this larger system for purposes of privatization is a mistake that is not easily reversed and runs the risk of overusing maintenance when fleet management might be more cost effective.

Know Your ABCs

In this case ABC stands for *a*ctivity *b*ased *c*ost accounting. Most public operating budgets and financial statements break out cost data by department (e.g., police and fire). Within departments, budgets divide spending based on personnel and other than personnel services (OTPS). This breakout tells us little about how particular services generate costs for government. Without understanding the linkage between service provision and its costs, there is no justification for claiming that privatization saves money or is even cost effective. Similarly, there is no basis to justify in-house operation.

The major flaw in the rush to privatize highway-maintenance services in Massachusetts was the failure of the Weld administration to fully understand the real costs of its existing in-house operation. When Goldsmith came into office in Indianapolis, one of the first tasks of his administration was the institution of ABC accounting for all departments. An important reason for the success of the fleet service restructuring was its historically good cost-accounting database. The value of effective costing models and management information systems is too often underestimated, as are their costs. But, if over the long run, regardless of whether there is contracting or direct service provision, good public management is the key, then the costs of effective information and cost-accounting systems is a high-return investment.

Compare Privatization with In-House Operation by Using Avoidable Cost Accounting

Although ABC accounting is an improvement over traditional book-keeping, alone it cannot reveal the cost savings of change because it includes both overhead and direct operating costs. In essence, it is a fully allocated accounting system. As we saw in the case of the Foothills Transit Zone, fully allocated cost-accounting can lead to a significant over-statement of savings. As the situation in Santa Barbara, California, demonstrated, it even makes possible privatizations that actually increase public expenses and still permit claims of savings. There is widespread professional agreement that cost comparisons in situations of privatization should be made on an avoidable-cost basis. If there is no avoidable-cost savings in the short run, it is unlikely, though not impossible given the systemic reality of public-contracting dynamics, that there will ever be any real long-term savings from the privatization.

Fully Address the Reality of Transaction Costs

Careful specification of the service, understanding its cost structure, and a proper avoidable cost model are necessary management tools, but they are not sufficient. When contracting is considered, there must be meaningful consideration of transaction costs. Contract markets are not spot markets. Only rarely do they neatly fit into the category of classical contracting. As a result, factoring an assessment of transaction costs into the decision-making process is important. Although not easily quantified, these costs must be carefully considered when privatization is contemplated. Too often, transaction costs are ignored. But, as we have seen over and over again, these costs do not disappear. They merely grind the privatization initiative to a halt at some future point, leaving taxpayers stuck with higher costs and fewer alternatives.

The economics of organization teach us that when a service is frequently or regularly used, providing it internally because of the transaction costs generated by supervising outside providers often pays. This is especially true if the service requires highly specialized equipment and/or especially skilled labor. Once these specific assets are controlled by the outside service provider, the public agency loses the ability to bargain for an efficient price or more effective service. The greater the degree of control over the needed assets, the more the contract price diverges from the actual cost of production. New York City pays the highest price in the country for contracted municipal school-bus service and has no cost-effective way to obtain access to alternative bus service. The assets, drivers and vehicles, are controlled by the contractors.

The more uncertain the service environment, the more difficult it is to create a contract with low transaction costs. Where risk is a major factor, it becomes almost impossible for government to avoid paying a risk premium (contingency cost built into the contract) to obtain competent work. However, when the government must pay such a risk premium, it should carefully consider in-house production as a preferable alternative.

With that much said, it is also important to bear in mind that we are not talking about a simple "either/or" situation. Technology changes and so do contract possibilities. Moreover, in an age of low-cost communications and information processing, it is especially the case that efficient network alternatives are viable possibilities. It is therefore vital that the full range of these possibilities be scrutinized when making decisions based on an evaluation of transaction costs.

Recognize that Public Contracting Is Different from Private Contracting

One appeal of public contracting is its apparent similarities to private contracting, but these similarities are just that—more apparent than real. The comparison is misleading. Public contracting is always tightly constrained by accountability rules that are designed to ensure that public money is spent on the intended public purpose and can scarcely be otherwise. Without tight regulation, money spent in the name of the people is easily diverted to the pockets of public officials or power brokers who fashion the contracts, as well as to the contractors themselves, instead of adding value for the citizenry. That is the abiding story from the time of the construction of the New York County courthouse down to the construction of the Westchester County Medical Center parking structure.

As a result, public agencies are not free to pursue deals with the flexibility of the private sector. Public agencies must always be prepared to justify the contracts into which they enter. Losing bidders have the right to challenge the winning bid and even force reversal of the agency's decision, even when the initial decision is in the best interests of the citizenry. Although officials and contractors frequently bemoan how red tape ties their hands, we need to recognize this inflexibility as the price to be paid to avoid moral hazards and give all bidders a fair opportunity to win public contracts. Even in the best of circumstances, public contracting for services is a second-best option that is always more problematic than the situation in the private sector. The costs of these constraints should be honestly estimated in any privatization decision.

Compare *Three* Alternatives

Too often the public decision on privatization is treated as an "either/or" decision. When this occurs, it essentially involves casting up the policy choice as a comparison between an "imperfect" government and an "ideal" contract market. As the experiences recounted in this book have demonstrated, private contracting is at least equally as imperfect as existing public service. The experience of the Indianapolis Fleet Services (IFS) shows that the relevant comparison must be between the agency as it now exists, contracting as it is likely to exist, and direct service provision as it can feasibly be improved (termed "best practice").

Once the choice is cast in that way, it no longer must be a zero-sum game that politically pits public employees against private contractors. Instead, rearrangements and permutations may be possible. Rye Brook, New York, went down the either/or path in 1995 but has since pulled back from that untenable position. Rye Brook realized that it had an improved set of options for providing itself with fire service and chose some of both. Instead of continuing to see itself as the passive purchaser of service from an outside party, Rye Brook became an active manager of a vital municipal service. The decision has given Rye Brook a richer menu of future options than the short list it thought it possessed when its initial feud with neighboring Port Chester led it to hastily try privatization.

Make Meaningful Employee Participation Possible

If best practice as the third alternative is to add to productivity or cut costs, then employees must be integral to the reorganization process. The experiences in Fort Lauderdale and Indianapolis illustrate this well. Although employee empowerment may be initiated in several ways, in an era of the popularity of privatization, it is most likely done via the competitive bid. If public officials seek to facilitate reorganization by staging a competitive bid, then the Indianapolis model is the correct precedent. Employees were brought into the managerial decision-making process in a manner that genuinely respected their knowledge and experience. That was also true in Fort Lauderdale where labor–management cooperation was the method of change. Although a different form, the collaborative substance was identical. By way of contrast, the "sink or swim" approach used by the Weld administration in Massachusetts that left employees essentially on their own to construct a bid is ultimately a sham. It does not build collaboration in pursuit of efficiency and high quality. It is at best a war of attrition and no one wins.

Employees must participate in the process from the very beginning. Often the most crucial decisions are made by the team that defines the scope of the restructuring task. Employee participation is critical at this stage because they, better than senior management and political leadership, understand the qualitative and quantitative portions of the service.

The employee team members asked to take part in the scoping decision must be chosen, not by management, but by the employees themselves. This is very important. In the best of circumstances, institutional change is difficult for everyone. If restructuring is intended to include a competitive bidding process at some point, the issue of trust becomes even more crucial.[1] Recognize that no matter how much leadership tries to avoid it, there is inevitably a high degree of mistrust and suspicion built into the initial stages of any institutional change process. If all parties believe that they have played a meaningful role right from the start, they are more willing to take risks and identify with the result, no matter how painful some of the short-term adjustments are.

Management is a learned skill. Employees who are asked to take part in a bidding process for their work must be trained to view that work in an analytic top-down manner along with the bottom-up manner intuitive in their everyday work situation. The government should underwrite this training. It is an investment in the human capital of its workforce that more than repays itself in the quality of both the bid process and subsequent work.

Once employees are brought on board, they must be encouraged and permitted to look at all aspects of the task. They must be free to use their own special knowledge about the work and the freedom to redesign work as they see fit. The knowledge held by public employees is an untapped resource that can produce significant and rapid gains in agency performance. In a very real sense, the most valuable capital asset that any organization possesses is the knowledge and experience of its members. In effect, the most productive asset for good public service

---

[1] In terms of adjustments, it is important that management make clear to workers from the outset that if the process leads to a very fundamental change in the organization they personally will not be hurt. No one rationally assists in cutting their own throat.

walks out the agency door every night. Only a leadership that respects its employees can access the full productivity of that capital.

Once the process starts, management must be attentive to employee complaints about how existing rules and procurement practices hinder the performance of their jobs. Political leadership must be prepared to help the restructuring committee cut through red tape.

A corollary to the previous point is that overhead must be on the table. Frequently, overhead, not direct service costs, makes public service more costly. Restructuring can often be more effective than privatization because it can provide ways to meaningfully reduce overhead. Contracting without internal reorganization simply replaces direct service costs with outside resources. Beyond the most unskilled service work, there is little or no wage savings margin in that tradeoff. But, public services with a high proportion of low-skilled labor are a small proportion of the total cost of public service. The bulk of public costs resides in the tasks performed by more highly skilled labor.

Within those services, the largest potential for savings often can be found within the overhead of the agency. Public bureaucracies, like sedentary people, tend to accumulate fat around the middle. I recall one of my consulting jobs at a major transit agency several years ago in one of the largest cities in the United States. Labor and management were sitting around the table attempting to redesign work in the mold of best practice. One of the union officials noted that when he began work at the agency ten years earlier he reported to one supervisor. He currently reported directly to *five* different people! Cutting this type of overhead may be difficult because it means confronting middle managers, some of whom are also political appointees. These are individuals who have become powerfully entrenched in midrange positions, many of which serve no useful organizational purpose. Crucial to Mayor Goldsmith winning over the line workers in the IFS to his competitive bidding style of restructuring was his demonstration of his willingness to eliminate superfluous middle management positions, even when it meant confronting political appointees of his own party. If the powers that be are willing to permit line employees to look at overhead, they frequently uncover some of the greatest sources of immediate savings.

Remove Politics from Contracting

Whereas restructuring is fundamental, contracting remains an integral part of public work. It is important that to the degree possible, public contract markets are made as efficient as possible. The most important step in this regard is the separation of public contracting from politics as much as possible. Although it is unlikely that this can ever be done completely, the situation may be vastly improved. One of the worst maladies of modern contracting is the corrosive impact of influence peddling on public officials. The potential for gain through shortcuts never abates. There is a special burden on those who espouse privatization to ensure that they are an equally strong voice in the battle against corruption and influence peddling. Nothing destroys a privatization more quickly than this sort of problem. Blame for the failure of the hospital parking-garage privatization in Westchester County, New York, must be laid at the feet of the former County Executive Andrew O'Rourke. Whether intentionally or inadvertently, he apparently looked the other way as one of his chief fundraisers and dealmakers, Albert Pirro, played both sides of the arrangement for personal gain. Staunch privatization advocates cannot have both contracting business as usual and reform, a lesson that Mr. Goldsmith fully absorbed but too many other advocates fail to grasp.

A simple first step requires that any firms and their principals who engage in public contracting are not free to contribute money to politicians who can influence contract policy or to buy gifts for officials who are important to the contracts decisions. After all, it is a free choice to engage in public contracting as a means of livelihood. This free choice also implies a moral responsibility by the contractors to keep the contracting system above board. Consequently, the issue of political free speech should not loom large. Too much public trust is at stake to permit standards of conduct between the agents of the buyers (the public sector) and the agents of the sellers (contractors) that are illegal or certainly not tolerated in wholly private transactions. Purchasing agents who take gifts or "kickbacks" from contractors lose their jobs, are fined, and are imprisoned. It is important that the integrity of the system be protected. A meaningful firewall that can effectively divide contracting from politics is thus a vital necessity. If contractors feel such restriction to be an infringement on their political right of free speech via influence peddling, they are always free to get into a new line of work.

Companies that engage in public contracting have occasionally been found guilty of bribery, price-fixing, and providing shoddy product. Ideally, the public-contracting process should have zero tolerance for such behavior or firms that have pleaded no contest to such charges. At minimum, other public officials should be made aware of the track records of firms with which they may do business. Firms found to have violated the law or have pleaded no contest should be, if not completely barred from all future public contracting, at least well known to future public officials. If a firm is innocent, then it should fight the charges. Money must not be worth more than reputation. The threat of permanent sanction creates such incentive. A national registry should be established to track firms and their principals that have been found guilty or pleaded no contest to charges related to public contracting. Given the high inherent risk of moral hazard in public contracting and the large amounts of taxpayer money at stake, there is no place in the field for business organizations with low moral standards. Improved information only helps to make markets more efficient. It also rewards those firms that play by the rules at the expense of firms that do not.

One of the worst aspects of public contracting is the revolving-door syndrome, in which officials who award lucrative public contracts leave public service shortly thereafter to work for the contractors to whom they awarded the contract. At times, legislation is enacted that requires a "decent interval" between the award of the contract and new employment, typically a one-year hiatus. That length of time is inadequate, and these rules need to be tightened significantly. Requiring a public official to wait three years before entering the industry in which he or she awarded contracts and five years before he or she could be employed by a firm that received a contract from the former public official would adequately protect the public treasury.

These rules are admittedly stringent. But, if there is a serious commitment to spending public money on private providers of public services, then the public has a right to know that penalties are stringent and that the firewall between politicians and contractors is equally strong. Symbolic fines, wrist slaps, and occasional bad publicity have not adequately deterred inappropriate behavior in the past, and these minor chastisements will not work any better in the future. If we cannot achieve political consensus on these provisions, then we are not really talking about a new age of public contract management. We are more likely preparing for a nostalgic stroll down memory lane back into the world constructed by Boss Tweed and his cohorts.

Privatization is too often pushed as an ideological proposition with little or no basis in good agency management (Feigenbaum and Henig 1997). The management of public services must be removed from the ideological battle about the size of government. They are properly two different realms. For our purposes, the issue of size is distinct from that of good management.

A simple separation of the two is easily mandated by requiring that before a privatization proceeds it must pass muster as a cost-effective, comparable-quality alternative. Thus, one of the most successful pieces of legislation is a Massachusetts law (Chapter 296 of the Acts of 1993). Popularly known as the Pacheco (or more formally, Pacheco–Manard) Act, it requires that all proposed privatization be subjected to a cost analysis (for background see Wallin 1997). The Office of the State Auditor carries out the work.[2] The law has permitted many privatizations to proceed, but it has also stopped some privatizations that would have been costly errors. The existence of the law essentially forces decision-making officials to move beyond the notion that privatization might work or that they thought it would be a good idea. It requires officials to do some real managerial homework. It permits impacted employees to submit proposals for work reform. In general, it forces privatization out of the realm of the ideological into that of the practical.

These rules summarize a broad range of initiatives that must be undertaken if genuine public sector reform is the goal: all are feasible but not equally probable, at least in the short term. Politics and economics always constrain the possible. Nonetheless, we must take heart from the experience of the progressive reformers who at the dawning of the twentieth century helped to fashion a workable if not perfect public sector. The reformers who carry out the work of building a responsive public sector in the twenty-first century always need to think just one step beyond conventional wisdom about what is possible.

---

[2]Notably, for purposes of cost comparison the state auditor in Massachusetts requires the use of avoidable cost accounting. See Rule 3 above (for more detail see Commonwealth of Massachusetts, Office of the State Auditor, March 1994).

Bibliography

Adler, Moshe. 1999. "Been There, Done That: The Privatization of Street Cleaning in Nineteenth Century New York." *New Labor Forum* 4 (spring/summer): 88 – 99.

Ahlbrandt, Roger S. Jr. 1973a. "Efficiency in the Provision of Fire Services." *Public Choice* 16.

———. 1973b. *Municipal Fire Protection Services: Comparison of Alternative Organizational Forms.* Beverly Hills, Calif.: Sage.

American Federation of State County and Municipal Employees District Council #61 and Blue Collar Workers Union Local 1961. N.d. *An Investigative Study.*

American Public Transportation Association. 1988. *Privatization: Is a Level Playing Field Possible?* Tape Transcription, tape #88-19. Session held at the 1988 Annual APTA Meeting, 2 – 6 October, Montreal, Quebec, Canada.

Aries, Nancy. 1996. "Beyond Individual Heroes: Emerging Networks in Biomedical Research and Development." Prepared for the Council on Biomedical Research and Development. New York: New York Academy of Medicine.

Arrow, Kenneth Joseph. 1974. *The Limits of Organization.* Fels Lectures on Public Policy Analysis. New York: Norton.

The Atlanta Constitution. 1999. "Private Prisons Present Public Risk." 6 January, A12.

Barrett, Wayne. 1993. "The City Scandal That Won't Go Away." *The Village Voice,* 13 April.

Bates, Eric. 1999. "CAA, The Sequel." *The Nation,* 7 June, 22.

Belluck, Pam. 1999. "As More Prisons Go Private, States Seek Tighter Controls." *The New York Times,* 15 April, A1.

Belman, Dale L., and John S. Heywood. 1993. "Job Attributes and Federal Wage Differentials." *Industrial Relations* 32, no. 1 (winter): 148 – 57.

Bernstein, Andrea. 1997. "M.T.A. Thwarts Giuliani and His Investigation into Lockheed Contract." *The New York Observer,* 30 June – 7 July.

Braggs, Rick. 1999. "Contractor Found Guilty in Trial of ValueJet," *The New York Times,* 7 December, A21.

Bubrick, Christine Elizabeth. 1997. "What's Competition Got To Do With It?: An Analysis of Trade Waste Collection in New York City." Master's thesis, Columbia University.

Canadian Urban Transit Association. 1991. Operating Characteristics of Member Systems.

————. 1996. Competitiveness of Urban Transit, Public or Private Operation: Guidelines for Assessing the Options.

Cascio, Lynne. 1995. "Battle Continues to Rage Over Costs of Fire Department." *The Daily Times*, 12 December, 3A.

————. 1998. "Rye Brook, Rural/Metro Fire Ends Ties." *The Daily Times*, 11 March, 1A.

Cities Action Clinic, State and Local Government Labor–Management Committee Conference. 1996. "How the Fort Lauderdale Public Services Water Pipe Committee Jointly Analyzes In-House Costs for Laying Pipe." Panel discussion attended by author. 18 November, Fort Lauderdale, Fla.

City of New York, Department of Investigation. 1993. The Recommended Award of the Parking Violations Bureau Privatization Contract to Lockheed I. M. S. New York.

City of New York, Office of the Comptroller, Bureau of Management Audits. 1989. Audit Report on the New York City Department of Transportation: Comparison of In-House vs. Contractor's Resurfacing Costs. Document no. MC88–201. New York.

————. 1995. Audit Report on the New York City Department of Transportation: Comparison of In-House vs. Contractor's Resurfacing Costs. Document no. EU94–164A. New York.

City of New York, Office of Management and Budget. 1990. Contracting-In Cost Comparison Manual: A Guide to Determining Cost-Effectiveness. New York.

Coase, Ronald H. 1937. "The Nature of the Firm." *Economica* 4 (November): 386–405.

————. 1960. "The Problem of Social Cost." *Journal of Law and Economics* 3: 1–44.

Commonwealth of Massachusetts, House Post Audit and Oversight Bureau. 1994. *Interim Report: Review of Essex County Privatization*. Boston, Mass.

Commonwealth of Massachusetts, Office of the State Auditor. 1994. *Guidelines for Implementing the Commonwealth's Privatization Law*. Boston, Mass.

————. 1995. Privatization of the Maintenance of State Roads in Essex County, October 7, 1992 to October 6, 1993. Document no. 93–5015–3. Boston, Mass.

Coopers & Lybrand. 1991. *RTD/Foothill Transit Zone: Review of Marginal Cost Analysis Approach*. Los Angeles, Calif.: Southern California Rapid Transit District.

————. 1996. *Independent Assessment of Massachusetts Highway Maintenance Privatization Program*. Prepared for the Executive Office of Transportation and Construction.

Cormier, A. E. 1996. "Let's Set the Record Straight on the 'Privatization' of Transit." Press Release from the Canadian Urban Transit Association, June.

Cox, Wendell, and Jean Love. 1990. "A Public Purpose for Public Transit." *Policy Study #207* (January). Los Angeles, Calif.: Reason Foundation.

Cox, Wendell, and Samuel A. Brunelli. 1992. *America's Protected Class: Why Excess Public Employee Compensation Is Bankrupting States*. Washington, D.C.: American Legislative Exchange Council.

Crain's New York Business. 1995. "DA Should Probe Why Businesses Stay with Cartel." 10 July, 8.

Crooks, Harold. 1993. *Giants of Garbage: The Rise of the Global Waste Industry and the Politics of Pollution Control*. Toronto, Canada: James Lorimer & Co., Publishers.

D'Adamo, R. Raleigh. 1985. "Westchester's Public/Private Partnership in Transit: A Decade of Experience." Paper presented at the APTA Annual Meeting. Los Angeles, Calif.

David M. Griffith & Associates. 1994. "Request for Proposals for Fleet Management & Maintenance Services for the City of Indianapolis," November.

———. 1995. "City of Albany: Phase II Report of the Citywide Management Audit."

Davies, Matt. 1999. "Folkloric Legends." *The Journal News*, 20 May, 10B.

Deakin, Simon, and Jonathan Michie. 1997. "The Theory and Practice of Contracting." In *Contracts, Co-operation, and Competition: Studies in Economic Management and Law*, 1–39. Oxford: Oxford University Press.

Demsetz, Harold. 1993. "The Theory of the Firm Revisited." In *The Nature of the Firm: Origins, Evolution and Development*, ed. Oliver E. Williamson and Sidney G. Winter, 159–78. New York: Oxford University Press.

DeNucci, Joseph. 1996. Letter to James Kerasiotes, 26 June.

Denver RTD. 1996. Comprehensive Annual Financial Reports of the Regional Transportation District.

———. 1996. RTD Bus Cost Model Documentation.

Donahue, John D. 1989. *The Privatization Decision: Public Ends, Private Means*. New York: Basic Books.

Donovan, Joseph, William Gay, Candace Neufeld, Alan Siegel, and David Wuertz. 1989. *Fire and Emergency Medical Services Assessment: Scottsdale, Arizona*. Prepared for the City of Scottsdale, Ariz. Herndon, Virginia: University City Science Center.

Dublin, Larry. 1995. "Rye Brook Board Signs Contract for Fire Services, Privatization Deal Ends Partnership with Port Chester." *The Daily Times*, 23 December, 1A.

———. 1998. "Aid Pact in Peril in Rye Brook." *The Daily Times*, 4 January, 1A.

Ernst & Young. 1991. Evaluation of the Foothills Transit Zone, Fiscal Year 1990 Report to the LACTC.

Fallows, James. 1981. *National Defense*. New York: Random House.

Fantauzzo, Stephen. N.d. "Competitive Government: A Labor Perspective of the Indianapolis Model." AFSCME Council 62.

Federal Register. 1984. Volume 49, no. 205, Washington, D.C., 22 October.

———. 1989. Volume 54, no. 73, Washington, D.C., 18 April.

Feigenbaum, Harvey, and Jeffrey Henig. 1997. "Privatization and Political Theory." *Journal of International Affairs* 50, no. 2 (winter): 338–55.

Fire Advisory Panel. 1989. Fire Advisory Panel Report to Scottsdale City Manager Jorge Carrasco. 22 May, Scottsdale, Ariz.

Flash, Cynthia. 1988. "Sun City to Dismiss Rural/Metro." *Scottsdale Progress*, 17 September, 3.

Gelarden, R. Joseph. N.d. "City Workers Outbid 3 Firms for Contract." *The Indianapolis Star*, 1.

Glaberson, William. 1998. "Experiment in Private Fire Protection Fails for a Westchester Village." *The New York Times*, 13 March, B1.

Gold, Steven D., and Sarah Ritchie. 1992. *Compensation of State and Local Employees: Sorting Out the Issues*. Albany, N.Y.: National Commission on the State and Local Public Service.

Gomez-Ibanez, Jose A., and John R. Meyer. 1993. *Going Private: The International Experience With Transport Privatization*. Washington, D.C.: The Brookings Institution.

Hammond, Ken. 1995. Memorandum to Allyn Waggle, 22 February.

Hanlon, Martin D. 1993. "Privatization of Human Services: Personnel Consequences of the Dual Service Delivery Model." Paper prepared for the Western Regional Science Association Annual Meeting, February, Wailea, Hawaii.

———. 1999. "Running on Two Tracks: The Public and Private Provision of Human Services." *New Labor Forum* (spring/summer): 100–109.

Harrison, Bennett. 1994. *Lean and Mean: The Changing Landscape of Corporate Power in the Age of Flexibility.* New York: Basic Books.

Harvard University, John F. Kennedy School of Government. 1993. *From Public to Private: The Massachusetts Experience: 1991–1993,* Student Report (April). Cambridge, Mass.

Higby, David. 1995. "Privatize Trash? A Cautionary Tale; An Incinerator in Washington County, NY Led to Political Corruption, Corporate Greed and Environmental Problems." *The Nation,* 3 July, 14.

Hinchey, Maurice D. 1986. Organized Crime's Involvement in the Waste Hauling Industry. A Report from the Chairman to the New York State Assembly Environmental Conservation Committee based on the Committee's 1984 Hearings and Subsequent Staff Investigation. Albany, N.Y.

Hirschman, Albert O. 1970. *Exit, Voice, and Loyalty; Responses to Decline in Firms, Organizations, and States.* Cambridge, Mass.: Harvard University Press.

Holstrom, Bengt, and Jean Triole. 1989. "The Theory of the Firm." In *Handbook of Industrial Organization,* ed. R. Schmalensee and R. Willig. Volume I. Amsterdam: North-Holland.

Holstrom, Bengt, and John Roberts. 1998. "The Boundaries of the Firm Revisited." *Journal of Economic Perspectives* 12, no. 4 (fall): 73–94.

Institute for Local Self-Government. 1976. Data in Robert W. Poole. 1980. *Cutting Back City Hall.* New York: Universe Books.

International Association of Fire Fighters. N.d. *Privatization Primer.* Washington, D.C.: International Association of Fire Fighters.

———. 1990. *Analysis of Fire and Emergency Medical Service Delivery: Scottsdale, Arizona.* Washington, D.C.: International Association of Fire Fighters.

International City Managers Association. 1990. *1989 Municipal Yearbook.* Washington, D.C.: International City Managers Association.

Kemper, Peter, and John M. Quigley. 1976. *The Economics of Refuse Collection.* Cambridge, Mass.: Ballinger Publishing Company.

Kerasiotes, James. N.d. *A Proposal for Contracted Highway Maintenance.* Commonwealth of Massachusetts, Executive Office of Transportation and Construction. Boston, Mass.

Kitchen, Harry M. 1976. "A Statistical Estimation of an Operating Cost Function for Municipal Refuse Collection." *Public Finance Quarterly* 4, no. 1 (January): 56–76.

———. 1992. "Urban Transit Provision in Ontario: A Public/Private Sector Cost Comparison." *Public Finance Quarterly* 20, no. 1 (January): 114–28.

Klein, Benjamin. 1993. "Vertical Integration as Organizational Ownership: The Fisher Body–General Motors Relationship Revisited." In *The Nature of the Firm: Origins, Evolution and Development,* ed. Oliver E. Williamson and Sidney G. Winter, 213–26. New York: Oxford University Press.

Kohn, Brian. 1999. "Hospital to Buy Garage." *The Journal News,* 4 February, B1.

Kostro, Charles. 1994. Letter to Thomas Hammond, 14 February.

———. 1995. Letter to Frank Borgia, 6 October.

KPMG Peat Marwick. 1991. *Denver RTD Privatization Performance Audit Update: July 1990–June 1991, Final Report.* Report prepared for the Denver Colorado Regional Transportation District.

Langosa, Gerry. 1992a. "Mayor Halts Work on Garage." *Indianapolis News,* January.

———. 1992b. "Belmont Site Renovation to be Diverted to Jail Use." *Indianapolis News,* 14 February.

Lazard Freres & Co. LLC. 1996. Wackenhut Corrections Corp.: Company Report.

Local 285, SEIU. 1995. Union Workers as In-House Contractors. Interim Report.

Macneil, I. 1974. "The Many Futures of Contracts." *Southern California Law Review* 47: 696–816.

———. 1978. "Contracts: Adjustment of Long Term Economic Relations Under Classical, Neoclassical and Relational Contract Law." *Northwestern University Law Review* 72: 854–905.

Martin, Lawrence. 1993. "How to Compare Costs Between In-House and Contracted Services." *How to Guide #4* (March). Los Angeles, Calif.: Reason Foundation.

McCorkhill, John. 1992. "Keep Em Rollin." *CEMD Pit Stop,* February/March.

———. 1995. Inter-department Communication to Steve James and Dominic Mangine, 27 February.

McDavid, James C. 1985. "The Canadian Experience with Privatizing Solid Waste Collection Services." *Public Administration Review* (September/October): 602–8.

Ménard, Charles. 1995. "Markets as Institutions Versus Organizations as Markets? Disentangling Some Fundamental Issues." *Journal of Economic Behavior and Organization* 28: 161–82.

Milgrom, Paul, and John Roberts. 1988. "An Economic Approach to Influence Activities and Organizational Responses." *American Journal of Sociology* 94 (supplement): S154–79.

Miles, Raymond E., and Charles C. Snow. 1992. "Causes of Failure in Network Organizations." *California Management Review* 34, no. 4 (summer): 53–72.

Morrison, Patrick. 1992. "Garage Project Will Continue with New Plans to Save Money." *Indianapolis Star,* 14 February, 1–2.

National Fire Protection Association. 1992. "US Fire Experience." In *International City Managers Association, 1992 Municipal Yearbook.* Washington, D.C.: International City Managers Association.

North, Douglass. 1984. "Transaction Costs, Institutions, and Economic History." *Journal of Institutional and Theoretical Economics* 140 (March): 7–17.

Osborne, David, and Ted Gaebler. 1992. *Reinventing Government: How the Entrepreneurial Spirit Is Transforming the Public Sector.* Reading, Mass.: Addison-Wesley Publishing Company.

Peskin, Robert. 1991. Letter to Jack McCroskey, 11 February.

Pickup, Laurie, et al. 1991. "Bus Deregulation in the Metropolitan Areas." *Oxford Studies in Transport.* Aldershot, U.K.: Avebury.

Poole, Robert W. 1980. *Cutting Back City Hall.* New York: Universe Books.

Porter, Carol. 1987. Memorandum to Neal Shearer, 9 December.

Powell, Walter W. 1990. "The Transformation of Organizational Forms: How Useful Is Organization Theory in Accounting for Social Change?" In *Beyond the Marketplace: Rethinking Economy and Society,* ed. Roger Friedland and A. F. Robertson, 301–29. New York: Aldine de Gruyter.

Price Waterhouse. 1989. Metro-Dade Transit Agency: Private Enterprise Participation Program Evaluation—Six-Month Report.

————. 1990. Private Enterprise Participation Evaluation—Second Six-Month Report. Prudential Securities. 1996. Wackenhut Corrections: Company Update.

Raimondo, Henry J., ed. 1992. "Contracting-Out Services in the New Jersey Department of Transportation." Prepared for the Policy Research Seminar (July), Eagleton Institute of Politics. New Brunswick, N.J.: Rutgers University.

Rehfuss, John. 1989. *Contracting Out in Government: A Guide to Working with Outside Contractors to Supply Public Services.* Jossey-Bass Public Administration Series. San Francisco, Calif.: Jossey-Bass Publishers.

Richmond, Jonathan. 1992. "The Cost of Contracted Service: An Assessment of Assessments." Prepared for the Los Angeles County Transportation Commission (July). Boston, Mass.: MIT Center for Transportation Studies.

Rocky Mountain News. 1988. "Bill Would Privatize RTD Bus Operations." 9 January, 12.

Rural/Metro Corporation. N.d. Self-titled promotional brochure.

————. 1988. Rural/Metro Audit: Human Resources Analysis—Management Response. 28 July, Scottsdale, Ariz.

————. 1996. *1995 Rural/Metro Financial Report, Note # 7.* Scottsdale, Ariz.

Ryan, Andy. 1987. "Public vs. Private Testing Buses in Miami." *Mass Transit,* January/February.

Salanié, Bernard. 1998. *The Economics of Contracts, A Primer.* Cambridge, Mass.: The MIT Press.

Sappington, David E. M., and Joseph Stiglitz. 1987. "Privatization, Information and Incentives." *Journal of Policy Analysis and Management* 6, no. 4: 567–82.

San Mateo County California Transit District Budget Department. 1993. *Fully Allocated Cost Analysis Plan: For Fiscal Year 1993–94 Budget.* San Mateo, Calif.

Savas, Emanuel S. 1977. *The Organization and Efficiency of Solid Waste Collection.* Lexington, Mass.: Lexington Books.

————. 1987. *Privatization: The Key to Better Government.* Chatham, N.J.: Chatham House Publishers.

Savas, Emanuel S., and Christopher Niemczewski. 1976. "Who Collects Solid Waste?" In *The Municipal Year Book,* 167–72. Washington, D.C.: International City Management Association.

Schuckel, Kathleen. 1992. "Give Us a Chance, Union Says." *Indianapolis News,* 31 January.

Schumpeter, Joseph A. 1947. *Capitalism, Socialism, and Democracy.* New York: Harper Brothers.

Sclar, Elliott. 1997. *Paying More, Getting Less: The Denver Experience with Bus Privatization 1990–1995.* Prepared for the Amalgamated Transit Union.

Sclar, Elliott, and Mel Watkins. 1994. *Urban Bus Transit Privatization (in Canada): A Look at the Record.* Prepared for Amalgamated Transit Union, AFL-CIO/CLC.

Sen, Amytra K. 1970. *Collective Choice and Social Welfare.* San Francisco, Calif.: Holden-Day.

Sexton, Connie Cone. 1988. "Sun City Awarded Fire Pact." *Phoenix Republican,* 22 December, B1.

Shaller, Michael. 1991. *Reckoning With Reagan: America and Its President in the 1980s.* New York: Oxford University Press.

Smith, Bruce. 1992. "Mayor Meets with Bond Analysts, Rating Houses Upbeat About City." *The Indianapolis Star,* 16 February, 16.

Smothers, Ronald. 1997. "Ex-Official In Newark Is Convicted." *The New York Times*, 22 March, 25.

South Eastern Pennsylvania Transit Authority (SEPTA). 1997a. Meeting of Union and SEPTA officials, 11 September. Attended by Elliott Sclar.

———. 1997b. Paratransit ADA/Shared Ride Weekly Consolidated ADA/Shared Ride Expenditures Report 59701 for Month Ending April 26, 1997.

———. 1997c. Response to query from Allstate Transportation concerning SEPTA's desire to impose a minimum hourly operator compensation rate requirement on outside contractors. Handout.

South Eastern Pennsylvania Transit Authority (SEPTA) Board. 1997. Resolution re: Authorization to Approve a General Release and Settlement Agreement with Triage, Inc., in the Form of Amendment No. 2 to the Existing Paratransit Agreement.

State of California, Office of the State Auditor. 1996. *State Contracting Reforms Are Needed to Protect the Public Interest.* Sacramento, Calif.

State of Colorado, House of Representatives. 1996. *House Bill 96–1360.*

State of New Jersey, Commission of Investigation. 1989. *Solid Waste Regulation.* Trenton, N.J.

Stett, Charles "Skip." 1996. Interview by author. Via telephone. 6 September, Larchmont, N.Y.

Stevens, Barbara, and E. S. Savas. 1977. "The Cost of Residential Refuse Collection and the Effect of Service Arrangement." In *The Municipal Year Book*, 200–205. Washington, D.C.: International City Management Association.

Stevens, Barbara J. 1984. *Delivering Municipal Service Efficiently: A Comparison of Municipal and Private Service Delivery: Technical Report.* Washington, D.C.: The United States Department of Housing and Urban Development, Community Development and Fair Housing Analysis Division.

Teal, Roger. 1985. *Transit Service Contracting Experience and Issues.* Transportation Research Board Record 1036: 28–36. Washington, D.C.: TRB, National Research Council.

———. 1987. "Transportation Privatization: Experience and Issues." *Urban Resources* 4, no. 1: 7–12.

———. 1988. "Public Service Contracting: A Status Report." *Transportation Quarterly* 32, no. 2 (April): 207–22.

United States Department of Commerce, Bureau of the Census. 1992. *1990 Economic Census.* Washington, D.C.

United States Office of Management and Budget. 1990. *A-76 Circular.* Washington, D.C.

U.S. Secretary of Labor's Task Force on Excellence in State and Local Government Through Labor–Management Cooperation. 1996. *Working Together for Public Service.* Washington, D.C.: Government Printing Office.

Vagnier, John, and Elliott Sclar. 1993. Fully Allocated Cost Comparisons and Avoidable Cost Models for Four Subcontracted Projects Utilizing Project Inspectors in District 11, Ohio Department of Transportation in FY 1991 and 1992. Prepared for the Ohio Civil Service Employees Association.

Wallin, Bruce A. 1997. "The Privatization Process: Lessons from Implementation and Development." *Public Adminstration Review* (January).

Walsh Cab Company. 1996. Chapter 11 Bankruptcy Petition filed by Walsh Cab Company t/a Access Paratransit. Eastern District of Pennsylvania, Bankruptcy Court.

Williamson, Oliver E. 1985. *The Economic Institutes of Capitalism*. New York: New York Free Press.

——. 1988. "Corporate Governance and Corporate Finance." *Journal of Finance* 43: 567–91.

——. 1993. "The Logic of Economic Organization." In *The Nature of the Firm: Origins, Evolution and Development*, ed. Oliver E. Williamson and Sidney G. Winter, 90–116. New York: Oxford University Press.

——. 1996. *The Mechanisms of Governance*. New York: Oxford University Press.

Wilson, David McKay. 1994. "Med Center Parking Rates to Rise, Increase of at Least 27 Percent Provokes Protests." *The Daily Times*, 19 November, 1A.

——. 1997a. "Med Center, Garage Owner Discuss Sale." *The Daily Times*, 2 May, 1A.

——. 1997b. "Hospital Visitors Say Parking Fees Make Dollars, Not Sense." *The Daily Times*, 16 June, 1A.

——. 1999. "Albert Pirro Brokered Many Big Deals in Region." *The Journal News*, 25 February, A2.

Wines, Leslie. 1996. "High Order Strategy for Manufacturing." *Journal of Business Strategy* (July/August): 32.

Womack, James P., Daniel T. Jones, and Daniel Roos. 1990. *The Machine that Changed the World*. New York: Macmillan.

Woolhandler, Steffie, and David Himmelstein. 1991. "The Deteriorating Administrative Efficiency of the US Health Care System." *New England Journal of Medicine* 324, no. 18 (2 May): 1253–58.

Index

Italic page numbers indicate tables.

Access Transit, Inc., 112–13
Activity-based cost accounting, 144, 159
ADA. *See* Americans with Disabilities Act, 1992 (ADA)
Adler, Moshe, 153–54
Administrative. *See* Management
Adverse selection: in contracting, 107–14; definition of, 107–8
AFSCME. *See* American Federation of State County and Municipal Employees (AFSCME)
Albany, N.Y., privatization of vehicle maintenance, 116–18, 146–47
American Federation of State County and Municipal Employees (AFSCME), 116, 137–38, 147–48
Americans with Disabilities Act, 1992 (ADA), 110
American Transit Corporation (ATC), 66
Anecdotal evidence, value of, 13, 156
APCOA, Inc., 104–7
Arm's-length relationship, definition of, 101n
Asset specificity, in government contracting, 118–21
ATC. *See* American Transit Corporation (ATC)
ATC/Vancom, Inc., 86, 87
Atlantic Express, Inc., 114
Audit and Oversight Bureau of the General Court (Massachusetts), 33
Avoidable cost accounting, in calculation of overhead, 65, 66–68, 160

Baker, Dean, ix
Baltimore, paratransit services in, 112n
Benetton, Inc., 124
Big government. *See* Government, big
Biotechnology industry, relational contracting in, 125
Blue collar services, privatization of, 56–57
Blue Collar Workers Union, 116
Brunelli, Samuel A., 60
Bureaucratic costs vs. external transaction costs, 16–19. *See also* Transaction-cost economics
Burton, Nancy, 117
Busing in Canada, privatization of. *See* Canadian bus service privatization

California Bus Association, 66
Canada: health care costs in, 92; paratransit services in, 112n
Canadian bus service privatization: analysis of studies on, 50–55; market size vs. privatization rate, 50–51, *51;* operating cost vs. system size in, 51–55, *53, 54;* ridership patterns and, 51, *52;* studies on, 49
Canadian Urban Transit Association, 50, 51n
Capital costs vs. operating costs, 35–36
Capitalism: and disruptive nature of profit motive, 126–27; historical instability of, 1; mid-twentieth-century theories for reform of, 1–2; renewed faith in, 2; strengths and weaknesses of, 2; U.S. faith in, vii. *See also* Market(s)

Central Equipment Management Department (CEMD), City of Indianapolis, 132–34

Communist Russia, development of markets in, 100

Competition among government contractors: as cost control incentive, viii, 11–12, 61–62, 69, 145–46; costs of, 92–93; difficulty of maintaining, 12–13, 48, 70, 75, 83, 92–93; inherently monopolistic ventures and, 14, 83; levelness of playing field in, 9–11; in oligopolistic markets, 69–70, 71–72, 84–93; political agenda underlying, 3–4; reform of public agencies via, 15, 69; specialized services and, 18–19, 91; and standard market model, 8–9, 47

Complexity of real life, and standard market model, 15–16

Computer industry, relational contracting in, 125

Conceptual framework, importance of having, 13

Conservatives: agenda of, 4, 11, 13, 94; frustrations of, 3; shortsightedness of, 46; success of, 6, 95. *See also* Ideology in privatization debate

Construction services, consumers of, 62

Consultants, and corruption, 105–6, 121

Contract(s): complexity of, 13–14, 101–2, 154; contingency funding in, 108–9; evaluation of bidders in, 109–14; incentive and penalty clauses in, 117–18, 122; ineffectiveness of, 128–29, 156; percent of public money dispensed via, 157; and politics, 164–67; public vs. private, 161–62; relational, 121–28; third party help in negotiation of, 106–7; transparency in, 106

Contract(s), classic (complete), 101–2

Contract(s), incomplete: characteristics of, 102–3; and opportunism by contractors, 103; problems with, 103–21

Contracting efficiency, in transaction-cost economics, 98

Contract markets vs. spot markets, 18–19

Contract(s) with government: complexity of, 13–14, 101–2, 154; corruption in, 48, 105–6, 121, 151–55, 161, 164–67; fixing market-structure problems with, 90–91; politics in, 10–11, 12, 86–87, 87–88, 164–67; in practice vs. theory, 101–29. *See also* Government contractors

Cooperation between contracting parties. *See* Relational contracting

Cooperation programs between labor and management. *See* Labor-management cooperation programs

Coopers and Lybrand, Inc., 39–41, *40,* 66

Corruption in public contracting, 48, 105–6, 121, 151–55, 161, 164–67. *See also* Performance, monitoring of

Cost(s): capital vs. operating, 35–36; difficulty of measuring, 28, 37; importance of measuring, 44, 144, 159, 167; of managing public workers vs. contractors, 146; types to be considered, 63–64. *See also* Activity-based cost accounting; Avoidable cost accounting; Overhead costs; Transaction cost(s)

Cost effectiveness, importance of embracing, 95

Cost-plus contracting: vs. direct supply of services, 83–84; spiraling costs of, 122

Cox, Wendell, 60

Cutting Back City Hall (Robert Poole), 11

David M. Griffith & Associates, 139, 147

Decker, Peter, 81

Defense spending, as abuse of public treasury, 70

Delivering Municipal Services Efficiently (Barbara Stevens). *See* Los Angeles, HUD privatization study of

DeNucci, Joseph, 41

Denver Colorado Regional Transportation District, 67

Denver public transportation, and oligopolistic markets, 84–89

Department of Motor Vehicles (DMV), efficiency of, 21

Department of Public Works (DPW), Albany, N.Y., 116–17

Dinkins, David, 153

Dispute resolution, in relational contracting, 123–24

Distribution of wealth, in standard market model, 7, 8

DMV. *See* Department of Motor Vehicles (DMV)

DPW. *See* Department of Public Works (DPW), Albany, N.Y.

Economic power, tendency toward concentration of, 10–11

Efficiency, economic, and redistribution of wealth, 8
Efficiency of workers, public vs. private sector, 60, 61–62, 62–63, 68
Elections, political pressure of, viii
Employees. *See* Workers, public
England. *See* United Kingdom
Equity. *See* Social equity
Ernst and Young, Inc., 66
Excludability of goods: definition of, 23–24; and public goods and services, 24
Expansion vs. outsourcing, efficiency of, 16–19
Experience goods, definition of, 106
External benefits: definition of, 25; importance of evaluating, 44; of publicly provided goods and services, 25
External costs, and publicly provided goods and services, 25

FAA. *See* Federal Aviation Administration (FAA)
FAC. *See* Fully allocated cost accounting (FAC)
Fantauzzo, Stephen, 137–38
Federal Aviation Administration (FAA), 17
Federal Express, Inc., and public vs. private service providers, 21, 22–23, 25
Fire protection: cost of, 72; cost of in Scottsdale, Ariz., 73–77, *74*, 82; history of, 26–28; privatization lessons learned from, 82–84; and risk aversion, 78–79, 81; in Rye Brook, N.Y., 79–82
Foothill Transit Zone (FTZ), 66–67
Fort Lauderdale, Florida, privatization of pipe laying service, 71–72
Foster-Wheeler, Inc., 119, 120–21
Freedom Transit (SEPTA), 113
Free enterprise. *See* Capitalism
Frequency of business transaction, and cost efficiency, 98
FTZ. *See* Foothill Transit Zone (FTZ)
Fully allocated cost accounting (FAC), in calculation of overhead, 64–65, 66–68

Ghent, N.Y., 21–22
Giuliani, Rudolph, 89–90, 153
Gleason, Gary, 65
Glendale, Ariz., fire protection costs in, *74*
Golden Gate Bridge and Transit District, 66
Goldsmith, Steven, 11, 130–31, 134–37, 143–45, 148, 164

Goods and services, categories of, 23
Government: contemporary attitude toward, 3; loss of faith in, viii, 2
Government, big: citizens' suspicion of, viii; possibility of shrinking, 4; rise of, viii, 1. *See also* Welfare state
Government agencies. *See* Public services and agencies
Government contractors: and corrupt practices, 48, 105–6, 121, 151–55, 161, 164–67; fairness of competition among, 9–11; and maintenance of equipment, 115–16; as percent of federal workers, 6; political donations and, 165; remedies for subpar performance, 13–14. *See also* Competition among government contractors; Contract(s) with government; Privatization
Government role, public opinion of, 4
Government workers. *See* Workers, public
Greyhound Lines, Inc., 115
Grosvenor Bus Lines, 87
Guile, in transaction-cost economics, 97

Hamilton, Alexander, viii
Hard Lessons: Public Schools and Privatization (Century Foundation), ix
Harrison, Bennett, 124
Hawthorne effect, 149
Health care, competition in, 92
Highway construction, inspection of, 62–63
Highway maintenance, privatization in Massachusetts, 29–44
Home remodellers, and relational contracting, 124–25
House Post Audit and Oversight Bureau (Massachusetts), 33
Houston, Tex., public transportation in, 84n
HUD. *See* U.S. Department of Housing and Urban Development (HUD)
Human services, importance of organization goals in, 127

IDA. *See* Industrial Development Agency (IDA), N.Y.
Ideology in privatization debate, 4, 29, 44, 46, 94, 128, 131, 138, 148, 156. *See also* Conservatives
IFS. *See* Indianapolis Fleet Service (IFS)
Incentives for contractor. *See* Moral hazard
Incentives for public employees, 130–31, 140–41

Incomplete contracting, information asymmetry in, 103
Indianapolis Fleet Service (IFS): attempted privatization of, 134–38; history of, 132–34; incentive program at, 130–31, 140–41; lessons drawn from, 143–50, 162; responsibilities of, 132; restructuring of, 138–41; successful restructuring of, 140–43, *141, 142*
Industrial Development Agency (IDA), N.Y., 119–20
Industrialization, and rise of big government, 1
Information asymmetry: adverse selection problems in, 107–14, 121; in incomplete contracting, 103; moral hazards in, 114–18; principal-agent problems in, 103–7; 97
Information costs, and transaction-cost economics, 96
Inspection of work. *See* Performance, monitoring of
Institute for Local Self-Government, 73
Institutional economics, new, 99–101, 100n
Institutions, as constraint on economic behavior, 99–101
Interim Report Review of Essex County Privatization (1994), 33–40

James, Sharpe, 151
James, Stephen, 139
Johnson Controls, Inc., 140
Jones, Daniel T., 124–25
Just-in-time manufacturing, 124–25

Kerasiotes, James, 33, 41, 43
Kingsbury Township, N.Y., 119
Kitchen, Harry M., 49–55
Koch, Edward, 153
Kostro, Charles, 33–34, 36, 37, 38
KPMG Peat Marwick, Inc., 67, 86

Labor-management: cooperation programs, 42n, 43, 71; benefits of, 131–32, 146, 162–63; at Indianapolis Fleet Service, 130–31, 134–35, 138–45; long-term viability of, 149. *See also* Workers, public, cooperative relations with
Laidlaw Transit, Inc., 66, 86, 87–88
Libertarian Reason Foundation, 11
Lockheed Corporation, and political corruption, 152–53

Los Angeles, HUD privatization study of, 55–56; analysis of, 56–59; findings of, 56, *56;* purpose of, 55; services compared in, 55–56
Los Angeles County Transportation Committee, 66, 67

Madison, James, viii
Mail delivery: social benefits of, 25. *See also* U.S. Postal Service (USPS)
Maintenance of equipment: cost of, 158–59; government contractors and, 115–16. *See also* Vehicle maintenance
"Make-buy" decision, 16–19; definition of, 16
Managed care organizations, and profit motive, 127
Management: expertise in private vs. public sector, 83–84; privatization of, 32, 44–45, 78, 91; training workers in, 163; trimming middle levels of, 139, 164
Mangine, Dominic, 135–37, 139
Market(s): contract vs. spot, 18; and contracting of extended services, 19. *See also* Capitalism; Competition among government contractors
Market contraction in public service contracting, 70
Market entry barriers: and competition, 70; in standard market model, 9; transaction costs and, 16
Market model, standard, 6–9; and competition among government contractors, 9–11, 47; issues in, 8–9; oversimplicity of, 12–13, 47, 156; problems with, 94; and theory of organizational change, 15–16
Market structure: fixing problems in, 90–91; importance of understanding, 70
Massachusetts, privatization of highway maintenance in: bidding process in, 30–32, 42–43, 109; capital costs vs. operating costs in, 35–37; conclusions about, 44–46, 159; cost-effectiveness of, 35–41, *39, 40;* interim report on, 33–40; management problems in, 34–35; political background of, 29–30; principal-agent problems in, 35; success of, 32–33; unions and, 41–44, *42*
Massachusetts Institute of Technology, 67
MassHighway, and privatization of highway maintenance, 30, 31, 33, 34, 35, 37, 38

Mattison, Jackie R., 151
Mayflower, Inc., 86–87
McCorkhill, John, 134, 135–37, 138–39, 140, 142, 144, 148
McCroskey, Jack, 67
MDTA. *See* Metro-Dade Transit Agency (MDTA)
Mesa, Ariz., fire protection costs in, *74*
Metro-Dade Transit Agency (MDTA), 114–16
Metropolitan Transportation Authority (MTA), N.Y., 153
Middlesex Corporation, 32–33, 34
Miller, Mannix, Lemery, and Pratt, Inc., 119
MLS/Ryder, Inc., 140
Monitoring of performance. *See* Performance, monitoring of
Monopolies, tendencies toward, 10–11
Moral hazard: in contracting, 114–18; definition of, 114; in fire protection, 78–79, 81, 82
Morningside Heights, N.Y., 20
Motivation, individual, vs. theory of organizational change, 15. *See also* Incentives for contractor; Incentives in privatization debate
MTA. *See* Metropolitan Transportation Authority (MTA)
Mucha, Zenia, 153

National defense, as pure public good, 24
Nethercott, Bill, 81
New institutional economics, 99–101, 100n
New York City: cost of street repaving in, 57–59; oligopolistic markets and, 89–90; political corruption in, 153; privatization of school busing in, 89–90; privatization of solid waste collection in, 48–49; privatization of street cleaning in, 153–54
New York City Transit Authority (NYCTA), 9
New York County Courthouse, 151–52
Nike, Inc., 124
NYCTA. *See* New York City Transit Authority (NYCTA)

Office of Private Sector Initiatives, 64
Office of the State Auditor (OSA), State of Massachusetts, 30, 33
Ohio highway inspection contract, privatization of, 62–63
Oligopolistic markets, competition among government contractors in, 69–70, 71–72, 84–93

Operating costs, vs. capital costs, 35–36
Opportunism: costs of thwarting, 98, 103, 156–57; in transaction-cost economics, 97
Organizational goals, importance of considering, 127
Organizations: complex responses of, 16; need for theory of, 95–96; theory of, and standard market model, 15–16; theory vs. reality of privatization in, ix–x, 101–29
O'Rourke, Andrew, 104, 107, 165
OSA. *See* Office of the State Auditor (OSA), State of Massachusetts
Output of public service, importance of delineating, 157–59
Outsourcing vs. expansion, efficiency of, 16–19
Overhead costs: and avoidable cost accounting, 65, 66–68, 160; and fully allocated cost accounting, 64–65, 66–68; in service-restructuring negotiations, 138, 164
Oversight of performance. *See* Performance, monitoring of

Pacheco-Manard Act, 167
Paratransit services: in Baltimore, 112n; and evaluation of contract bidders, 110–14; in Toronto, 112n
Pareto, Vilfredo, 8
Pareto optimum, 8; and institutional economics, 100
Performance, monitoring of: and contract market structure, 91; cost of, 50, 62–63, 116, 117, 160; in highway construction, 62–63; in Massachusetts highway maintenance privatization, 34–38; in New York City, 48–49; and opportunistic behavior, 97, 103, 156–57; and price collusion, 48; in publicly provided services, 29–30; and stability of contractors, 113; structural considerations in, 34. *See also* Corruption in public contracting
Personnel costs, and privatization, 59–62
Peskin, Robert, 67
Phoenix, Ariz., fire protection costs in, *74*
Pirro, Albert, 105–6, 165
Political climate, current, 3
Political discourse, vagueness of, vii
Political donations, and government contractors, 165

Politicians: as catalyst for action, 144–45; rhetoric of, vii
Politics: in contracting process, 10–11, 12, 86–87, 87–88, 164–67; in privatization debate, 4, 29. *See also* Conservatives; Ideology in privatization debate
Poole, Robert, 11
Post Office. *See* U.S. Postal Service (USPS)
Price, in market model, 6–7
Price Waterhouse, Inc., 115
Principal-agent problems, in contracting, 103–7, 154
Prison privatization, costs in, 122
Private Enterprise Participation (PEP), in Miami region, 114–16
Private goods: characteristics of, 23–24; and market economy, 24
Private vs. public service providers: efficiency of, 20–21; reasons for having, 23–26
Privatization: arguments for, viii, 4, 11–13; cost savings of, 68; current bias toward, 29; definition of, viii, 3; earlier attempts at, 153–56, 157; effectiveness of, 155; vs. improvement of public services, 5; at management vs. task level, 32; need for hybrid version of, 128–29; as rhetorical tool, vii; savings from, 29; theory vs. reality in, ix–x, 101–29; U.S. faith in, vii. *See also* Competition among government contractors; Contract(s); Government contractors; Market model, standard
Privatization and Public Hospitals (Century Foundation), ix
Privatization debate, opportunities provided by, 5
Privatization movement: benefits of undermining, 13; as catalyst for change, 145, 149–50; and measurement of costs, 28–29; and past privatization efforts, 155–56; publications of, 48; and unions, 59
Production, in market model, 7
Productivity, factors affecting, 145
Profit motive, disruptive nature of, 126–27
Progressivism: possibility of renewing, 95; rise of, 1
Public action. *See* Progressivism; Social equity
Publicly provided goods: definition of, 24–25, 26; fire protection as, 26–28; reasons for existence of, 24–26
Public opinion: of public servants, 21, 131; on role of government, 4
Public schools, social benefits of, 26
Public servants, public opinion of, 21

Public services and agencies: complexity of improving, 5, 156–57; complexity of services rendered by, 25, 158–59; delineating output of, 157–59; efficiency of expansion vs. outsourcing, 16–19; efficiency vs. private service providers, 20–21; irreplaceable expertise of, 45; reasons for having, 23–26; reforming via competition, 15, 69; reforming vs. scrapping of, 45, 94–96, 162; relational contracting in, 125–26; uniqueness of contracts for, 161–62. *See also* Reform of public services; *specialized services*
Public transportation: in Denver, 84–89; in Houston, Tex., 84n; privatization of, 64; and publicly provided goods and services, 25, 26. *See also* Canadian bus service privatization; Paratransit services
Public workers. *See* Workers, public
Purchaser-vendor relationship, 13–14; importance to success of contract, 14–15

Rationality: in new institutional economics, 99; in transaction-cost economics, 97
Reagan, Ronald Wilson, 3, 55, 64, 114
Reason Foundation, 67
Reform of capitalist system, mid-twentieth-century theories of, 1–2
Reform of public services: avenues to, 45, 94–96, 162; savings from, 71; suggested rules for, 157–67; techniques and benefits of, 162–64. *See also* Indianapolis Fleet Service (IFS); Labor-management cooperation programs
Regional Transportation District (RTD), Denver, Colo., 85
Relational contracting: advantages of, 121–23, 128–29; companies currently employing, 124–25; complexities of, 126; keys to effective use of, 126–28; in public agencies, 125–26; situations appropriate for, 123–24
Relationship of vendor to purchaser, 13–14; importance to success of contract, 14–15
Repaving of streets, privatization of, 57–59
Revolving door syndrome, 166
Rivalrousness of goods: definition of, 23–24; and public goods and services, 24
Robber barons, and rise of big government, 1

Roob, Mitchell, 138
Roos, Daniel, 124–25
RTD. *See* Regional Transportation District
    (RTD), Denver, Colo.
Rural/Metro, Inc., 72–77, 77–78, 79–82,
    90, 103–4
Russia, collapse of communism in, 2
Rutnik, Douglas, 153
Rye Brook, N.Y., fire protection in, 79–82,
    99

Sabretech, Inc., 17
Salaries of workers, public vs. private sector,
    59–62
San Diego biotechnology industry, relation-
    al contracting in, 125
Santa Barbara Metropolitan Transportation
    District, privatization experience, 65
School busing in New York City, oligopolis-
    tic markets and, 89–90
Schools, public, social benefits of, 26
Schumpeter, Joseph, 2
Sclar, Elliott, ix
Scottsdale, Ariz., fire protection cost in,
    73–77, *74*, 82, 90, 103–4
SCRTD. *See* Southern California Rapid
    Transit District (SCRTD)
SCT. *See* Sonoma County Transit (SCT) pri-
    vatization experience
Search goods, definition of, 106
Sen, Amartya, 8
SEPTA. *See* Southeastern Pennsylvania
    Transportation Authority (SEPTA)
Service Employees International Union,
    145
Services, categories of, 23
Services to be provided, definition of:
    importance of accuracy in, 23, 41, 44,
    81–82; inability to arrive at, 28, 38–39
Silicon Valley, relational contracting in, 125
Smith, Adam, 8
Smith, Barney, Upham, and Harris, Inc., 119
Social equity: and inevitability of socialism,
    2; vs. productivity, 2; and publicly pro-
    vided goods and services, 25; and uni-
    versal mail service, 25
Social institutions, as constraint on eco-
    nomic behavior, 99–101
Socialism: advocates of, 1–2; inevitability of,
    2
Solid waste collection: privatization in New
    York City, 48–49; privatization in
    Washington County, N.Y., 118–21; priva-
    tization movement and, 48

Sonoma County Transit (SCT) privatization
    experience, 66
Southeastern Pennsylvania Transportation
    Authority (SEPTA), 111, 113–14, 122
Southern California Rapid Transit District
    (SCRTD), 66–67
Soviet Union, collapse of communism in, 2
Specialized services, and market competi-
    tion, 18–19
Spot markets vs. contract markets, 18–19;
    and contracting of extended services,
    19
Stanley, Ralph, 64
Statistical significance, 53
Stett, Charles "Skip," 136–37, 138, 139
Stevens, Barbara J., 55–59
Stolzenberg, Edward, 104, 105
Street cleaning, privatization in New York
    City, 153–54
Success, personal, in market model, 8
Sun City, Ariz., fire protection costs in,
    77–78
Supervision of contracts. *See* Performance,
    monitoring of
Supply chain management, 124

Tammany Hall, 152
Taxes, political pressure to limit, viii
Technological constraints, and contract
    performance, 14
Tecom, Inc., 140
Tempe, Ariz., fire protection costs in, *74*
Theories of organization, need for, 95–96
Theory vs. reality in privatization, ix–x,
    101–29
"Third way" reformers, 2
Toronto, paratransit services in, 112n
Transaction, as unit of analysis in transac-
    tion-cost economics, 98
Transaction cost(s): importance of calculat-
    ing, 63–64, 160–61; vs. internal bureau-
    cratic costs, 16–19; and market entry, 16
Transaction-cost economics: advantages of,
    97; history of, 96; rationality in, 97; and
    relational contracting, 128; transaction
    as unit of analysis in, 98
Transparency in contracts, 106
Trash collection: privatization in New York
    City, 48–49; privatization in Washington
    County, N.Y., 118–21; privatization
    movement and, 48
Trilateral governance in contracting, 103
Trust in working relationships, importance
    of, 146–47

Tucson, Ariz., fire protection costs in, *74*
Tweed, William Marcy, 152
Tweed Ring, 152

UMTA. *See* Urban Mass Transportation
    Administration (UMTA)
Unions: anti-privatization efforts of,
    137–38; and effective public agencies,
    59; and highway maintenance in
    Massachusetts, 41–44, *42;* privatization
    movement and, 59; and school busing
    in New York City, 89
United Kingdom: postal service privatiza-
    tion in, 158; public transport privatiza-
    tion in, 88
United States, faith in capitalism, vii
Urban Mass Transportation Administration
    (UMTA), 64, 65–66
Urban transit. *See* Public transportation
U.S. Department of Housing and Urban
    Development (HUD), labor cost data,
    59. *See also* Los Angeles, HUD privatiza-
    tion study of
U.S. Department of Transportation, 64
U.S. Office of Management and Budgets, 67
U.S. Postal Service (USPS): and public vs.
    private service providers, 20–23, 25, 44;
    social benefits of, 25

ValueJet crash (1996), 16–18
Vehicle maintenance: complexities of,
    158–59; privatization in Albany, N.Y.,
    116–18, 146–47. *See also* Indianapolis
    Fleet Service (IFS); Maintenance of
    equipment
Vendor-purchaser relationship, and impor-
    tance to success of contract, 13–14,
    14–15

Wackenhut Correctional Corporation, 70
Walsh Cab Co., 112–13
Ward, George, 34
Washington County, N.Y., privatization of
    solid waste disposal in, 118–21
Wastewater treatment, as inherently
    monopolistic, 14
Wealth, optimization in standard market
    model, 7–8
Weld, William, 29–30, 33, 36, 42, 159
Welfare state: loss of interest in, 3; support-
    ers of, 2. *See also* Government, big
Westchester County, N.Y.: privatization of
    medical center parking in, 104–7, 118,
    165; privatization of public transport in,
    88–89
Westchester County Association of Fire
    Chiefs, 81
White collar services, privatization of,
    57–59
Williamson, Oliver E., 103
Witzeman, Louis, 72
Womack, James P., 124–25
Wood, Robert, 136
Workers, public: cooperative relations with,
    59, 134–35, 146–49; cost of managing,
    vs. contractors, 146; efficiency vs. private
    sector, 60, 61–62, 62–63, 68; feeling of
    powerlessness among, 144–45; incen-
    tives for, 130–31, 140–41; privatization
    of, 3–4; public opinion of, 21, 131;
    salaries vs. private sector, 59–62. *See also*
    Labor-management cooperation pro-
    grams; Unions

"Yellow Pages" test, 29, 32
Youngtown, Ariz., fire protection costs in,
    77–78